The Beginning

The Beginning

EUROPEAN DISCOVERY AND EARLY SETTLEMENT OF SWAN RIVER
WESTERN AUSTRALIA

R. T. APPLEYARD & TOBY MANFORD

UNIVERSITY OF WESTERN AUSTRALIA PRESS

First published in 1979
by the University of Western Australia Press, Nedlands W.A. 6009
Reprinted with amendments 1980

Agents: Eastern States of Australia and New Zealand: Melbourne University Press, Carlton South, Vic. 3053; United Kingdom and Europe: International Scholarly Book Services (Europe), a division of Abacus Books Ltd, Abacus House, Tunbridge Wells, Kent TN4 OHU, England; U.S.A. and Canada: International Scholarly Book Services Inc., Box 555, Forest Grove, Oregon 97116.

Photoset by University of Western Australia Press, printed in Western Australia by Frank Daniels Pty Ltd, and bound by Printers Trade Services, West Perth.

National Library of Australia
Cataloguing-in-Publication data

Appleyard, Reginald Thomas, 1927-
    The beginning: European discovery and
    Early settlement of Swan River . . .

    Index
    First published, 1979.
    ISBN 0 85564 184 3

    1. Swan River settlement, Western Australia — History.
    I. Manford, Toby, 1936- , joint author. II. Title.

994.1'102

Contents

Plates

Figures

Introduction

This book had its 'beginning' about a decade ago when we began research on the history of Fremantle port. We soon realized, however, that dearth of publications on Western Australia's economic and social history made it necessary for us to broaden the research base in order to study Fremantle in the depth we believed it deserved. During this phase we identified two aspects of the state's early history which required more attention than they had hitherto been accorded. First, a systematic examination of all information on the western coast of the southern continent sent back to Europe by Dutch, French and British maritime explorers since the early seventeenth century was necessary in order to appreciate how and why the area's unenviable reputation for danger and sterility had been acquired, and why the entire western coast remained unclaimed and unsettled until 1829. Second, it became necessary to explain why first settlers made many and widespread explorations of the mainland within months of their arrival at Swan River, when they had been told before embarkation that Swan River itself had extensive tracts of fertile land suitable for agriculture. These and other aspects of early European contact with the western coast have been carefully researched for both the Fremantle study, and also for our separate forthcoming book on maritime and terrestrial exploration of Western Australia.

Broader-based research for the Fremantle study also required careful analysis of events leading to the British government's decision in 1828 to annex the western coast and establish a settlement at Swan River when experience suggested that it was a misplaced decision. For this reason, we became especially interested in the role played by James Stirling, the British naval officer who visited Swan River in 1827 and saw the potential for European settlement that others had missed. His effusive report was instrumental in the government's decision to make at Swan River a unique colonial experiment whereby first settlers were granted land on the basis of value of selected capital goods and stock brought from England. It is our view that a careful study of the reasons for this decision, and of the characteristics of settlers who responded to the offer, and the difficulties they experienced on arrival at Fremantle where nothing had been done to facilitate their resettlement, is necessary in order to understand the important formative years of Fremantle port.

An invitation to contribute a volume to the sesquicentenary series provided us with a timely opportunity to place long-term research aside for a while, and to suggest ideas which we hope will stimulate thoughtful discussion during the year of celebrations. We gratefully acknowledge financial support from the Australian Research Grants Committee, Fremantle Port Authority and the University of Western Australia. The Surveyor-General of Western Australia's cartographers drew most of the unacknowledged figures in this book (including Figure 3.1). Librarians and their staff at the University of Western Australia library, Battye Library, the Western Australian Art Gallery, the Public Records Office and the British Museum (London), the Aylesbury Archives, the Bibliothèque Nationale (Paris), the Musée d'Histoire Naturelle at Le Havre, the Maritiem Museum (Rotterdam), the Algemeen Rijksarchief (The Hague), the Australian National Library and the Mitchell Library provided much information and advice. We are grateful to Ian Berryman who gave us access to letters he had discovered during many years research in London; to Ann Parry who gave us research notes from her book *The Admirals Fremantle*; to Lord Cottesloe and Commander John Fremantle who gave us access to their family papers; to Harry Turner, author of *The Gilt Dragon Incident*, for unpublished notes; and to Gerard Rousilles who assisted with translation of French manuscripts. We are also indebted to Commander Andrew David of the British Hydrographer's Office; to Günter Schilder of the University of Utrecht; to Madam Marie-Louise Hemphill of Paris; and Neil Jarvis of the Western Australian Department of Education for suggestions and criticism during early stages of the research. Amongst colleagues at the University of Western Australia, Ronald Berndt, Sylvia Hallam, John White, Jim Sewell, Margaret Pitt Morison, Pamela Statham and Leslie Marchant have been especially helpful. Research assistants over the years—Mary Ahern, Chris Heagney and Jan Moore—have provided indispensable service, and for typing so expertly many rough drafts we wish to thank Margery Clegg, Caroline Baird and Pat Andrews. Seeing this book through press has been a pleasure because Eric Hinchliffe and Naomi Zeffertt have been so helpful and cooperative. Finally, we wish to acknowledge the patience and forebearance of Iris and Tony, our spouses, who have acted as sounding boards for many ideas, sometimes in the dead of night!

Despite the great assistance and support of these and many other persons, responsibility for accuracy of fact and interpretation is ours alone.

R.T.A. & T.M.

1
Discovery

They call her a young country, but they lie:
She is the last of lands, the emptiest,
A woman beyond her change of life, a breast
Still tender but within the womb is dry.
                                    A. D. HOPE.

To those Europeans who discovered it, Western Australia's coastline, though diverse, seemed uniformly arid and monotonous. The rugged cliffs of Euclonia, the granite headlands of the south coast and the low sandhills of the north-west are but variations on a theme Oscar Spate has called 'impressive by its very consistency in monotony, at once coarse in texture and very subtle in its modulations; but rarely smiling'.[1] The unsmiling western face attracted few and repelled many. Unlike other continents, there were no snow-capped mountains, no wide rivers winding through fertile plains and no lush vegetation to welcome the mariner who had sailed for weeks across what Henry Handel Richardson called 'the bleak and windy desert of the seas'.[2] Instead, he found shores which were, and mostly still are, uninviting in the extreme. The vegetation was stunted, prickly and grey-green, and with few exceptions (which early visitors failed to recognize) bore no edible fruit. Water, that indispensible commodity for mariners, was difficult if not impossible to find on large portions of the coast. Coastal lowlands, and especially their rivers, were not easily explored and the Aborigines encountered in northern parts were often warlike and wore no adornments to show that the land contained gold, silver and other precious metals.

I

As we know it, and as it was seen at the fringes by non-Aboriginal visitors, Australia's topography is passing through a stage of evolution which has lasted millions of years. From Cambrian times of 500 million years ago to the Tertiary of one to forty million years ago, southern land masses, contorted and convulsed by the earth's cooling, took shapes which bore no resemblance to Australia's present outline. Only about forty million years ago, during a period called the early Pleistocene Ice Age, did the familiar shape emerge. Then, towards the end of this age, when Bass Strait was shallow, the Tasmanian Aboriginal arrived and, a little later, the Australian Aboriginal.[3] The climate then was very wet, and large herbivores still existed; but as the great ice sheets melted so water levels rose, widening Bass Strait and probably separating the Australian land mass from Asia. By late Pleistocene small volcanoes were still active but with the passing of the Ice Age came desiccation. The probable final stage has been graphically described by Edgeworth David:

> Lake Eyre ceases to overflow into Lake Torrens. Its waters shrink and become saline, or even entirely disappear. As we survey from our 'time machine' the garment of green which overspreads Australia, we realize that a great hole is forming at its centre, widening fast with time. That hole is a desert . . . . Aridity [comes] to more than a quarter of Australia, and even the coastal zones become drier than before. The great marsupials, their supplies of food and water dwindling, perish in thousands, bogged around the dwindling mud springs and the shrinking waterholes. Once more, as in Cretaceous time, Eastern Australia is isolated from Western Australia, not as then, by sea, but now by desert.[4]

The legacy of this long weathering process is a continent with very little variation in topography. Unlike Europe, no Great Alpine Storm raised young folded mountains. If, as Spate imaginatively conjectures, Australia had central mountain ranges high enough to carry glaciers and snowfields, the north would reproduce the conditions of monsoon Asia. Or, even if the present relatively low eastern highlands of Australia were concave to the Pacific, instead of parallel and close to it, there would be great perennial rivers in temperate and subtropical latitudes.[5] The facts, alas, are otherwise. An 'uplifting' which did occur on the western side of the continent in the Pleistocene raised the huge shield of pre-Cambrian strata by a mere 360 m. 'A traveller in central West Australia', observes Griffith Taylor, therefore 'sees a landscape which has not materially altered since Pliocene times'.[6] Most of the western state is a vast truncated upland, known as the Great Plateau of Western Australia; a monotonous, flat landscape which, except along the coast where plains have formed as a result of weathering along the edges of the shield, is simply a massive peneplain eroded down over millions of years. Though hills reach 1200 m they are merely residuals of erosion or fault blocks (Fig. 1.1).[7]

Because the landscape is very flat, and rainfall generally modest, the state's drainage basin is also very limited. Only a small part of the land is drained by seaward-flowing rivers: in the Kimberleys and North-West, rivers hundreds of kilometres long flow infrequently and for short periods; and in the South-West, shorter rivers flow from the scarp across the coastal plain. The major part of the land has very low rainfall which is either absorbed into inland basins or has no surface drainage at all. As there is only a small area above 600 m altitude, differences in climate are due mainly to latitude, and compared with other continents, the latitude range (12°-38°s) is rather small. Rainfall is governed by two wind streams—the westerlies, which blow with regularity, and the monsoons in the north during summer. The westerlies, which sweep across the Indian and Southern oceans, move to the north in winter and bring consistent rains to the lower western and southern coasts. The northern regions of the state receive most of their rainfall during sum-

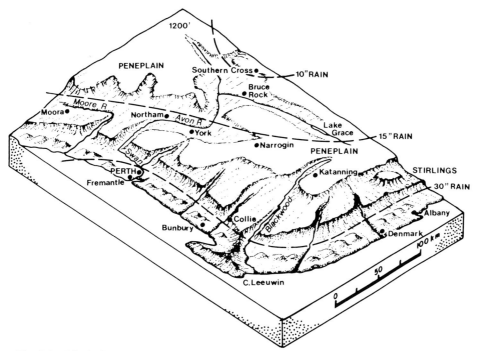

Fig. 1.1 Block diagram of Swanland. [Adapted from Griffith Taylor, *Australia*, p. 191]

mer when monsoons, having originated in tropical seas, move in a south-westerly direction with increasing force. Regularity of rain-bearing winds means that the South-West receives over 760 mm of rain mainly during winter months and the Kimberleys receive falls exceeding 1270 mm between October and April. In the remainder of the state, rainfall is light and irregular.

Because rainfall is the main determinant of Western Australia's vegetation, incidence of vegetation varies considerably. Trees belong to one of two genera—in the outer (coastal) zone, eucalyptus, and in the inner zone, acacia—and even though there are many species of both, the lack of genera, together with the flat landscape, gives both the state and the continent a uniqueness unshared by other land masses.[8] Even well-vegetated areas such as the south coast are concealed from mariners by sand dunes, which host only stunted hardy plants able to sustain strong westerly winds, or granite outcrops which bear little or no vegetation.

II

Australian Aborigines have lived upon this old and rarely smiling continent for over 40 000 years. Where they came from, when and how, will probably remain uncertain, although in recent years anthropologists and pre-historians have made considerable progress in piecing together fragmentary evidence to support plausible theories. As these early ancestors and their descendants moved across the

continent—Australia's first explorers—forming tribal communities which, in time, differed according to the sophistication and skills of the members and variations in vegetation, rainfall and soils, so the earth itself changed. After the Pleistocene Ice Age, when changing sea levels altered both the size and shape of the continent, migration from the Asian mainland in primitive craft would have been more difficult than when the continent was larger and the channels separating Asia were narrower. Climatic conditions were much colder, and would have influenced internal migratory patterns, thus explaining why man appears not to have penetrated the higher and colder south-eastern alpine regions of Australia. Archaeological research has uncovered artefacts which suggest life-styles rather different from those often attributed to Aborigines. They could have been adept fishermen (a large cord for this purpose was unearthed at Lake Mungo, New South Wales); they ground seeds and fruit (an 18 000-year-old grinding-stone was discovered in the Kimberleys); they baked food in ovens and made ceramics (a 30 000-year-old piece recently discovered ranks amongst the world's oldest); at Koolanda Cave on the Nullarbor Plain finger-markings on thousands of square metres of soft limestone walls, estimated at 20 000 years old, attest to early artistic expression; and at Devil's Lair in south-western Australia beads and pendants 30 000 years old have been discovered.[9]

During the long intervening period between the Pleistocene and the arrival of Europeans, Aborigines penetrated most of the continent. Even though probably 85 per cent are genetically interrelated, 'tribes' developed distinct languages which few other tribes could understand. Comprising groups of families numbering between twenty and fifty persons, they developed efficient techniques for hunting game and harvesting seeds and yams. Nomadic in the sense that they moved about designated territory, their lives were directed to seeking food, acquiring necessary skills and accepting clear patterns of job responsibility. Ever ready with a spear, which was part of himself, and rarely out of his hands so that he could, at a moment's warning, catch whatever animal crossed his path, Aboriginal man was a hunter of the greatest dexterity.[10] Aboriginal women collected yams, nuts and berries which, in regions where game was scarce, may have provided up to 80 per cent of the tribe's diet.

Their dispersal throughout the continent, writes Mulvaney, 'their responses and adjustments to the challenges of its harsh environment, and their economical utilisation of its niggardly resources, are stimulating testimony to the achievements of the human spirit in the face of adversity'.[11] In all parts of the continent, and especially in those parts where food was scarce, he 'knows intimately all the habits of the creatures around him, for without this knowledge his spears and his skill would be useless. He must track with stealth . . . imitate the sounds of animals and birds, understand the directions of the wind and the importance of the seasons in hunting'.[12] Just as they preserved plants which bore fruit, not spoiling a bush by over-picking nor collecting all the roots on a yam plant, so they also understood the need for both agriculture and animal husbandry. Recent research by Sylvia Hallam on

Pl. 1.1 (facing page) A Western Desert family sets out for another waterhole, 1964-65. [Courtesy of B. Tonkinson, through permission of R. & C. Berndt]

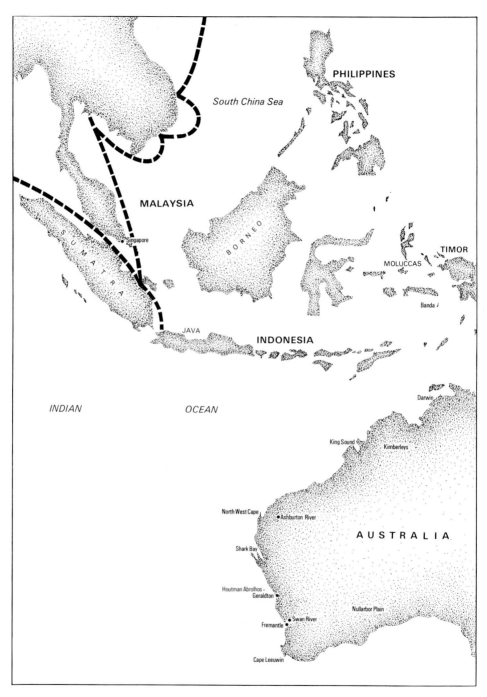

Fig. 1.2 South-East Asia and Western Australia, showing the route presumed to have been taken by Cheng Ho.   [Based on a map by L. P. Thomas, *History Today,* July 1975]

Aboriginal life in south-western Australia confirms that 'fire-stick farming'—
burning the bush on a regular basis first to scare out kangaroos which could be easily
captured, and later to catch other kangaroos which returned to feed on new, green
shoots—has been practised for centuries.[13] They were genuine farmers, concludes
Hallam, who modified the structure and distribution of floral and faunal communities with effects on the landscape which 'may have been more crucial than we
can yet fully appreciate'. Mulvaney also seeks reappraisal of their skills and
sophistication. They were not as parasitic of nature's bounty as has sometimes been
suggested, he writes, nor is it true that they never saw the connection between seed
and germination. In many respects, he concludes, they were innovators. Though
their life-style was nomadic, it was 'controlled nomadism', the degree of mobility
depending mainly on climate and vegetation. In less favoured areas, which describes
much of Western Australia, they had to move more frequently and over greater
distances, sometimes travelling for a whole day to reach the next waterhole. In fertile pockets, such as the Swan and Murray river valleys in the South-West, their
needs could be met from abundant food supplies and hence mobility was less than in
arid areas. Just as landscape conditioned their living so it affected their physiques.
The Western Australian desert people, write the Berndts, are short, thin and wiry
from constant movement in search of food, whereas in the north, towards the coast,
they are bigger boned, taller and heavier.[14]

Not only did Aborigines develop a close affinity with the land, but because of its
'climatic unpredictability, with its whimsical bounty and famine',[15] they also
developed a rich ceremonial and mythological life. Tribes occasionally congregated
with others for ceremonies, a contact which led to a gradual but steady interchange
of ideas and techniques. There is ample evidence that a large-scale and complex
trade developed from tribe to tribe across the continent from north to south, thus
enlarging the array of artefacts, tools and weapons available to each and at the same
time enlarging their experiences and vision.[16] Even so, they had few material comforts although a great deal of leisure to devote to art, myth and ceremony.

Thus when the first Europeans to visit the north-western side of the continent saw
near-naked Aborigines (but seldom their women and children, who were discreetly
hidden nearby) waving their spears in anger, they did not, and could not be expected
to, appreciate either the reasons for their nakedness or their demeanour. To European traders of the seventeenth century they were wretched, warlike savages,
although to later visitors, especially the French and British of the nineteenth century
who spent some time on the south-western coast and who approached Aborigines
with greater respect and interest, impressions were generally more favourable. But
whatever European visitors thought, the Aborigines were children of an old, ancient
and very significant culture. 'They grew, loved and died believing themselves to be
part of a comprehensible and universal scheme arranged primarily for their benefit.
There was no real strangeness, no grappling with essentially unknown elements, nor
unforeseen conditions. They were sure of themselves, and of the culture in which
they had grown; they could cope with all they met, all they saw and all they heard.'[17]
This sureness and ability to cope, the legacy of 40 000 or more years as sole oc-

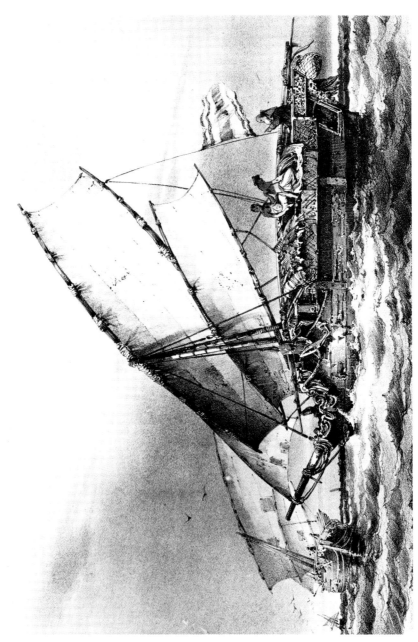

Pl. 1.2 Makassan proas at Raffles Bay. [Le Breton lithograph from J. S. C. Dumont d'Urville, *Voyage au Pôle Sud et dans L'Océanie . . . Atlas Pittoresque*, Vol. 2, plate 114]

cupants of the Australian mainland, was to be sorely tested by the arrival of out-
siders with alien cultures and values.

III

Who arrived first and where he landed are questions impossible to answer, and
probably irrelevant, but as early as the thirteenth century, a full three centuries
before the arrival of the first Europeans, Asian traders may well have sailed
southwards from the continent and landed somewhere on Australia's northern
shores. Chinese are believed to have been the first visitors. To press their claim, a
Chinese scholar has cited calculations by Confucius during 592-553 B.C. based on
observations made by Chinese savants in Australia, adding that they maintained
sporadic contact with the continent for the next 2000 years. The claim is conjectural;
there is firmer basis for the same scholar's assertion that Chinese were actually in the
vicinity of Darwin in A.D. 1432.[18] For example, it is known that Cheng Ho, the fifteenth century traveller, was in Timorese waters within a few hundred kilometres of
the continent, and may well have landed (Fig. 1.2);[19] and that Chinese traders were
active in Javanese ports during the fourteenth century.

Arab 'adventurers' were also in the region (Malaysia and Sumatra) during the
fourteenth century and by 1515 merchants were operating a prosperous rice em-
porium at Banda only a few hundred kilometres from the Australian continent.[20]
They were capable and inquisitive seamen and it is not unlikely that while trading in
island waters they, with the Chinese, either deliberately explored to the south or
were blown ashore during the monsoon season. Whether the islanders themselves
knew about, and landed on, the continent either by accident or design before the
coming of Chinese and Arab traders is not known, although Manning Clark contends that the Javanese and all who lived on the south coast as far east as Timor were
afraid to proceed more than 5 km out of sight of land for fear of being drawn into
the abyss of Pausengi from which there was no return.[21]

Even so, it is almost certain that by A.D. 1700 Makassan fishermen were exploiting
the rich trepang grounds off the north and north-western coasts of Australia.
Trepang, or bêche-de-mer, a small marine animal known as sea-cucumber and used
mainly in soups, was in great demand in China, and Makassan fishermen were
prepared to take the risks, real and imagined, in crossing the Timor Sea in small but
seaworthy proas to harvest it (Plate 1.2). Leaving their island on monsoon winds in
summer, and returning on the south-east trades in late May (see pp. 3), they spent a
great deal of time ashore on Australia boiling down their catches.[22] Archaeological
research by I. M. Crawford in the Kimberleys and by C. C. Macknight in Arnhem
Land indicates that boiling-down sites were usually chosen for protection against attack by Aborigines—with whom relations were uncertain, ranging from poor to
quite good. It is believed that Makassans occasionally took one or two friendly
Aborigines back to Makassar and, if this is true, they would have brought back to
their tribal brothers astounding tales of things hitherto neither seen nor experienced.

According to Mulvaney and the Berndts the presence of Makassan fishermen on the Australian mainland during the eighteenth and part of the nineteenth centuries had a profound influence on Aboriginal culture. They introduced the dug-out canoe and metal implements; Aborigines learned and used Makassan words, grew beards, smoked pipes; and Aboriginal art, ceremonies and mythological symbols clearly reflect the visitors' influence. Although contact was regular, it was only seasonal. Makassans built stonework around their boiler sites and dug wells, but they returned home at the end of each season with their catch and all their fishing-gear.[23] They probably did not explore the Australian continent beyond its mangrove fringe and, as if to confirm their mistrust of Aborigines, only remained in Australia on a year-round basis after 1824 when the British government established protective outposts near the fishing-grounds.

Through overland trade with the far east, *Europeans* of the thirteenth century gradually increased their knowledge of that mysterious region of the known world. The writings of Marco Polo were a landmark in this process. Not since the days of Alexander the Great had so much information about the east been disseminated in Europe. Returning home (from China) along the coast of Cochin China (see Fig. 1.2), and making careful observations of all he saw, the great Venetian traveller also heard, and recorded, from Arab traders tales concerning islands which lay to the south. The terms 'Java Major' and 'Java Minor' appear frequently in Marco Polo's writings about this region. Unlike his detractors and his followers, Marco Polo was fairly precise about what he understood by these terms. Java Major referred to what was known about Java and what was assumed concerning land beyond it. At that time even the south coast of Java was unknown to his informants. The term Java Minor referred to the island of Sumatra.[24] Other travellers such as Nicolo de Conti used the same terms but in his case Java Minor did not represent Sumatra. The confusion which followed amongst cartographers and scholars was caused partly by Marco Polo using the word 'Java' to refer to Cochin China, and although he apparently did not provide any maps of the region, many appeared when he and de Conti returned to Europe. On some maps Java Major appeared as a large southern continent; on others it referred to Java itself with other islands 'thrown here and there at random'.[25] Most significant for speculation concerning the existence of a southern continent was the map on which Austral regions called *Terra Australis* envelop the south pole and 'extend in the correct longitude sufficiently North to warrant the supposition of a knowledge of the Australian continent'.[26]

The imaginative maps were consistent with Marco Polo's vivid descriptions of land described to him by Arab traders. For example, 'Locac' was rich in timber and fruit with a delicious flavour. Gold was 'abundant to a degree scarcely credible' and the people exported shells to other countries, where they were used as money. On another island the people, governed by a king, had established a thriving trade in spices and drugs. Alas, however, as McIntyre shows, Locac was not Australia but Siam and the other islands probably Malaysia and Singapore.[27]

The influence of Marco Polo's writings on European speculation concerning land south of Cochin China lasted for nearly three hundred years. During this period,

Pl. 1.3   Marco Polo in the Land of Pepper.   [Courtesy of Bibliothèque Nationale, Paris]

and before Europeans themselves discovered the land mass which is Australia, other travellers, many like the Franciscan monk, Odoric, who visited Java in the fourteenth century (thus coming much closer to Australia than did Marco Polo), added to the speculation concerning whether a continent lay in southern climes and what it might be like. The Muslim trader, El Edrisi, also contributed to speculation when he told of a large, uninhabited country south of Borneo containing large birds. Perhaps, writes McIntyre, there is credence in his story in that the Aboriginal population of Australia at that time was probably sparse and that the birds he referred to could have been the non-flying emus. In this regard, he notes, the word 'emu' *(ema)* is an Arabic word.[28]

The first contact with the western coast of *Terra Australis* by Europeans could well have been made by Portuguese traders who formed the vanguard of European expansion overseas in the fifteenth century. At that time Arab traders held a monopoly on trade with the spice-rich islands of the East Indies. Spices were required in Europe to preserve meat, which had to be slaughtered during winter time when feed was short. Though salt was the most common preservative, spices were

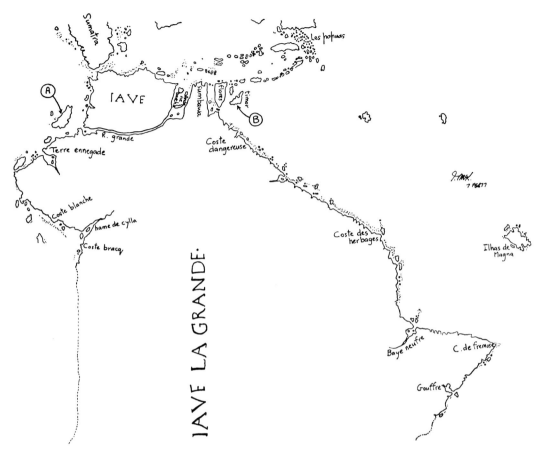

Sumatra

Les papuas

IAVE

A

B

R. grande

Terre ennegade

Coste
dangereuse

Sumbawa
Flores
timor

Ilhas de
Magna

Coste blanche

hame de cylla

Coste des
herbages

Coste bracq

Baye neufre

C. de Fremose

Gouffre

JAVE LA GRANDE

Fig. 1.3   Cartographic detail from 'Dauphin Map'.   [Courtesy of Ian McKiggan]

also in demand, especially cloves, which grew only on a few islands of the Moluccas.[29] Overland routes to spice depots on the Asian mainland (e.g. Malacca) were effectively blocked by the Turks, so towards the end of the long and bitterly fought Crusades between Christian and Moslem, Portuguese mariners, encouraged by their incredible leader, Henry the Navigator, searched for a sea-route to the spice islands. With each successive voyage down the west coast of Africa, in primitive ships crewed by superstitious and unwilling sailors and aided (if that is the word) by primitive instruments, one of their number—Bartholemew Diaz—finally reached the southern tip of the African mainland. Several years later, in 1495, Vasco de Gama followed Diaz's course and then rounded the Cape, sailed northwards along the east coast of Africa and across the Indian Ocean to the Malabar coast. Within a few years the Portuguese had blockaded Arab traders from the Moluccas and held a monopoly until late in the sixteenth century when, with the rise of northern European maritime powers, they in turn were replaced by the Dutch.

Fig. 1.4 'Jave' and 'Jave la Grande' after removing east coast distortions. [Courtesy of Ian McKiggan]

Whether, during the long period that Portuguese traders dominated the East In- dies, their mariners explored the southern continent, either deliberately or accident- ally during monsoon storms, is a question which until quite recently received answers based mainly on speculation. During the last few years, however, K. G. McIntyre and Ian McKiggan have provided evidence and arguments which show that the Portuguese knew a great deal more about the Southland than had been hitherto imagined. Starting with McIntyre's 'speculative argument' that the Por- tuguese navigators Cristovas de Mendonca and Gomes de Sequeira were exploring the coast during the 1520s, McKiggan then provides 'formal proof' with carto- graphic evidence. The important Dauphin Map of 1536 had depicted Jave la Grande as a huge land mass south of 'Jave', in much the same way as cartographers of the thirteenth century had depicted Marco Polo's information. The Dauphin Map, however, contains many detailed inlets and islands on its eastern and north-western sides, which led McKiggan to conclude that they may have been added by someone who had visited the region. McKiggan then corrected the navigators' cumulative longitudinal errors on the basis that these would have been greater in higher latitudes, and produced a revised map which is remarkable in its accurate depiction of the Australian continent. 'Jave la Grande', he concludes, 'is a map of Australia, and moreover, is an incredibly accurate one' (Figs. 1.3 and 1.4).

The Dauphin Map is a composite of at least three maps, details of the eastern coast having been provided by Mendonca during a voyage in about 1522. Thus almost 250 years before Cook, Mendonca not only sailed down the eastern coast, but identified over fifty inlets and rivers and over fifty islands, many of which were missed by Cook. He then entered Bass Strait and sailed westward as far as the present South Australian border, which was the longitude which separated Spanish (eastwards) from Portuguese (westwards) territory. Mendonca was therefore 'trespassing' on the Spanish division for his entire voyage, which probably explains why he could not claim authorship of the map. He apparently did not find any products on the coast which could be 'pillaged or traded', and so there was no follow-up expedition.

That part of the Dauphin Map depicting north-western Australia to King Sound was probably made by Sequeira during a voyage in 1525, and the part from King Sound to Shark Bay by others who followed him a few years later. At Shark Bay the cartographer of the Dauphin Map, lacking any information on the coast beyond that point, simply dropped a dotted vertical line to the bottom of the map. Unlike Mendonca, however, Sequeira was sailing in Portuguese waters; but like Mendonca he did not find any products on the Kimberley coast which he could pillage or trade. Indeed, what he discovered, concludes McKiggan, 'was, if anything, worse' than Mendonca had found.[30]

IV

It is to the Dutch, however, that credit is given for systematically revealing the shape and terrain of Western Australia's coastline. In early voyages to the East Indies their vessels followed the Portuguese route—around the Cape, north along the east coast of Africa or the east coast of Madagascar, across the Indian Ocean to India and thence to Java—and thus experienced the same hazards: contrary southeast trade winds; frequent becalming in the tropics, when the scorching sun melted the very pitch in the planking of their vessels, causing cargo to rot; and loss of crew through scurvy. Thus when Henrik Brouwer, one of the Dutch East India Company's mariners, who later became its governor-general in Batavia, pointed out in 1610 that prevailing westerly winds at high latitudes might provide a quicker and therefore less costly route to the Indies, he was sent in two vessels to prove his hypothesis. Brouwer's voyage was highly successful. On leaving the Cape he sailed east at about 36° latitude until he reached what he believed was the longitude of Sunda Strait, whereupon he turned north and on favourable winds reached his destination. His voyage took a mere six months compared with twelve or more by vessels using the old route. The route's viability was soon confirmed by other East

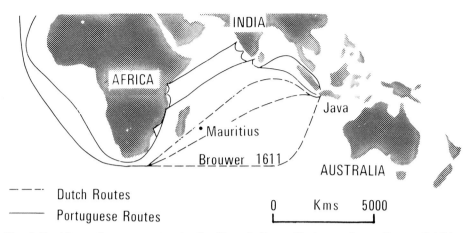

Fig. 1.5 Alternative sea routes to the East Indies. [Redrawn from Günter Schilder, *Australia Unveiled*]

Indiamen, and in 1617 the company gave its formal approval by issuing a *Seynbrief* (instruction) that in future all its vessels would use the new route (Fig. 1.5).[31]

Article thirteen of the *Seynbrief* instructed masters to sail eastwards from the Cape for one thousand Dutch miles before turning northwards, and warned that if they altered course before covering that distance they ran the risk of being driven off course and possibly becalmed, one of the very hazards the new route was intended to avoid. However, the new route was not so easily followed as Brouwer's experience had foreshadowed. The chronometer, essential for accurately calculating longitude, had not been invented and distance travelled eastwards could be estimated only by dead reckoning and/or with the aid of a primitive log-line.[32] There is even some doubt whether *Seynbrief* article thirteen referred to the German mile (5358 metres) or the Snellius mile (7158 metres).[33] In view of these difficulties and uncertainties, it was inevitable that sooner or later a vessel would underestimate distance travelled eastwards and its northern path would therefore be obstructed by the then unknown western coast of *Terra Australis*. In October 1616 Dirck Hartog in *Eendracht* (Concord) was the first Dutch master so to err. About half way on his northern tack to Batavia he sighted and landed on an offshore island which still bears his name, by a mainland which on subsequent Dutch charts bore the name of his vessel.[34]

The use by Brouwer of winds hitherto unknown was a major landmark in the discovery, exploration and settlement of Australia. In the century which followed Dirck Hartog's discovery, Dutch East India vessels, using the Brouwer route, progressively revealed the shape of the western coast. As landmarks and offshore reefs were discovered, so they were incorporated into the changing Dutch charts. Their contact with the coast was, however, a love-hate relationship from the start. On the one hand, the new route was quicker and healthier than the old Portuguese route; on the other, the coastline where vessels made their landfall was generally barren, dangerous and lacking in much-needed water, vegetables and fruit. Far from being a welcome sight, the coast became merely a convenient landfall signifying to relieved mariners that they were about to begin the final leg of their voyage to Batavia. Lacking adequate navigation aids, many vessels were wrecked when they unexpectedly came upon the coast and with each loss the company generally warned masters to avoid the area. For example, when *Batavia*, carrying passengers and bullion, was wrecked on the Abrolhos islands in 1629 and, during a five months' incarceration on the low, barren and rocky reefs, many passengers and crew were murdered by mutineers, the company instructed its captains to avoid the area.[35] At one time the rugged cliffs of Shark Bay, and at another the North West Cape, proved to be reasonably safe landfalls. Both were high and therefore visible well out to sea and, unlike the ocean off Geraldton (lat. 28° 46') and Fremantle (31° 57') were not obstructed by offshore reefs.

Eager to reach Batavia as quickly as possible and discharge their cargoes, not many masters loitered on the Western Australian coast and even fewer went ashore. Those who did were generally searching for survivors from lost vessels. Being mariners, not scientists, their observations on Aborigines, flora and fauna were at best superficial and invariably misleading. Thus on the basis of information accumulated by the Dutch East India Company during the seventeenth and early eighteenth centuries, very few officials recommended that the land should be claimed and settled. In addition to their disappointment at the scarcity of edible provisions, mariners were often repelled by the appearance and warlike attitudes of the Aborigines they encountered, especially those met on the northern and north-western coasts. Tasman's instructions reflected the experience of many Dutch traders: Aborigines were to be treated with kindness and caution, 'seeing that it is well known that the Southern regions are peopled by fierce savages'.[36] Perhaps if Aborigines had revealed traits similar to the Javanese, the Dutch might have been more persistent.

The coast from the Abrolhos islands to the Kimberleys became familiar to Dutch mariners because it was on their track to Batavia. The southern coast was not, although the Dutch no doubt realized that the colder southern climate would probably contain richer vegetation and possibly an array of edible foods not found on the north-western coast. Soon after Dirck Hartog discovered the western coast in 1616, the vessel *Leeuwin* (master unknown) discovered the south-west tip of the continent. He had probably miscalculated his easting and although officials were annoyed that his voyage took so long, they nonetheless were interested in his discovery.[37] Five years later (1626), Frans Thyssen in *'t Gulden Zeepaerdt* (Golden Seahorse) accidentally discovered and explored the south coast east of Cape Leeuwin. Reaching the Cape in January, he sailed eastwards along the southern coast for over 1600 km, naming the landmass Nuytsland in honour of the company official aboard his vessel.[38] His report was clearly more favourable concerning the potential of what he had seen than the reports of masters who had visited the north-western coast; and many years later Joan Pieter Purry, at one time a servant of the company, published a book in which he recommended the establishment there of a Dutch settlement (Fig. 1.6). The climate was favourable, he wrote, Javanese labour could be used to cultivate crops; gold and silver might be discovered and, most important, annexa-

AANMERKINGEN;

Betreffende de Kuſt der

KAFFERS,

En het Landt van

PIETER NUYTS:

Ten opzigte van de nuttigheit, die de
OOSTINDISCHE COMPAGNIE,
van dezelve voor haaren Koophan-
del zoude konnen trekken.

t'A M S T E R D A M,
By R. en G. WETSTEIN, 1718.

Fig. 1.6 Title page of Purry's publication recommending establishment of a Dutch settlement on the south coast of Western Australia

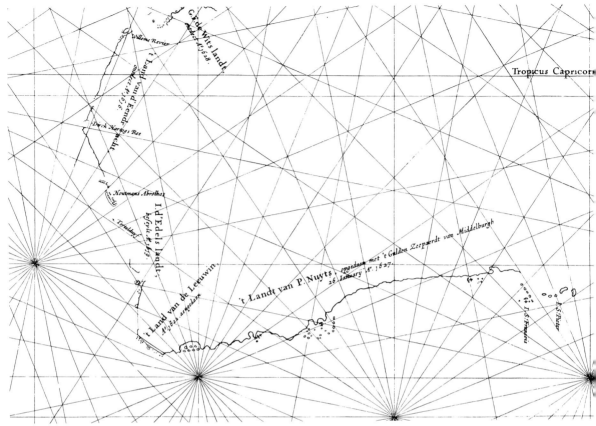

Fig. 1.7 The Gerritsz map of 1628

tion would forestall emerging French and British ambitions for the area.[39] Purry had revealed uncanny perception but the company was not convinced and his plan for settlement of the southern coast came to nought.

By 1628, therefore, the shape and dimensions of present-day Western Australia were well known to the Dutch. In that year Hessel Gerritsz, chief cartographer of the V.O.C. (Dutch East India Company), drew a detailed map which incorporated information from charts and journals handed to the company by captains at the termination of their voyages. His map was updated and reproduced in 1628 (Fig. 1.7).[40] Then between 1642 and 1644 Abel Tasman, perhaps the best-known Dutch explorer of the Southland, circumnavigated the continent, though well clear of the coast for most of the voyage, and by touching the southern tip of Tasmania, delineated the continent's potential size (see Fig. 1.8). Making a continuous coastline from the 'small pieces' revealed by predecessors, he proved the continuity of the north-western side to 22°S (near North West Cape). The instructions for his 1644 voyage were to proceed southwards from Willem's River (probably the Ashburton) to the Abrolhos islands, recover lost treasure from the *Batavia* and then search the mainland for two survivors put ashore by Captain Pelsaert when he returned to the wreck with a rescue vessel in 1629. While there, he was to 'take possession of the land' by erecting a structure with an inscription declaring his 'fixed intention to send a body of men thither by the first opportunity to secure this property by founding a settlement there'.[41] It is not known whether Tasman fulfilled the instruction.

Until 1658 knowledge of the western coastline between the Abrolbos islands and Cape Leeuwin was fragmentary, mainly because it lay too far south to be an appropriate landfall, and it was known to contain dangerous reefs similar to those at Abrolhos. Knowledge increased in 1658 with the visit of the vessels *Waeckende Boey* (Watchful or Wakeful Buoy) and *Emeloort* (named after a fairy city of Emeloord at the bottom of the sea, whose bells are said to ring a warning when storms are nigh) in search of *Vergulde Draeck* (Gilt Dragon), which had been lost on the coast near 32°S. Instructed to rescue survivors and to salvage as much merchandise—especially coins—as possible, and to chart the coast carefully, the captains of these vessels were also instructed to find out whether the land was inhabited and, if so, to try and establish trade with Aborigines. They were also instructed to take formal possession of all the places they discovered. The vessels reached the coast in February 1658, having been separated on the voyage from Batavia, discovered wreckage of the *Vergulde Draeck* near Ledge Point (107 km north of Fremantle) and made contact with a small group of Aborigines. Again, it is not certain whether the land sighted was claimed; and although the expedition did not find any survivors, at least the *Vergulde Draeck's* fate was confirmed. The captains' reports also confirmed that land in the region of Rottnest Island was no more hospitable than the coast further north, and that reefs were a hazard for vessels that came close inshore.[42]

The possibility that land near 30°-32°S might be suitable for a settlement nonetheless persisted in official minds during the remainder of the seventeenth century. With the loss of the vessel *Ridderschap van Hollandt* between the Cape of Good Hope and Batavia in 1694, it was decided to send three vessels to search for survivors on the islands of St Paul and Amsterdam in the southern Indian Ocean and along the coast north from Rottnest Island, and at the same time to assess the area's agricultural potential. Willem de Vlamingh reached Rottnest Island in *Geelvinck* in December 1696. Parties landed on the mainland a few miles north of the entrance to Swan River and trekked eastwards in mid-summer heat, across sand-dunes, limestone outcrops and scrub, to what they first thought was a salt lake. Vlamingh was not impressed with the area; it contained no good country and the coast for hundreds of miles northwards was bare and desolate.[43]

Though Dutch vessels continued to use the safer parts of the western coast as a landfall, nothing more was discovered to make company officials change their minds concerning the suitability of any part for European settlement. Thus, after more than a century of contact, the Dutch forsook the opportunity to claim the western side, perhaps the whole, of what A. D. Hope has called the last of lands.[44] Their lack of interest had been caused by a number of reasons: monotonous and inhospitable landscape; lack of water and vegetables; dangerous maritime reefs, which had caused the loss of many passengers, crew and cargo; the absence of precious

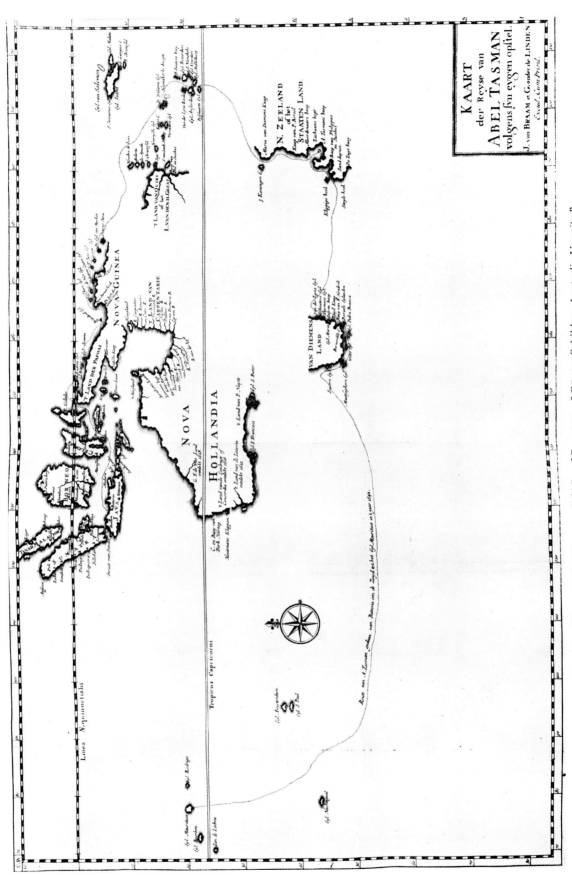

Fig. 1.8 Chart of Abel Tasman (1644).   [Courtesy of Günter Schilder, *Australia Unveiled*]

metals and gems; the general aloofness and occasional hostility of nomadic Aborigines, who were never considered potential workers for Dutch outposts; and the absence of strategic and military reasons for annexing the coast ahead of rivals.

V

French and British interest in Western Australia began seriously in the eighteenth century, although even before a southern continent had been discovered by Europeans, some Frenchmen were convinced that one existed. In 1503-04 the French explorer de Gonneville, blown off course in a storm near the Cape of Good Hope, took refuge in a land which he described as fertile and inhabited by hospitable people.[45] For centuries afterwards Frenchmen seemed to be obsessed with the desire to rediscover de Gonneville land. Some had already concluded that the arid western coast of the southern continent could not be the place described by de Gonneville. Others still supported the medieval theory that a southern continent had to exist in order to 'balance' land in the northern hemisphere.[46]

Thus, in 1738 the French sent de Lozier Bouvet, a navigator and colonial governor, to explore southern lands further, his secret instruction being to discover Austral lands and to survey and take possession of all places he considered suitable for settlement. Though Bouvet was not successful, Spate is of the opinion that his significance as a maritime explorer has been seriously underestimated. He foreshadowed Cook and was his equal as an explorer if not as an achiever.[47] Then in 1772, following a resurgence of French interest in southern seas, an expedition in two vessels under Kerguelen set out from the Ile de France (Mauritius) to search for de Gonneville land. On reaching land far to the south-east of the Cape of Good Hope, Kerguelen thought he had found the missing continent.[48] Before hurrying back to France to report his exciting discovery, and in accordance with instructions, he despatched the second vessel of his expedition, *Gros Venture*, under the command of St Allouarn, eastwards across the Indian Ocean to the southern continent just to make sure that no further land lay between the two 'continents'. St Allouarn reached Cape Leeuwin on 17 March 1772, where he tried, but failed, to go ashore. On his voyage north along the coast he probably sighted Garden Island, sailed on to Shark Bay, where on March 29, at Dirk Hartog Island, he took possession for France of 'the land to the north-west' of their anchorage (Fig. 1.9). Too ill to take part in the ceremony, St Allouarn died soon after. His annexation aroused little interest in Paris, where debate still raged over the genuineness of Kerguelen's discovery.[49] In fact, Kerguelen had discovered only an island (which still bears his name) and after an official inquiry was imprisoned for his deception. Thereafter, the French appeared to lose interest in trying to rediscover de Gonneville land.

Despite Britain's long-standing interest in southern lands, lack of funds and sea power prevented her from mounting long-distance explorations. However, in 1688 a British adventurer named William Dampier visited the north-western coast of Australia. His reports led to a government-sponsored expedition being sent there in 1699 under his leadership. Dampier's journals did not encourage the government to

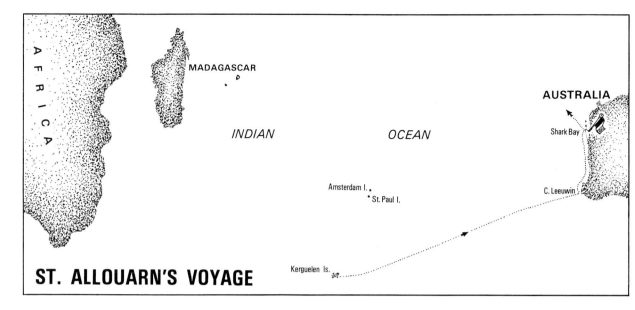

ST. ALLOUARN'S VOYAGE

Fig. 1.9 The route taken by St Allouarn, 1772

Above: St Allouarn sailed *Gros Venture* from Kerguelen Is. to Cape Leeuwin, thence to Shark Bay

Right: A facsimile of Rosily's chart of Shark Bay, dated 1 April 1772, showing where the French flag was raised and the land claimed for France. A party landed at the northern end of Dirk Hartog Island (A), where possession was taken of 'The land to the northwest' of their anchorage. St Allouarn then investigated waters between Bernier and Dorre islands (C) and the mainland (D) before leaving the continent for France

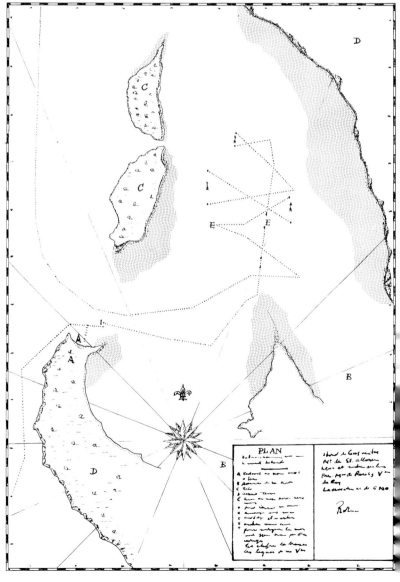

make any further exploration, although literary and scientific circles in England were especially interested in what he had recorded. At the time, England was involved in the wars of Spanish Succession and it was not until the mid-eighteenth century that interest in southern lands was reactivated. This was not because the French had claimed to have rediscovered de Gonneville land, nor because St Allouarn had claimed part of the western coast of the Southland for France, but because of James Cook's 'discovery' of the eastern coast of the Southland, although for some time it was uncertain whether Cook had discovered the eastern side of a *second* continent, separated from the western coast of the Dutch by a channel—an idea that had been put forward by many geographers following Tasman's voyage of circumnavigation in 1644.[50]

For sixty years after Cook's discovery, French and British explorers visited the western coast in 'pairs', a situation not entirely coincidental. Both nations were at war for much of the period and even when the Napoleonic Wars ended in 1815, each nation remained understandably suspicious of the other's motives and intentions for the area, especially its unclaimed parts. Eighteen years after Cook, the British government established a convict settlement at Port Jackson. This gave a new importance to the south-western coast because vessels of supply were obliged to sail near its shores on their voyages from England. When the new settlement at Port Jackson was but a year old, and experiencing unexpected difficulties, it was visited by La Pérouse, the great French explorer of the Pacific. After leaving the colony to continue his exploration, La Pérouse was never seen again by Europeans.[51] His disappearance was deeply felt in France and several expeditions were sent out to find him. The first was led by Bruny D'Entrecasteaux, ex-governor of Ile de France and probably the most experienced French captain in far eastern navigation. In addition to this central objective, D'Entrecasteaux was also instructed not to ignore the possibility that de Gonneville land, despite the débâcle caused by Kerguelen, might yet exist in the southern Indian Ocean. In the vessels *Recherche* and *L'Espérance*, not good seaworthy craft but the best available, the expedition reached Cape Leeuwin on 5 December 1792. Though essentially scientific in objective, the expedition was instructed to survey the southern coast east of Cape Leeuwin as if it were 'discovering it for the first time', and to find out what was produced and how it compared with American regions in the same latitude (Fig. 1.10).[52] D'Entrecasteaux was well aware that the southern coast was the most important tract of unexplored territory known to exist in the south seas. On his eastward exploration he was unable to enter King George Sound but sighted Cape Riche, the Recherche archipelago and Esperance bay, where he landed. Constantly sailing against strong easterly winds, and unable to find adequate supplies of water, he soon concluded that the coast was unattractive and was therefore not surprised that Nuyts (on Thyssen's 1627 expedition) had given no details of it, 'the aspect of which is so uniform that the most fertile imagination could find nothing to say about it'.[53] When water became critically short, and there seemed to be no likelihood of finding a safe anchorage, he terminated his coastal exploration and on 3 January 1793 headed for Van Diemen's Land. In less than a month D'Entrecasteaux had explored 1450 km of the southern

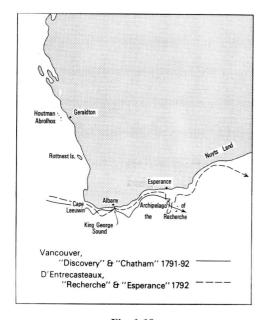

Fig. 1.10

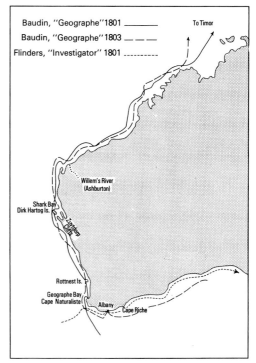

Fig. 1.11

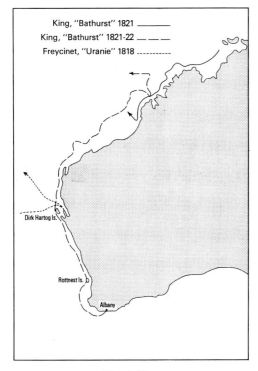

Fig. 1.12

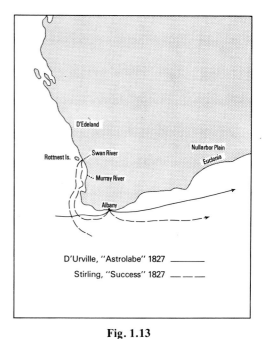

Fig. 1.13

Figs 1.10-1.13 Coincidal French and British exploration of Western Australia

coast. Had he continued, as planned, he would have discovered the strait which separates the continent from Van Diemen's Land. In fact, he predicted its existence[54] and this was verified a few years later by the English explorers Bass and Flinders. Though D'Entrecasteaux failed to find any sign of La Pérouse, either on the Australian coast or in the Pacific, his scientific achievements on the voyage were considered significant.

. D'Entrecasteaux's British counterpart on the southern coast was George Vancouver, who, on his way to explore the north-western coast of America, decided to investigate the south-western corner of the Australian continent rather than by-pass it.[55] Perhaps luckier than his predecessors, Vancouver was able to enter what they had missed—a magnificent harbour, which he promptly named King George the Third Sound in honour of his sovereign. He also took possession of the land seen 'north-westward of cape Chatham, so far as we might explore its coasts'.[56] During his two weeks' stay at the Sound he explored and named surrounding bays and islands, and made short inland explorations, from which he concluded that only some of the rather scrubby land was suitable for agriculture.[57] Vancouver's detailed charts of the coast eastward to Termination Island (long. 121° 52'), where he left the coast, were of great value to British mariners who followed him. But more important was his discovery of King George Sound (Plate 1.4), a harbour with great potential not only as a base from which shipping bound for the eastern colonies could be protected, but as a source of supplies. Until his discovery, no other part of the western coast offered such a safe anchorage, ample supplies of food, fresh water, timber and some agricultural potential.

Nearly a decade was to pass before French and English explorers visited the western coast again. Strongly supported by the influential Joseph Banks, who had been with Cook at Botany Bay,[58] Matthew Flinders's voyage to the antipodes in *Investigator* was motivated as much by Britain's concern to protect her trade as by her interest in scientific discoveries. The British government had been especially troubled by news that the French had already sent an expedition to the region under the command of Nicolas Baudin, ostensibly for scientific purposes but with other motives in mind—a reasonable suspicion, since the two countries were still at war.[59] Indeed, the powerful British East India Company had told the government that a French base on the western side of New Holland, if established, would menace their trade in the area.[60] Having already been to Port Jackson on an earlier voyage, Flinders was well aware of the political issues, especially the significance of a foreign base on the western coast for the defence of shipping bound for Port Jackson. He was also aware of the widely held hypothesis that Australia could be two continents, the eastern and western coasts separated by a north-south channel, and that this could be verified only by careful exploration of the entire southern coast.[61]

Investigator sailed from England during July 1801, about two months after the Baudin expedition reached Cape Leeuwin. With Vancouver's charts to guide him, Flinders found King George Sound where he stayed a month making observations, exploring the hinterland and making friendly contact with Aborigines. He confirmed Vancouver's view that there was not much potential for extensive agriculture

Pl. 1.4 View from the anchorage in King George Sound, by J. Sykes, midshipman on Vancouver's expedition. [Produced from one of Sykes's paintings, with the sanction of the Controllor, H.M. Stationery Office, and of the Hydrographer of the Navy]

although fresh water, timber and seafood—indispensable for seamen whose previous port of call would often have been two months earlier—were there in abundance.[62] Sailing eastward in the wake of Thyssen and D'Entrecasteaux, Flinders charted the coast with great care. A superb navigator, he was determined to make his survey so complete that there would be little else for others to do. Taking *Investigator* so close inshore that 'breaking water on the shore should be visible from the ship's deck . . . and no river or opening could escape being seen', he concluded that the land he saw was not suitable for settlement and that a channel did not separate the eastern and western sides of the continent.[63] In a voyage full of incident, perhaps the most remarkable was his meeting with Baudin at Encounter Bay on the southern coast. Both men were respectful, but suspicious, of the other, and for good reason.

The motives of the French in mounting the Baudin expedition were unclear at the time mainly because the nation was still at war with Britain and secrecy was an official byword; 'mistrust and suspicion poisoned all fields of human endeavour'.[64] There can be no doubt, however, that the gathering of scientific information was a major objective. One of the best-equipped expeditions ever to leave France, it included a team of scientists carefully chosen on the basis of achievement and promise and representing all the significant professions of the day. But there was also much talk of commerce and settlement. The Institut National considered that the results of the expedition would have scientific as well as political interest, thus inferring that parts of the unclaimed continent could be suitable for a French settlement—a remark made to Napoleon in the hope of gaining his favour and support.[65]

Instructed to explore all parts of the continent, Baudin was to give special attention to the south-western coast between Cape Leeuwin and Swan River, which, it was noted, 'has not yet been examined; and it is one of the parts of this coast . . . which demands to be investigated'.[66] The French were well aware of Vlamingh's discoveries, and Baudin was given St Allouarn's charts to guide him along the south-western coast. Shark Bay, on the basis of existing knowledge, also merited 'examination in some detail, at least with respect to the anchorage, because it is the only bay in this area which appears to offer some shelter for ships'.[67] In two vessels, *Géographe* and *Naturaliste*, the expedition sighted Cape Leeuwin on 17 May 1801, sailed north for about 100 km and rounded a cape which they named Naturaliste, and entered a bay which they named Geographe, where, much to the scientists' delight, several days were spent ashore exploring, collecting samples, sketching, observing Aborigines and investigating their huts and sacred grounds.[68] Although the vessels left Geographe Bay together for Rottnest Island, only *Naturaliste* anchored there. *Géographe*, with Baudin abroad, sailed close to the island, but as the winter sea was very rough, he decided to continue northwards rather than risk shipwreck on uncharted reefs surrounding the island. The enforced stay there by *Naturaliste*'s crew and scientists was not a happy one. Boats were lost in trying to land on the islands, some men became ill after eating what they thought were walnuts, and there was unanimity concerning the danger of surrounding reefs. Nor was their six-day expedition up the 'river of Swans . . . discovered in 1697, by Vlamingh' very rewarding.[69] They spent much time and effort pushing their boat across the bar at the river's mouth and across mud flats further up river. The report of this expedition by Joseph Bailly, the mineralogist, makes no reference to the area's suitability for settlement, but it does warn of dangerous reefs and the inaccessibility of the river.

Baudin spent nearly four years on the Australian coast, during which the scientists made careful observations of the land and its people, before returning to Rottnest Island on his way back to France. On the basis of what he had been told by crew and scientists aboard *Naturaliste*, he did not bother to send a boat ashore on the mainland, declaring that it was 'not worth the trouble of stopping there'. Thus when Baudin finally left the area for France—sadly never to reach it—he too warned of the dangerous reefs and declared that Swan River 'offers no resources at all'.[70] A great deal of scientific information was acquired and thousands of samples were collected and sketches made during this important expedition. However, great loss of life amongst scientists and crew owing mainly to scurvy and tropical diseases (one of which caused Baudin's death) and ill-will and lack of respect between Baudin and the scientists, seriously impeded *esprit de corps* and therefore achievement. When the vessels finally reached le Havre separately some four years after they had sailed midst a euphoria of expectation and excitement, there was little interest, and certainly not the excitement and anticipation normally accorded returning expeditions of discovery. François Péron, the naturalist (in collaboration with Charles-Alexandre Lesueur, the artist), and Louis de Freycinet, the sub-lieutenant, published books several years later which were of great interest to scientists, but the government of the day did not hear anything from members of the expedition to encourage them to send another vessel to claim for France any parts of the unclaimed western coast of the continent.[71]

Fourteen years later, Freycinet returned to 'complete unfinished scientific tasks' at Shark Bay.[72] By this time the Bourbons had been restored in France, the wars with Britain were over and Freycinet, with the backing of Louis XVIII and the Ministère de la Marine (the French equivalent of the Admiralty), was determined to restore his country's reputation for scientific discovery and, no doubt, provide his government with further information on the suitability of Shark Bay for settlement.[73] His explorations inland from Shark Bay were restricted by lack of food and water (Fig. 1.12), despite his success in distilling sea water into fresh (Plate 1.5). The bay itself was described by Freycinet's wife, who had stowed away on his vessel, as arid and miserable; threatening reefs discouraged visitors and the land was forbidding, desolate and 'a frightful abode!', judgements supported by others on the expedition.[74] Apparently there was again little official interest in Freycinet's discoveries. He only confirmed the west coast's unenviable reputation, which helped influence the British to avoid the area and establish a base later at King George Sound on the southern coast.[75]

Freycinet's British counterpart on the western coast was Phillip Parker King, son of a former governor of New South Wales and the first Australian-born maritime explorer. Like Flinders, he was a superb navigator and seaman. In *Mermaid*, and

Pl. 1.5 The camp of *Uranie* at Shark Bay, showing Louis de Freycinet's apparatus for distilling water (1817).   [Courtesy of National Library of Australia]

later *Bathurst*, vessels not much larger than modern ferries and much less comfortable, he spent more than three years exploring the Australian coast.[76] On his first visit to the south-western corner in 1819 he by-passed Swan River because sickness had reduced to four the number of crew able to keep watch. On his second visit in 1822 he spent some time at King George Sound, then sailed around Cape Leeuwin and, on the voyage to the by now much-visited Rottnest Island, confirmed French descriptions of a sandy coast with only slight vegetation. He too was not impressed by the island; unable (like the French) to find water there he declared that only Cunningham, the botanist, had derived any advantage from the visit.[77] Accepting (as had Baudin) Bailly's report that Swan River held nothing of importance, he did not land there. Noting the dangerous offshore reefs, he reassured British officials that the area held nothing worth the trouble and expense of annexing.[78] Perhaps the most important aspect of King's voyages concerning Swan River is that he was accompanied by the young Lieutenant John Septimus Roe, who was destined to play a major role in the administration of a colony established there by the British government seven years later.

VI

The final, and in many ways the most exciting—certainly the most crucial—phase of this saga of uninterest began in October 1826 with the arrival at King George Sound of the Frenchman, Dumont d'Urville, in *Astrolabe*. He had been sent to southern seas to confirm whether wreckage recently discovered at Vanikoro Island (Solomons group) was of La Pérouse's vessel. En route, he was to explore the southern Australian coastline, note good anchorages, collect scientific samples and make astronomical observations.[79] D'Urville spent eighteen days at King George Sound (Plate l.6), where he took on fresh water and made a careful assessment of its potential as a port before sailing on to Western Port (Victoria) and Port Jackson.[80]

On March 1 of the same year, Lord Bathurst of the Colonial Office in London wrote to Governor Darling of New South Wales reminding him that he had already

Pl. 1.6   Painting by de Sainson of a party from the d'Urville expedition taking on water at King George Sound (1826).   [Courtesy of Art Gallery of Western Australia]

sent him instructions to survey Western Port as a suitable site for a British settlement (Fig. 1.14). If Darling had already completed the survey, and the site was suitable, he was to despatch convicts there to clear the land in readiness for future settlers. Lord Bathurst's letter also instructed Governor Darling to take steps to procure accurate information on Shark Bay, if it should be thought advisable to establish a penal settlement there to which convicts 'whose offences might not require their rigorous confinement in Norfolk Island' might be sent.[81] Bathurst thought that if Shark Bay was a suitable site, then Moreton Bay (Queensland) could become a place for prisoners who had been convicted for the first time of offences in the settlement, and Port Macquarie, which was presently fulfilling that purpose, could be 'thrown open to general Colonisation' as had been suggested by Sir Thomas Brisbane in his despatch of 21 May 1825.[82]

What was the reason for Lord Bathurst's follow-up letter? Why the request for more information about Shark Bay when all that was known suggested that it would be an entirely unsatisfactory site for a penal settlement? Lord Bathurst's reasons were revealed in a private letter to Darling of the same date: 'The sailing of two French ships on a Voyage of discovery [*Thétis* and *Espérance*, commanded respectively by Bougainville and du Camper] have led to the consideration how far our distant possessions in the Australian Seas may be prejudiced by any designs which the French may entertain of establishing themselves in that quarter, and more especially on that part of the coast of New South Wales which has not as yet received any Colonists from this Country.'[83] The British-claimed part of the continent was specified as all land *east* of a line drawn at 129° longitude, i.e. the same longitude decided by Papal decree in the sixteenth century to separate Portuguese and Spanish territory.[84] Although Lord Bathurst thought that the western side of the continent was for the most part barren and that the French would therefore be unlikely to form an establishment on it, he was very concerned that they might encroach on the eastern side at Western Port unless his government established a settlement there (Fig. 1.14).[85] This was not the first time the French had shown interest in that part of the continent. When Baudin left Port Jackson in 1804, where he had stayed many months, the then governor (King) sent a vessel to trail him southwards with instructions to thwart attempts he might make to claim parts of Van Diemen's Land.[86] Once Bass and Flinders had confirmed that Van Diemen's Land was an island, Western Port assumed strategic significance as a base on the northern side of the strait from which shipping could be protected or, if the port fell into French hands, harassed.

Lord Bathurst's concern was not entirely misplaced. In November 1825 secret intelligence had revealed French intentions of forming a colony to which criminals might be sent. 'Several places have been under consideration . . . but the general opinion has been favourable to New Holland, both as regards the climate and the little opposition that is to [be] apprehended from the natives. ——'s opinion is asked as to the probability of England making any objections. Only a very small part of the country is occupied by England; and there is space enough for every state to send colonies without their interfering with each other.'[87] But the British were in no mood

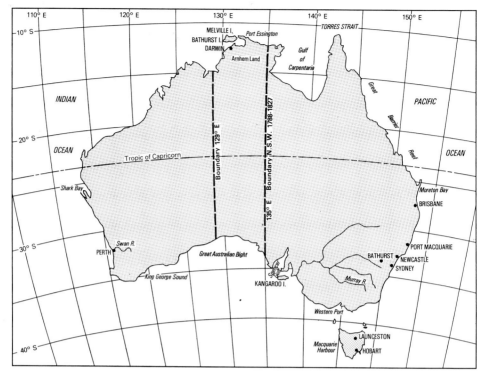

Fig. 1.14 Map of changing boundary of the Colony of New South Wales, 1788-1827.
[Redrawn from J. J. Eddy, *Britain and the Australian Colonies 1818-1831*]

to share the Australian continent with France. In addition to expressing his concern
that French vessels were cruising in Australian waters, Lord Bathurst pointed out to
Governor Darling that his letter (of 1 March 1826) had 'carefully avoided any expression which might be construed . . . as an admission of there not having been a
pre-occupancy by us, before the French may have attempted to establish themselves
there: and you will regulate your language accordingly.' In confirming British-
claimed parts of the continent (i.e. east of longitude 129°), Bathurst also wanted it
made quite clear to the French that the non-claimed parts were also British![88]

Bathurst's pen ran hot that month. On the eleventh he wrote again to Darling instructing him that, before making the survey of Shark Bay, he should survey the
land bordering King George Sound and, if the soil there was found to be good, and
if circumstances 'in other respects' were favourable, he was to establish a settlement
there first. Bathurst already had had second thoughts about the suitability of Shark
Bay, for he confessed that all information available (possibly including Freycinet's)
indicated that it was 'extremely barren'. King George Sound, on the other hand, in
addition to physical advantages, was on the track of vessels from England and thus
enjoyed an easy communication with Port Jackson, from where, presumably, it
would be governed.[89]

Governor Darling responded to Lord Bathurst's correspondence on October 10. In reporting on preparations already made for establishing a settlement at Western Port, he tried hard to discourage Lord Bathurst's plans for King George Sound and Shark Bay. The land around *both*, he argued, was 'perfectly barren and desolate of vegetation', and even if the French established settlements there they would find them difficult to maintain. Pointing out that settlements at both places would be difficult to govern from Sydney, he claimed that even King George Sound would be totally unfit for a settlement, even a penal settlement; that communications with Sydney would at all times be tedious and difficult, and during the months when contrary winds were strong, 'hardly practicable'. Shark Bay, he wrote, would be 'still more difficult' to govern.[90] It was therefore with great reluctance that Darling obeyed orders and made arrangements for the Sound to be examined.

During November 1826 preparations were under way in Sydney for the departure of *Fly, Amity* and *Dragon* to Western Port and King George Sound. Parties for each place would comprise two officers, eighteen rank-and-file and twenty convicts, with supplies sufficient for six months. Major Lockyer, the officer who would be in charge of King George Sound, had been instructed to make an early report so that Governor Darling could 'determine as to the expediency of establishing' a penal settlement there. In a private letter to Lord Bathurst, Darling reported having given instructions to both Lockyer and Captain S. Wright concerning British claims to the territory. Should they be questioned, presumably by the French, on the 'western Boundary of this Government', especially if it was pointed out that *published* maps were marked through the centre from north to south, and that Governor Darling's commission adopted that line as the western boundary, they should state that the British nevertheless have 'an indisputable right to the Sovereignity [*sic*] of the whole Territory'.[91]

Lockyer sailed for King George Sound in the brig *Amity* on 9 December 1826. His instructions concerning the stance to be taken if he met the 'French Discovery Ships' are worthing noting. If they called at the Sound he should 'be careful to regulate [his] language and Communications with the Officers, so as to avoid any expression of doubt of the whole of New Holland being considered within this Government, any division of it, which may be supposed to exist with the designation of New South Wales being merely ideal, and *intended only with a view of distinguishing the more settled part of the Country*' (our emphasis).[92]

Amity had been gone for less than a month when d'Urville's *Astrolabe*, not *Thétis* and *Espérance*, sailed into Port Jackson, having called at both King George Sound and Western Port. Although d'Urville insisted that his expedition had purely scientific objectives, there were many disbelievers in Sydney Town. Some claimed that the French had already raised their flag in both places,[93] and even Governor Darling, on being told by d'Urville that he intended proceeding to New Zealand, wrote the Colonial Office that he would not be surprised if the French intended establishing themselves in those islands. It is fortunate, noted the troubled Darling, that H.M. warships *Warspite, Success* and *Volaze* were at anchor in Sydney Cove (Plate 1.7) and that *Fly* had already left for King George Sound, 'as [d'Urville] may in Conse-

Pl. 1.7 Coming to anchor off Sydney Cove (1826). [Courtesy of Mitchell Library]

quence be more circumspect in his proceedings than he otherwise would have been'.[94] The commanding officer of *Success*, one of the three ships at anchor in Sydney Cove, was James Stirling, who had been sent from England with instructions to disestablish a British settlement at Melville Island in northern Australia and re-establish it at a more appropriate place in the same region.

During the Napoleonic Wars, which ended in 1815, Holland was cut off from her trading-posts in the East Indies and, as Blainey shows, actually lost Java and the Moluccas to the British, who were not slow to trade in goods which previously they could only do illicitly.[95] Cheap cotton goods and metal-ware, for which British manufacturers were renowned, were greatly demanded by natives. Then in 1819 Britain possessed Singapore, an ideal base for its commercial invasion of the Indies from the west. No such port existed at the eastern end of the islands, and the Australian mainland, already annexed as far west as 129°, was an ideal location for a port from which a commercial invasion could be mounted from that direction. As already noted (p. 9) northern Australian waters were rich in trepang, a small marine animal which had been harvested by Makassan fishermen since about 1700 and which yielded considerable revenue to Dutch traders when sold in China.[96] The British therefore decided to establish a trading-post at Melville Island in 1824 mainly in response to a convincing proposal articulated by a trader named William Barnes in a letter to Under-Secretary Horton of the Colonial Office on 15 September 1823. Such a post, argued Barnes, if established near the fishing-grounds, would supply island fishermen who stayed on the mainland for several months of the year with muskets, cutlery, white cloth and other necessities. The powerful Committee of Merchants trading to the East Indies had also been persuaded, partly by Phillip Parker King, who had visited northern waters during 1819-20, that the proposed settlement would be of great benefit to manufacturers in the United Kingdom, and if the settlement was also a military station, it would protect trade at a time when the retention of Singapore by the British was uncertain.

John Barrow, secretary of the Admiralty, gave the proposal his full and influential support, having also been persuaded by King.[97] Thus, during August 1824 Captain Gordon Bremer of H.M.S. *Tamar*, accompanied by a supply ship, left Sydney to establish a post at Port Essington (see Fig. 1.14). Finding no supplies of fresh water there he sailed further westward and established the post, serviced by convicts, at Fort Dundas on Melville Island.[98] Barrow was delighted. He claimed it would become another Singapore and suggested that it be colonized either by the government or by an association of individuals.[99] In May 1825 the Committee of Merchants even suggested that settlers enter the outpost and clear it for cultivation.[100] For reasons which seem obvious, the Melville Island settlement was never a success. Though its existence relied on the visit of fishing-fleets, it had been situated too far from the fishing-grounds and so not one sail was seen during the five years that a watch was manned at the port. The soldiers at Melville Island, notes Uren, had already experienced enough difficulties in the tropical climate to know that an agricultural settlement there could never succeed. Their reports of unfriendly natives, tropical diseases and the wreck or capture of the *Lady Nelson* sent from the island to

Timor for supplies, sealed the outpost's fate.[101] Before the Committee of Merchants' proposal could be acted upon, the British government decided to send an officer from England to find a more suitable location for the northern settlement.[102] Captain James Stirling had been chosen for the task.

2

James Stirling

In giving my opinion of the Land seen on the Banks of Swan River, I hesitate not in pronouncing it superior to any I ever saw in New South Wales east of the Blue Mountains, not only in its local character but in the many existing advantages, which it holds out to Settlers . . .

CHARLES FRASER

Naval links in the Stirling family were strong. James Stirling's maternal grandfather was an admiral and his uncle (Charles Stirling) a rear-admiral who, after James entered the Navy as a volunteer at age twelve, exercised considerable patronage which contributed to his nephew's rapid promotion.[1] Indeed, James's second posting was to H.M.S. *Hercules* in the West Indies, the vessel commanded by his uncle. This patronage was repeated several times during James's early career until Uncle Charles was prematurely relieved from the service following a court martial on charges of corrupt practices. James Stirling was only fourteen years of age when he tasted battle for the first time—against French and Spanish fleets off Cape Finisterre, three months before Trafalgar, a battle he missed because his ship had been sent elsewhere. He then saw action in South America, returned to England and served in the North Sea and Mediterranean, where, at age eighteen, he was promoted to the rank of lieutenant. His first permanent command (*Brazen*, a sloop of 28 guns) coincided with the outbreak of war in the United States in 1812. Under Stirling's command, *Brazen* successfully harassed both forts and shipping near the mouth of the Mississippi River.

While patronage had assisted Stirling's promotion, his successful tour in American waters, followed by service in North America, where he also protected British merchant shipping, and in the eastern Atlantic, stamped him as a naval officer worthy of promotion on the basis of efficiency and leadership. When war with France ended in 1815, his retirement from active service was inevitable. Three years later he was retired on half pay with the rank of captain, a status held for eight years during which (1823) he met and married sixteen-year-old Ellen, the daughter of James Mangles, high sheriff for Surrey and a director of the East India Company. The couple lived in Surrey for two years before James was recalled to the active list and given command of *Success*, a new vessel of 28 guns.[2]

Stirling was still a young man when he sailed from Portsmouth on 25 January 1826 with instructions first to take a supply of currency to Sydney and then sail north to disestablish the Melville Island garrison. The arrival of *Success* brought to three the number of British warships at anchor in Sydney Cove. Normally such an auspicious event in that small, remote British settlement would have been gaily celebrated, but the commodore, Sir James Brisbane, lay gravely ill; and even before his death an 'event of a different kind'—the arrival of *Astrolabe*, the French man-of-war commanded by d'Urville—caused Sydneysiders further concern.[3] While Stirling did not seem unduly disturbed by d'Urville's presence (he paid him a courtesy call and invited him to dine aboard *Success*), he was clearly very interested in the reasons why Governor Darling had sent expeditions to Western Port and King George Sound but not to Swan River.

For eight years James Stirling had been living close to his father-in-law, a director of a company holding far-reaching monopolistic powers over trade in the Indian Ocean. During this period they must have discussed the possible implications of the western part of the Australian continent being unclaimed, and that when it was claimed, Swan River would be the most likely place to establish a settlement. It is also likely that, on his long voyage to Australia, Stirling spent many hours thinking out a convincing case for visiting Swan River* while he was in Australian waters.[4] How else could he have devised and presented to Governor Darling a lucid and well-argued document proposing such a visit only six days after persuading the same governor that mid-summer was an inappropriate time to be disestablishing the settlement at Melville Island?[5] Within days of receiving Stirling's submission, Darling sent it to London with the covering note that, because Stirling had shown 'numerous and important' advantages of establishing a settlement on the west coast, he had given him permission to sail to Swan River and ascertain whether the region was as suitable as the proposal had led him to suppose.[6]

Why had the governor been so impressed? Because Stirling had cleverly argued his case on the basis of 'professional observation', and concluded that there was 'no position, *nautically considered* which presents such attractions' as Swan River (our italics),[7] a conclusion which Darling was unable, or unwilling, to dispute.[8] In arguing that the direction and velocity of winds in the Indian Ocean greatly favoured the establishment of a settlement on the western coast, Stirling only reaffirmed Hendrik Brouwer's discovery in 1610 that, by following prevailing westerly winds in high latitudes across that ocean, Dutch Indiamen would secure a quicker passage to the East Indies. Brouwer, however, had warned mariners that they must not sail too far west before turning north (one thousand Dutch miles was his estimate); Stirling showed that the same westerlies would carry vessels to the shore of New Holland and, at about 28° (near Geraldton), would unite with the south-east trades, thus assuring vessels which leave ports in this vicinity of fair winds and speedy voyages to ports in the northern Indian Ocean and beyond. Swan River was ideally located for vessels to take advantage of these prevailing winds. Aside from the advantage of being about three weeks 'closer' to Europe and Indian Ocean ports than Port Jackson, vessels bound from Swan River to Indian Ocean ports would take six weeks less than vessels bound from Port Jackson to the same ports. The reason was obvious

* By 'Swan River' we mean the islands, surrounding coast and river.

Pl. 2.1 Portrait of Captain James Stirling. [Courtesy of Mitchell Library]

Pl. 2.2 Engraving of General Sir Ralph Darling. [Courtesy of Mitchell Library]

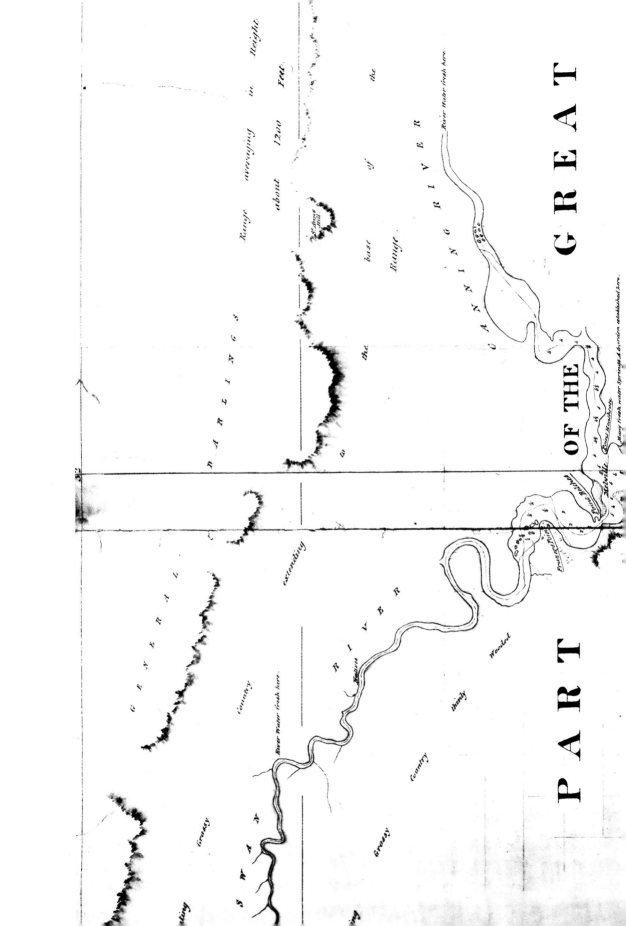

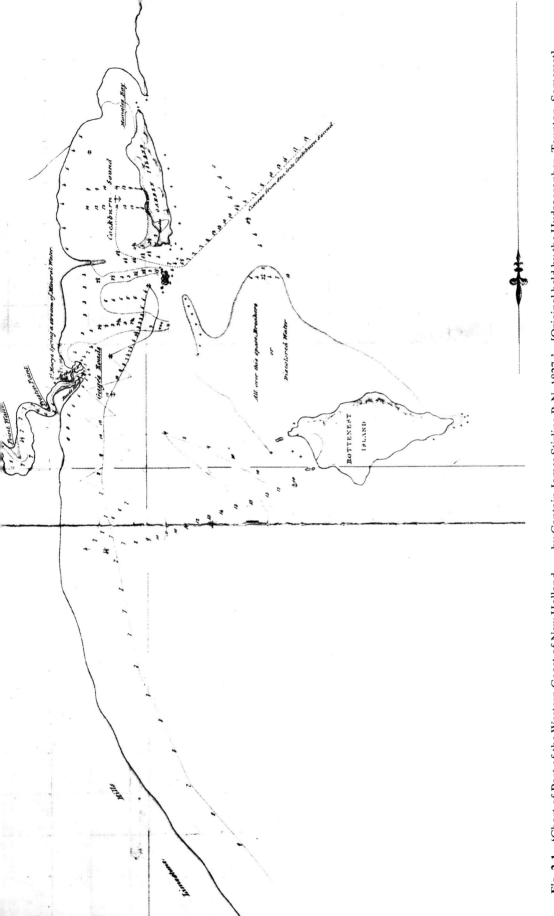

Fig. 2.1 'Chart of Part of the Western Coast of New Holland . . . by Captain James Stirling R.N. 1827.' [Original held by the Hydrographer, Taunton, Somerset]

enough. The same westerlies which brought vessels so quickly across the Southern Ocean also prevented their speedy return.[9] Indeed, wrote Stirling, for the greater part of the year (only January and February excepted), merchant vessels simply could not beat against strong westerly winds and lee currents in the Southern Ocean, a fact which Governor Darling had already warned the Colonial Office would make it difficult for him to supply the infant post at King George Sound.[10]

Because of its favourable location, a settlement at Swan River would, argued Stirling, have great advantages as a trading-post. For example, it was only a 'very little out of the Track of Ships bound to China, through the Eastern passages'.[11] The China tea-traders were lightly laden on their outward voyages because the Chinese had shown little interest in acquiring goods from Europe. Shipowners could therefore load their hatches with cargo for the proposed settlement at Swan River and in due course might find there articles suitable for the wants of the Chinese—oil, seal-skins, timber and trepang. Furthermore, crews would get much needed refreshments and rest after the long voyage. Shipowners would therefore obtain full cargoes for the entire voyage simply by making a slight detour from their normal tracks to include Swan River. Stirling omitted to mention, although Darling well knew, that most ships carrying convicts and stores to Port Jackson then sailed north as quickly as possible to China under charter to the East India Company.[12] A settlement at Swan River would simply 'capture' those China traders which took the Indian Ocean-eastern passage route.

Yet another advantage for a settlement at Swan River, argued Stirling, was that the generally fine weather and tranquil seas between it and India, Mauritius and the Malay Islands would allow small vessels to be used for trade—'an important advantage to a Young Colony where there is not Capital for the construction of large Ships'. He calculated that vessels could reach the Cape in six weeks and return in a month; reach Madras in three weeks and be back in a month; and reach Java in only ten days and be back in fourteen. These calculations were simply a preamble to Captain Stirling's trump card: the establishment of a naval and military station 'upon a grand scale' at Swan River to protect the colony and, more important, command India, the Malay Islands and all the settlements in New Holland. He carefully chose his justifying example: suppose an enemy fleet left Europe to attack the India station, it would sail down the western coast of Africa, round the Cape, go eastward to 80° longitude before hauling northward to India (see Fig. 2.2). If the British government, on hearing of the enemy fleet's departure, despatched a single vessel around the Cape and then eastward at high latitudes to Swan River, it could alert the fleet there, which, sailing on favourable winds, would encounter the enemy 'within a few days of its arrival in the Indian Seas'! The ensuing battle would presumedly see the British troops, fresh and vigorous after their sojourn at Swan River, victorious over the enemy troops debilitated by the long voyage and by scurvy.

Stirling set great store by the healthy and bracing climate at Swan River. Shark Bay, about 750 km to the north, which had been suggested as a possible site for settlement, was in Stirling's view much too hot for labour by Europeans; Swan

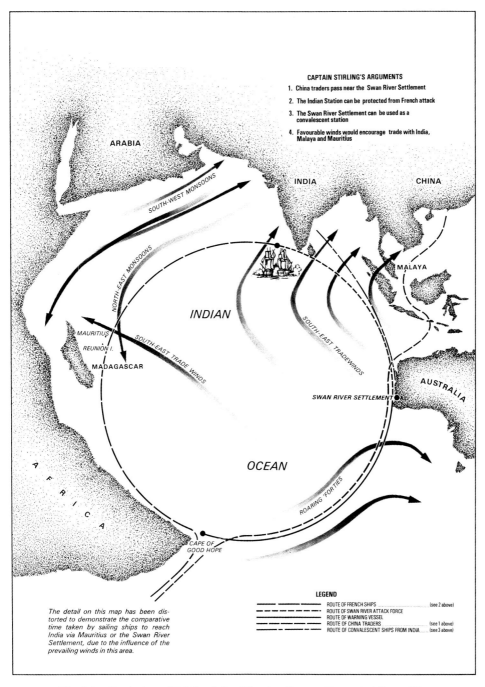

CAPTAIN STIRLING'S ARGUMENTS

1. China traders pass near the Swan River Settlement

2. The Indian Station can be protected from French attack

3. The Swan River Settlement can be used as a convalescent station

4. Favourable winds would encourage trade with India, Malaya and Mauritius

The detail on this map has been distorted to demonstrate the comparative time taken by sailing ships to reach India via Mauritius or the Swan River Settlement, due to the influence of the prevailing winds in this area.

LEGEND

ROUTE OF FRENCH SHIPS	(see 2 above)
ROUTE OF SWAN RIVER ATTACK FORCE	
ROUTE OF WARNING VESSEL	
ROUTE OF CHINA TRADERS	(see 1 above)
ROUTE OF CONVALESCENT SHIPS FROM INDIA	(see 3 above)

Fig. 2.2 Depiction of Stirling's justification for a settlement at Swan River

River, on the other hand, because of its favourable climate, would be an ideal convalescent station for troops stationed in India and for civil and military servants of the East India Company. If established, the convalescent station would render long and expensive voyages by sick Europeans from India to England unnecessary. The money spent at Swan River by convalescents would represent a source of income for free settlers and during the formative years Java or Timor could provide all the 'Necessaries of life'. The China traders would convey stores from England at a cheap rate and the troops at the naval and military station would provide adequate protection.

Stirling's observations on winds, currents and climate in the Indian Ocean were sound enough, although the manner in which he used these observations to justify the establishment of naval and convalescent stations at Swan River discounted wider economic and political issues. In arguing that because Swan River was on the same parallel as New South Wales it could be expected to produce grain for Mauritius, hemp for China and 'possibly coal and iron',[13] he ignored probable differences in climate, seasonal conditions, soils and geomorphology. Nor did he possess sufficient evidence to support the view that Swan River 'may hereafter be to the various Countries in India that which the Colonies in North America once were to the West Indian Settlements'. He did, however, admit that its 'soils and productions' were unknown, and as no British officer had yet explored the area, it was time one did. Finally, he sounded the note most likely to convince the worried governor: a French vessel of war was in Australian waters with objects not clearly understood, and an American vessel of war was seeking a place for settlement. Given its strategic location, and its assumed resources, Swan River was too important to fall into French or American hands.

Stirling had displayed fine capacity for clever argument. It was no wonder Governor Darling was impressed. In short, he had depicted Swan River as possessing all the ingredients necessary to become a major British settlement and naval station. A visit to the area could resolve the two unanswered questions: did it possess fertile soil and fresh water in sufficient quantities to support a settlement, and did it possess a safe anchorage for naval and merchant ships? Neither Vlamingh's nor Péron's journals (almost certainly read by Stirling)[14] suggested that he would reach affirmative answers.

His expedition left Port Jackson on 17 January 1827 and as if to underscore Governor Darling's warning to the Colonial Office that it would be difficult to service the new outpost at King George Sound from Port Jackson because of contrary winds in southern seas, the tender which accompanied *Success* and which had been equipped for coastal survey work and also carried provisions for King George Sound, was forced by heavy seas to turn back when south of Van Diemen's Land, leaving *Success* to make the journey alone. On rounding Leeuwin, Stirling's first sight of the western coast confirmed the reports of earlier navigators: 'the monotony of its outline, and the dusky hue of the meagre vegetation it supported' presented nothing attractive.[15]

They reached Rottnest Island on 5 March 1827 and would have gone directly to

Pl. 2.3   H.M.S. *Success* on Carnac Reef, 1830.   [Courtesy of Mitchell Library]

the mainland had strong breezes not forced them back to shelter about 2 km from the beach on the island's north-eastern shore. The next day Stirling again shaped his course for the mainland 'in anxious pursuit of the great object'—to find a safe anchorage—and brought *Success* to within a kilometre of the entrance to Swan River before moving away and dropping anchor further to the west-south-west (see Fig. 2.1). During these cautious manoeuvres he was relieved to discover that dark patches on the white sea bed were not rocks but seaweed. He was also relieved to find that the sea was free from coastal swell and that even a strong sea breeze caused only 'the slightest motion'. Prospects for finding a safe anchorage were encouraging but he was clearly apprehensive about prospects for his other objective—the barren downs immediately behind the mainland beach clearly bore marks of sterility so he decided to go ashore as soon as possible and find out what lay behind them. Before leaving, he instructed the master of *Success* to try and find a channel to the southward during his absence, for he had already resolved that it was the most likely place for a safe harbour. He then sailed his gig up-river for 8 to 10 km, apparently experiencing no difficulty in crossing the bar across the river's mouth, but recorded no observations on the landscape. On the master's return to *Success* his report on surrounding sandbanks and reefs encouraged Stirling to shift the vessel to what he deemed a safer, less exposed anchorage further westward. 'At Daybreak on the 7th we were accordingly on our way . . . . every precaution was adopted. An Officer, highly praiseworthy was sent ahead in a Boat; good leadsmen were in the Chains and the Ship's head directed towards the expected Channel' discovered by the master. Cautiously feeling his way through sandbanks and reefs, he brought *Success* close to

Carnac Island, where 'there were rocks and breakers which continued in succession as far as Rottnest, in short all around us rocks, Breakers or Land were visible in every point of the Compass'. Bailly, the mineralogist in *Géographe*, had made similar observations and concluded that all the islands from Cape Peron to Rottnest (including Carnac) were connected with reefs 'on which the sea breaks in many places [and] in some parts it is impossible for the smallest boat to find a passage'.

James Stirling was not a man to be deterred in his mission either by the reefs and banks surrounding *Success*, or by Bailly's warning. Even before the day was over he had taken a boat to Garden Island (see Fig. 2.1), where, between it and the main, he found and admired 'a Magnificent Sound'. Though yet to find a safe passage into it, he already knew he had found 'the great object' of his mission—the safe harbour necessary for Swan River to exploit its locational advantages. Anxious to reach his second objective, and satisfied that *Success* was anchored in perfect safety, he prepared to sail up the Swan River the following day. The party of eighteen in two boats, one of which took both Stirling and Charles Fraser (the colonial botanist from New South Wales), again apparently experienced no difficulty in crossing the bar at the river's mouth. 'The entrance', wrote Stirling, 'is flanked by two natural Piers or Heads.' The southern head (which he named Arthur Head, after the governor of Van Diemen's Land, who had accorded the expedition hospitality in Hobart), was 20 to 25 m high and obviously appeared to be an island, for he described it as 'connected with the Main Land by a Sandy isthmus bearing a Bay on each side'.

The aspect inside the heads was pleasant enough, but as the party moved up-river the banks became 'extremely beautiful and picturesque', enhanced by lofty trees and shrubs with 'bright green pendulous foliage'. In these idyllic surroundings they sailed on a favourable wind to Pt Belches (Mill Point), but beyond that point Stirling, like Heirisson of the French expedition before him, was soon grounded on the mud flats. The crew walked from shore to shore trying unsuccessfully to find a channel and then dragged their boats for 3 km until nightfall when, exhausted, and unable to find a camping-site, they spent the night in the boats stuck fast on the mud. The following day the gig was actually *carried* over the flats, although the cutter, despite the 'unremitting exertion' of crew from 5 A.M. to midnight, would not budge. The next day it too was carried 800 m downstream 'with the intention of sending her back' to the ship, but finding there a sandbank which provided better footing than the mud of the previous day, they steered her through the shoals to join the gig up-river. The discovery of a 'Spring of delicious Water' was especially welcomed after two days of such hard labour.

It was here that the party made their first contact with Aborigines. Three armed natives motioned to Fraser, alone in his boat about 90 m from the shore, to go away and despite Fraser's gestures of friendship and offering of gifts, 'they seemed angry at our invasion of their Territory, and by their violent gesture gave him reason to rejoice at the Space of water which divided them from the Boat'. Other European visitors to Swan River had seen evidence of habitation, and some thought they saw Aborigines on the river banks, but Fraser's was the first effective contact—an altercation during which Aborigines made a clear signal to the European interlopers that they were trespassing upon Aboriginal territory. Soon after, as the whole party was proceeding up-river from the flats, Stirling noticed two native boys 'peeping at us from behind trees', followed by others and then a whole tribe of thirty Aborigines. Stirling had decided beforehand that he would neither seek nor avoid contact, his objective being to prevent hostilities,

> for to approach a savage or to retire before him, I felt persuaded, would both produce the same results, in the one case leading him from fear to strike the first blow, and in the other, tempting him to make conquest of Enemies who, by retreating, exhibit symptoms of weakness and fear . . .

At first, the Aborigines on the river bank displayed great reserve but,

> as we made no Attempt to approach them, the Warriors followed us along the bank, the Women and Children retiring out of sight. The Woods now resounded with their Shouts, to which replied our Bugle with equal loudness and with more than equal melody. At this point, appearances wore a threatening aspect, for the Natives seemed much enraged, and I judged, from their violent gestures and the great noise they made, that we should shortly have a shower of spears. The River was here only 60 Yards across, and as they had the advantage of a bank 20 feet high, our situation put us much within reach of annoyance; we, however, pursued our course until the bank became nearly level with the Water, by which time they had assumed more confidence and began to mimic our Various expressions of 'How do you do?'; and at last we held up a Swan [shot earlier in the day] which seemed to amuse them, and, having cast it to them, they testified the greatest delight at the present; this led to an interview which proceeded upon amicable terms; we gave them various articles of Dress, a Corporal's Jacket, and three Swans, and received in return all their Spears and Womeras; at length we were forced to tear ourselves away, and they retired astonished at their acquisitions.

As the party sailed further up-river, Stirling noted how the sandy beaches and limestone cliffs of the coast had given way to flat, rushy shores and rising banks of grass and woodland. They sailed through 'a rich and romantic Country' and tied up near 'Steep red, brown and yellow Cliffs . . . and good red loam for their surface', from where parties sallied forth in various directions to explore the neighbourhood. Although away only two hours, the parties reported many traces of Aborigines and kangaroos, of prolific bird life and, most important, noted that the lower ground explored contained mostly 'deep dark coloured loam, devoid of clay or sand, and are usually clothed with grass'. For 25 km they sailed further on through open forest-like country resembling fields of grain because the high grass had been turned yellow by the sun. Throughout the following day (twelfth) there was little variation in soil and landscape until finally obstructions and shallow water prevented the boats from going further. If, before commencing the river expedition, Stirling had been satisfied that he had found his first object—a safe harbour—he had no doubt on the evening of the twelfth that he had also found his second: 'Here then on a high bank we pitched our Tent; the richness of the Soil, the bright foliage of the Shrubs, the

Pl. 2.4 'Swan River 50 Miles Up.' [A painting by J. W. Huggins, Marine Painter to His Majesty, from a drawing by J. R. Clause, surgeon on *Success*. Published as an engraving in the *Monthly Mirror* in 1829. Courtesy of National Library of Australia]

Pl. 2.5 Bivouac on the banks of Swan River. [Pencil & watercolour. Attributed to Frederick Garling. Courtesy of Art Gallery of W.A.]

Pl. 2.6 'View taken at the Commencement of the Freshwater—Swan River'. [Ink wash. Attributed to Frederick Garling. Courtesy of Art Gallery of W.A.]

Pl. 2.7 'View of the Flats, Swan River—Taken from Fraser's Point'. [Watercolour. Attributed to Frederick Garling. Courtesy of Art Gallery of W.A.]

Majesty of the surrounding Trees, the abrupt and red-coloured banks of the River occasionally seen, and the view of the blue summits of the Mountains, from which we were not far distant, made the scenery around this spot as bieutiful [*sic*] as anything of the kind I have ever witnessed.'

The next day, Stirling set off with a party towards the mountains. On top of a hill 11 km to the east he observed to the north, south and west 'an immense plain covered in general with Forest'. The following day (fourteenth), having returned to camp during the night, he divided the whole party into three expeditions. One, headed by Fraser, went eastward and reported finds of many 'curious and interesting' botanical specimens; another headed by Lieutenant Peter Belches and G. G. Heathcote, went northwards and found a 'considerable Lake of Fresh Water . . . near the foot of the Mountains'; Stirling's party travelled westward and found 'a bieutiful running brook, watering several hundred Acres of natural Meadow, covered even at this Season of the Year with rich, green, herbaceous grass'. Clearly confident that the vista of yesterday was no illusion, he planted seeds of various kinds including potatoes and peach trees on a tongue of land between the river and a creek, where there was 'rich soil of great depth'.

Having reached the date set for return (fifteenth), the party sorrowfully commenced the descent. Apparently having no trouble at the flats, they reached Pt Heathcote the following day, where they observed what the French had named *Entrée Moreau*, an 'Arm of the Sea [which] extended for 7 or 8 Miles to the S.S.E.' Belches was sent in the gig to explore the river (Canning), and on his return two days later, reported having followed it for 32 km. He found that it was fresh water and 'similar in every respect to the one we had just descended'. Towards evening on the eighteenth, the boats sailed down river and about midnight reached *Success*, having been away for ten days.

Before their departure, Stirling spent 'four days of exertion' exploring the channels and anchorages in and near Cockburn Sound and found all, or more than he could have wished. First and foremost, he discovered a channel of not less than 9 m from the open sea between Carnac and Garden islands into Cockburn Sound, the 'magnificent sound' he had discovered and admired before going on the mainland expedition. He also discovered a channel with a depth of 6 m from the ship's anchorage into Gage Roads (see Fig. 2.1), and explored the entrance to the Swan River[16] and the coasts and bays of Garden Island and the mainland. Before leaving—and as a seeming gesture of confidence that, on the basis of the very favourable report he intended making, the Colonial Office would soon establish a settlement at Swan River—he set free on Garden Island a cow, two ewes in lamb and three goats, 'where abundance of grass awaited them, and a large Pool of Water, which we had prepared for their use'. Thus, on March 21, fifteen days after he had reached the Swan River, James Stirling weighed anchor and sailed *Success* through the very channel into Gage Roads that he had discovered. Proceeding north for about 55 km he confirmed the reports made by the French and by King that the shore was sandy and sterile. Turning about, he sailed close to the shore after reaching Cape Bouvard, amazed at the regularity of soundings; at 48 km off shore, 55 m;

at 16 km, 27 m; at 3 km, 5 m—a gradation which was 'regulated with certainty and precision'—comments clearly directed to mariners who had been misled into believing that the coast there was unsafe.

Parties went ashore at Geographe Bay near where the French had landed in 1801. Stirling described the southern shores of the bay as flat and reckoned there to be swamps and lagoons behind the sandhills. Land to the eastward, however, looked very promising: undulating plain covered with large timber and stretching 80 km to the ranges. They found an anchorage on the western side of the bay secure from all winds except those from the north-north-west and north-east, and an abundance of timber and fresh water for ships. Indeed, at one spot, Belches found 'a source large enough to be called a River, gushing from the side of the Solid Limestone Rock and rushing to the Sea half a mile distant with a considerable noise'.

By March 25 Stirling, having stayed on the western coast to 'the very last day' of his orders, weighed anchor and set sail for King George Sound *en route* to Port Jackson. When he sailed into Port Jackson three months from the day he left, James Stirling had every reason to be immensely satisfied with his achievements. Not only could he confirm the favourable opinion he had formed of Swan River through 'professional observation', but he could also announce the discovery of a magnificent harbour and sufficient fertile soil to support a settlement. In his report to Governor Darling he wrote that the reported sterility of soil, the absence of fresh water and the impossibility of finding a safe anchorage on the western coast had been seen as 'unsurmountable objections' to its being settled. His exploration had shown this to be an inaccurate representation.

Much of Stirling's report on anchorages was devoted to those near Swan River simply because this was the area he considered most suitable for a settlement. The coast from Geographe Bay to Cape Bouvard contained anchorages suitable to the coasting trade; and Swan River and its environs contained several anchorages for large vessels. First, a 'good temporary anchorage' existed on the north-east side of Rottnest Island. Second, not far from the mouth of the Swan River was an 'excellent roadstead for Vessels of any Size, the Water is smooth, the bottom good, the depth from 3 to 12 fathoms, the communication with the Shore convenient and the access easy as well by night as day'. Though he realized that it was unprotected from winds from the north-north-west and west-north-west it was nonetheless an ideal anchorage, '. . . Superior in security to Table Bay [Cape Town] as well as in its closeness to the Shore, *and offering at all times facilities for landing or embarking*' (our italics). Further, he pointed out, just south of Arthur Head was a bay sheltered on all points, but unfortunately it had only 4 m of water and·was suitable only for small vessels.

But Stirling reserved his warmest accolades for Cockburn Sound and the passage into it of no less than 9 m. The Sound was deep (up to 27 m), the holding-ground good and clear and the anchorages protected from western and northerly winds by the island itself: 'I do not scruple to call it at all times perfectly Secure and available for Vessels of the greatest dimensions, as well as for any number of them.' He recognized that the distance from this Sound to Swan River was a distinct disadvantage for merchant ships with cargoes to deliver but expected that such vessels would anchor there only during north-west gales; '*at other times Gages Roads will be both safe and convenient*' (our italics). In time, the river itself would become the main anchorage for merchant shipping. The bar could be removed 'without difficulty or great expense', thus allowing vessels to sail only one or two kilometres inside to 'Natural Cliffs or Wharfs with 4, 5 and 6 fathoms close to their sides'. For several kilometres further on there was 9 to 15 m over a large expanse of water which, if it had an entrance, would become 'the first harbour in the World'. Furthermore, the river was 'tolerantly convenient' for navigation (his enthusiasm had been clearly dampened by experience at the 'flats') and could be rendered sufficient for the carriage of 'the products of an immense extent of Country'.

Although the country did not possess many spontaneous products of great value, its potential lay in what it *might* produce: cattle might graze on the abundance of natural grasses, and a shipbuilding industry flourish because of the variety and extent of timber. 'Situated in a Climate which admits of [European] Labour', wrote Stirling, and 'possessing great varieties of excellent Soil, well Watered by Springs, Creeks and refreshing Showers . . . it appears to hold out every attraction that a Country in a State of nature can possess.' Unwilling to specify exactly what might be cultivated at Swan River, he nonetheless noted its resemblance in all material points with that part of the states of America south of New York, thus implying some indication of its potential.[17] His observations on the soil and vegetation were confirmed, and no doubt influenced by Fraser the botanist who, in a separate report, wrote that although the white sand at the river entrance was sterile, inside the heads as far as Pelican Point, on the south side 'to the back Country as far as my observations led', the soil was at least two-thirds fine red loam of very considerable depth and capable of producing a garden and other light crops. Likewise on the northern side of the river. From 60 m inside the beach the soil changed to a fine brown loam, improving in quality until the hills were ascended, into a fine virgin earth capable of forming the finest compost. The small valleys, he wrote, were exceedingly fertile and capable of producing any crop. Eight kilometres east of the flats (Clause's Creek) the country changed to an 'extensive Plain of the richest description, consisting of an alluvial deposit, equalling in fertility those of the banks of the River Hawkesbury in New South Wales'. Beyond that, the country resembled the banks of rivers falling west of the Blue Mountains, varying alternatively on each bank from hilly promontories of red loam to extensive flats of the finest description. And as the river was ascended, the flats, which were several kilometres wide from the banks, increased in breadth to the base of the mountains. In summary, Fraser pronounced the land he had seen on the banks of the Swan River as superior to any he had ever seen in New South Wales east of the Blue Mountains, especially in the advantages it held out for settlers. The soil was superior, and because there were only an average 'ten trees to the acre', a settler could '*bring his Farm into a state of immediate culture*' (our italics). There was an abundance of springs producing water of the finest quality, and not only did the river provide carriage to the settlers' door, but there were also no impediments to land carriage. Stirling had indeed found a strong ally.

Stirling's observations on, and attitudes towards, Aborigines are also important. After making contact with about thirty on the upper reaches of the Swan River, one of his exploring parties in the hills then discovered deserted encampments which led Stirling to conclude that they frequented high ground only during winter; in summer they moved to the coast and engaged in fishing. They were active and handy in habit, and seemed to possess the qualities usually springing from such habits—bravery, vivacity and quickness, and temper alternating between kindness and ferocity. He vindicated his non-confrontation policy on grounds that retaliation would have come in the form of hostile action against future settlers, whereas his friendly actions had actually led to 'terms of amity with several Tribes'. But he also warned Governor Darling that while Aborigines might 'easily be attached to the interest and Persons of Settlers', care must be exercised because they are 'capricious and revengeful and always ready to resort to offensive measures'. His acknowledgement that the land belonged to the Aborigines was more than countered by the primary objective of his report—to recommend a European settlement at Swan River which Aborigines, inferior in arms and therefore unable to defend their rights, might help establish. Meantime, he believed that they viewed the European visitors simply as 'objects of new and excessive astonishment, and they were to us in some degree'.

Having shown that Swan River more than satisfied the two objects of his mission, Stirling then confirmed all the advantages he had claimed for it on the basis of professional observation. The China traders could now be assured of a safe and easily approachable anchorage for the greater part of the year and, like vessels bound from England to New South Wales, could find refreshment and goods for trade. An easy and profitable interchange would develop between the settlement at Swan River and other ports in the Indian Ocean because of favourable winds. Many valuable lives would be preserved if the East India Company made Swan River the site of an extensive hospital for Europeans. Finally, and probably most important to James Stirling, his discovery of an excellent anchorage for ships of war made viable his proposal that a military and naval station be established on a grand scale. Cockburn Sound, he wrote, was superior in convenience and more than equal in safety to Spithead. But haste should be the byword. Being the only port between Cape Leeuwin and Shark Bay, Swan River was far too valuable to be left to the French who, on learning of his discoveries, would surely have their interest in it rekindled.

Major Lockyer had been sent to King George Sound (several weeks before Stirling had reached Port Jackson from England during late November 1826) with instructions to make an early report to Governor Darling so that he could decide on the 'expediency of establishing a penal settlement' there (see p. 33). Stirling's call at King George Sound on his return from Swan River during April 1827 provided Lockyer with the opportunity to return aboard *Success* to Port Jackson. Lockyer had anchored at the Sound on Christmas Day 1826 near where Flinders had anchored on his voyage of discovery. With the few who had preceded him, and the thousands who followed him, Lockyer was greatly impressed by the fine, near land-locked harbour protected from all winds and heavy seas.[18] Though less enthusiastic about the agricultural potential of the hinterland than was Stirling about Swan River, he nonetheless reported to Governor Darling that sealers had told him there was 'excellent soil' along the coast towards Geographe Bay. The potential of King George Sound, he wrote, lay in the whale and seal trade but unless the government in Sydney took measures to restrict seal traders, this industry would be 'irreparably injured if not altogether destroyed'. He therefore proposed that the establishment at King George Sound be authorized to control the killing of seals by exacting a bounty on each kill, thereby affording revenue for the government. And, with Stirling, he wrote enthusiastically about the potential of the whale industry along the coast, which not only abounded in sperm whales but also contained several places where ships of any size could anchor in safety. Also with Stirling, he stressed the Sound's strategic location and warned that if it fell into the hands of an enemy, British traders plying the southern route to Port Jackson and Van Diemen's Land would be intercepted and greatly annoyed by the enemy's vessels of war. Although Stirling and Lockyer no doubt worked on their reports to Governor Darling during the long voyage across the Bight, there is no record of discussion between them.[19] Each intended recommending the development of a different site and was therefore probably unwilling to discuss in detail his experiences and discoveries, much less divulge the content of his report.

During the several weeks Governor Darling spent studying the two reports before sending them to Lord Bathhurst at the Colonial Office, he almost certainly had discussions with each author. Although his covering letters[20] tend only to summarize the conclusions reached by each, there is no doubt where his preference lay. Although Lockyer had travelled 56 km from the Sound into the interior, the soil he traversed was 'unpromising, and holds out no inducement to settlers', whereas at Swan River the country was 'favourable for cultivation, the soil in general being excellent'. Furthermore, he agreed that Swan River was an ideal place to send invalids from India and, because of its favourable location, the passage would take only thirty days—advantages which could not be matched by King George Sound. Although he made no reference to the fine natural harbour at King George Sound—perhaps its greatest natural advantage—he referred to the 'commodious and magnificent basin' in the Swan River and regretted that the bar prevented entry. He made no judgement on the relative attractions of Cockburn Sound, Gage Roads and other anchorages, leaving nautical men to decide whether these compensated 'for the inconvenient nature of the river'. Finally, he informed Lord Bathurst that he had not given any attention to Lockyer's proposals for a whale fishery and the preservation of seals simply because he did not have the means 'of carrying into effect any measures which it might be expedient to adopt'.

In clearly favouring Swan River as the location of a settlement on the western side of the continent, Governor Darling took the opportunity to reaffirm the difficulties he had experienced in servicing King George Sound. He referred to a letter he had sent to Colonial Secretary Hay in which he showed that direct communication between Port Jackson and the Sound was open only from January to March and 'even then is attended with extreme difficulty and uncertainty'. Lockyer's brig *Amity* had to put into Port Dalrymple and then Hobart for repairs caused by heavy seas. And the 'remarkably fine schooner' accompanying *Success* lost her rudder during the early part of the voyage and took three months to return to Port Jackson. These unfortunate incidents forced him to send a supply ship to King George Sound via the northern route through Torres Strait, a voyage which he expected would take at least three months. King George Sound was not Governor Darling's favourite outpost. If Swan River became the main settlement on the western coast, it could be serviced directly from either England or India and, as Stirling had pointed out, trade with countries in the Indian Ocean. One suspects that these issues weighed heavily in the governor's preference for Swan River. Though he agreed with Lockyer that an enemy at King George Sound could disrupt British trade with the eastern colonies, Darling was more positive about the seriousness of a foreign power at Swan River. Stirling's professional observations, backed by on-site inspection, confirmed Swan River's strategic position and he fully supported Stirling's warning that if the report found its way into French hands, His Majesty's government, if it entertained any intention of forming a settlement there, should lose no time in taking the necessary steps.

Captain James Stirling certainly lost no time in taking steps to become formally associated with Swan River. Within a few weeks of his return to Port Jackson, he wrote directly to Lord Bathurst at the Colonial Office and, on the basis of his successful investigation on the western coast of New Holland, sought the honour of becoming its superintendent should an establishment be formed there.[21] His application was warmly supported by Governor Darling, who described him as a very zealous officer who, from his conduct and character, would be 'well qualified for the situation he is desirous of obtaining'.[22]

3

Swan River Observed

*All were very shy, the Men, the Birds, the Swans, the Brent-geese, the
Crammed-gees, the Cockatoos, the Parakeets etc. The best of it is that
no vermin are found here: but during the day one is terribly tormented
by the flies.*

UNKNOWN DIARIST WITH THE VLAMINGH
EXPEDITION TO SWAN RIVER, 1697

Officials of the day who read Stirling's report could have been forgiven for believing
that he had not really visited the Swan River area described by his predecessors.
Almost everything they had written was critical, at best negative, mainly because
their reasons for being there were entirely different from Stirling's. None was an enthusiastic embryonic colonizer; two of the three were Dutch skippers sent in the
seventeenth century to search for vessels known or thought to be lost in the area; and
even though each had been instructed to report on landscape and vegetation, they
had neither the professional training nor the interest to provide anything more than
amateur observations. Neither was accompanied by a Charles Fraser. Charting
dangerous offshore reefs and finding lost vessels and survivors were their prime objectives, and each was professionally trained to achieve these. The third pre-Stirling
visitor was the French scientific expedition led by Nicolas Baudin. While the many
scientists on board the two vessels *Géographe* and *Naturaliste* were concerned
primarily with collecting and describing fauna, flora and minerals and observing
Aborigines, it had been made quite clear to Baudin before he left France that 'commerce and settlement' should not be entirely excluded from his interests and objectives while on the south-western coast of the Southland.

I

First European knowledge of the Swan River area, though very sketchy, came as a
result of Frederik de Houtman's expedition to Batavia. Eleven vessels left the
Netherlands in 1618 but, as happened so often, they were separated on the outward
voyage. Two of the fleet, *Dordrecht* and *Amsterdam*, left the Cape of Good Hope
together and sighted the Southland on 19 July 1619 at 32° 20'. According to Houtman's report to the Chamber in Amsterdam, they 'tried to learn more about this
land which seemed to them to be fertile, but they could not make a landing because

R

2

RS

R

31

S

R

RS

7

ROTTNEST ISLAND
THOMSON BAY
PORPOISE BAY
STRAGGLER ROCKS

S

16

4

R

29

CARNAC ISLAND

CHALLENGER PASSAGE

5

R

S

R

GARDEN

FIVE

20

ISLAND

Maritime explorers prior to Charles
Fremantle—Volkerson (1658) Vlamingh
(1696-97), the French scientists (1801) and
Stirling (1827)—approached the continent
from north of Rottnest Island. Each was
apprehensive about reefs to the west of
the island, but even more apprehensive
concerning the broken water extending
southwards (The Stragglers, Carnac and
Garden Islands). Volkersen, who sailed
northwards close to the mainland
searching for the *Gilt Dragon* also saw
dangerous offshore reefs. (See his chart
Fig. 3.2.)
None was comfortable while sailing his
cumbersome vessel in these dangerous
and uncharted waters. But when they
sailed away, westward beyond Rottnest
across the continental shelf they were
greatly relieved both by the regularity of
soundings, the increasing depth and the
sandy bottom.

S

S

R

33

FATHOM

8

POINT PER(

S

R

17

BANK

ROCKY SHORE   RS
ROCKY BOTTOM   R
SANDY BOTTOM   S

DEPTHS IN METRES

Fig. 3.1   Coastal physiography and bathymetry in the vicinity of Swan Ri

RS

*sible landing place of
...mingh's party.*

GAGE ROADS

SWAN RIVER

BANK

ARTHURS HEAD

MELIA

2

13

...BURN

BANK

COOGEE

R

RS

S

7

SOUND

CLARENCE
Landing place of Peel's settlers

S

2

S

MANGLES   BAY

S

5

SHOALWATER

LAKE
RICHMOND

R

BAY

S

PENGUIN ISLAND

WARNBRO   SOUND

S

12

of the heavy surf'.[1] Ten days later, when they thought they were far away from land, they sighted it again at 29°32'. It was low lying and broken by reefs so they took care to avoid it. The coast was seen again further north so Houtman concluded in his report that it must have been the same land mass which Dirck Hartog in *Eendracht* had discovered in 1616 at 22°, 23° and 25° south. In other words, the coast extended from 22° to 32°. These discoveries by the masters of *Dordrecht* and *Amsterdam* were later included in the famous Gerritsz map of 1627 and 1628 (see Fig. 1.7), and the coast they had sighted was named d'Edels landt after Jacob Dedel, who was supercargo (company representative) on the *Amsterdam*. As already noted, the mainland near Dirk Hartog Island had been named Eendrachtland after Hartog's vessel.

Dedel confirmed Houtman's statement that the land they had sighted on 19 July 1619 was a steep coast covered with dunes and in the interior of even height. They tried hard to land but were prevented by steep cliffs. Further north, where the coast provided better opportunities for landing, they were prevented by rough seas. Dedel knew that his large vessel was not suited for dangerous near-shore exploration and recommended that the coast be explored 'at a more favourable time [of the year] and with smaller ships'.[2] They had not seen any signs of human life while close to shore. If their latitude reading was correct, the masters of *Dordrecht* and *Amsterdam* had sighted the coast just south of Rottnest Island, or the island itself, the first Europeans to do so. Dedel's description of it as a steep coast was not accurate, but 'covered with sand dunes' was. Houtman recommended that the islands and shoals at 28°46', which bear his name, and which were also seen by the masters of *Dordrecht* and *Amsterdam*, should be avoided and that masters should make their landfall at 26° or 27°, which was a much safer area.

II

The next recorded occasion on which Europeans saw the Swan River area, and the first on which they landed, was under vastly different and tragic circumstances. On 4 October 1655 the jacht *Vergulde Draeck* and two other vessels sailed from the Netherlands for the East Indies with cargo, coins and passengers.[3] Skippered by Pieter Albertsz, and on her second voyage, she reached the Cape of Good Hope on 9 March 1656, victualled, unloaded cargo and four days later sailed for Batavia. She never reached her destination. Obviously miscalculating his easting, and possibly latitude, Albertsz drove her onto a reef off the western coast of the Southland just north of Rottnest Island between Moore River and Ledge Point on the night of 28 April 1656 (see Fig. 3.1). Of the 193 complement, seventy-five struggled to the mainland, including Albertsz and Abraham Leeman van Santwitz (known as Leeman), the understeersman (second officer).[4]

On striking the reef *Vergulde Draeck* burst open and only a few provisions were saved. Passengers and crew who perished were either killed by the impact or drowned. When the survivors had gathered ashore Albertsz decided to send a party to Batavia in the one schuyt (small boat) which had been saved from the wreck to report the tragedy and ask for a rescue vessel to be sent. In deciding to send Leeman in charge of the party, and remain himself on the mainland, Albertz was probably influenced by what had happened to the passengers and crew of *Batavia*, wrecked under similar circumstances twenty-seven years earlier on the Abrolhos islands.[5] On that occasion François Pelsaert, the skipper, sailed the boat to Batavia but in his absence many surviving passengers and crew were murdered by mutineers before the rescue vessel, commanded by Pelsaert, could return to the scene.[6]

In a truly epic journey, Leeman and his crew reached Batavia on 7 June 1656. The governor-general of the company immediately summoned his council, which decided to send the *Witte Valck* (White Falcon) and the *Goede Hoop* (Good Hope), then cruising in Sunda Strait, to the wreck site and rescue all the survivors and as much cargo, cannons and coins as possible. The skippers were also ordered to 'explore the repeatedly visited coast of the Southland where the Draeck is . . . and perfectly chart all the corners, bends, bays, rocks, sandbanks and shallows, so that we can use that for the benefit of the Company's [East] Indian trade . . .'[7] Unfortunately, the vessels sailed down the western coast during winter. Storms drove them apart and the *Witte Valck* struck such heavy seas that her master did not dare take her close to the land. However, a party from *Goede Hoop* managed to land near the 'mentioned latitudes' and explore several kilometres inland. But they too were struck by tragedy. Three crew were lost in the bush and another eight who were sent ashore to find them never returned, their boat having been later found smashed to pieces on the beach.

The governor-general and councillors in Batavia then decided to order the Cape station to 'detour' a suitable vessel on its way to Batavia to search for the survivors. *Vinck* (Finch) was considered suitable; she was small, flat-bottomed and could sail close to the dangerous western coast in relative safety. Her skipper was instructed to make for 32° 3'S where,

> according to the charts, many shallows of 100, 80 and less fathoms are to be found, as well as dunish land with trees and bushes. From there, sailing along the shore by day and heaving to by night, you will keep a close watch for any signs of fires or such from those poor, miserable people (also for any remains of the wreck) in order to release them from their misery, and to bring them back to Batavia . . . be very careful in approaching this Southland, using proper seamanship, that is if weather and wind allow such and if it can be done without risk.[8]

Provided with what primitive charts were available, the skipper was advised

> strongly to always keep the lead in hand near this Southland and to look sharp for all such lands, shoals, rocks and shallows as are yet unknown or undiscovered, keeping good record and making accurate notes or charts to be used after this by other Company ships that could come upon that coast.

Enclosed with the official papers were letters which had been written by 'the lost people' on the coast (presumably these had been brought to Batavia by Leeman), so that during the voyage south the skipper, Joost Jansz, could read them and thereby 'realise the better their Honourables' order and seriousness'.[9] Unfortunately, these

Pl. 3.1   The Cape of Good Hope. Detail of a late seventeenth century Dutch engraving

letters have been lost, for they no doubt contained much information on both the wrecking of *Vergulde Draeck* and the fears and hopes of the survivors—the first letters written by Europeans from the Swan River area and possibly the first letters written in the entire continent.

Vinck sailed from the Cape on 27 April 1657 and anchored by a reef near the mainland at 29° 7' on June 8. For four days Jansz sailed close to the shore but the winter was too boisterous to send a party ashore. At daybreak on the morning after Jansz anchored, he saw breakers on the reef and, ahead of them, the Southland which 'there showed as a low-lying coast with dunes'. Weighing anchor, he sailed along the coast 'but the weather began to become so much worse and the breakers on the coast were so violent, that it was a fearful sight to behold'.[10] Seeing his chances of landing getting 'less and less' Jansz abandoned his plans to go ashore and sailed on to Batavia.

The experiences of the skippers of *Dordrecht, Amsterdam, Witte Valck, Goede Hoop* and now *Vinck* finally convinced Governor-General Maetsuyker that June and July were not the best months to mount a rescue of survivors on the Southland at 31-32°S. Still very concerned for the safety of survivors, the next expedition was mounted during the summer. Meantime, the Cape station was instructed to divert all small Batavia-bound vessels to the wreck site, and told that January to March are the best months, for 'except for that season, this coast is unapproachable because of the strong winds'.[11]

A few days before Christmas 1657, the governor-general and his councillors in Batavia resolved to send the fluit *Waeckende Boey* and the galjoort *Emeloort*, in search of survivors from *Vergulde Draeck* and the lost eleven crew of *Goede Hoop*.[12] Captains Samuel Volckertszoon (Volkersen) and Aucke Pieters Jonck, with crews of forty and twenty-five respectively, left Batavia on New Year's Day, 1658. Leeman, the survivor of the wreck, had been appointed uppersteersman of *Waeckende Boey*.[13] The company's orders to Volkersen made it quite clear that the officials were as concerned about obtaining as much information as possible on the Southland as that survivors be found and brought back. He was to give special attention to navigational hazards along the coast, surveying

> all capes, forelands, bights, islands, rocks, reefs, sandbanks, depths, shallows, roads, winds, currents and all that appertains to the same, so as to be able to map out and duly mark everything in its true latitude, longitude, bearings and conformation.

He was also to find out all he could about the mainland and its inhabitants:

> You will moreover go ashore in various places and diligently examine the coast in order to ascertain whether or not it is inhabited, the nature of the land and the people, their towns and inhabited villages, the division of their kingdoms, their religion and policy, their wars, their rivers, the shape of their vessels, their fisheries, commodities and manufactures, but *specifically* [our emphasis] to inform yourselves what minerals, such as gold, silver, tin, iron, lead and copper, what precious stones, pearls, vegetables, animals and fruits, these lands yield and produce.

And finally, he was ordered to take formal possession of 'all places, lands and islands', entering into and making

> covenants with all such kings and nations as you will happen to fall in with, and try to prevail upon them to place themselves under the protection of the States of the United Netherlands, of which covenants and alliances you will likewise cause proper documents to be drawn up and signed.[14]

The governor-general's expectations of the Southland had been clearly conditioned by his knowledge and experience of the Java milieu in which he lived, and not much influenced by what was already known. Yet he may well have argued that the descriptions brought back by survivors of *Batavia* did not apply to the mainland,

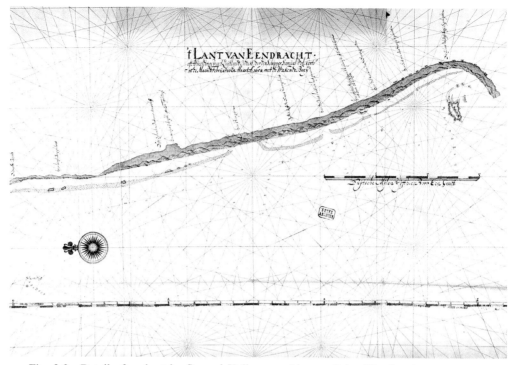

Fig. 3.2 Detail of a chart by Samuel Volkersen, skipper of the *Waeckende Boey* (1658), showing Rottnest Island and the spot where 'many signs of *Draeck* were found'. [Courtesy of Algemeen Rijksarchief, 's-Gravenhage]

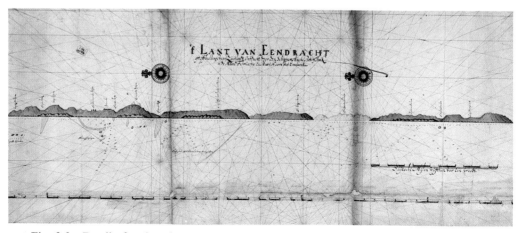

Fig. 3.3 Detail of a chart by Aucke Pieters Jonck, skipper of the *Emeloort*. Coast of the Southland north of Swan River. [Courtesy of Algemeen Rijksarchief, 's-Gravenhage]

especially further south, where the climate was more moderate and the likelihood of the kingdoms he envisaged being found was greater. The governor-general clearly wanted the land annexed to the Netherlands, no matter what Volkersen found there. He was therefore reminded, in no uncertain terms, that the company had invested heavily in the expedition and it wanted a careful record kept of all his actions and discoveries in order to 'obtain due and perfect knowledge of the situation and natural features of this region'.

Volkersen and Jonck were unequal to the task. From the start, they did not get on well together. *Emeloort* was a slower, less seaworthy vessel than *Waeckende Boey* and on the voyage south Volkersen recorded quite often in his journal the difficulties he was experiencing keeping the vessels together. Finally, on February 14 they parted company, Jonck believing that Volkersen had deliberately sailed away from him. Jonck appears to have been a cautious skipper, for he often headed out to sea and on only two occasions did he approach the shore and land boats.[15] Between them, however, Volkersen and Jonck provided important information of the south coast from as far south as 33° 20' (probably near Bunbury), where Jonck had touched and then sailed northwards. Volkersen touched the coast at Rottnest Island and continued his journey, and his charts to 23° 20'. They therefore met at least one of the governor-general's instructions. The charts they brought back were, for the time, accurate and detailed, special attention having been given to offshore reefs and landscape profiles (Figs 3.2 and 3.3).

It is to Volkersen, perhaps a more daring seaman than Jonck, that we are indebted for detailed descriptions of the Southland near the Swan River. It was sighted at 9 A.M. on 23 February 1658 at 31° 40'. Sailing past Rottnest Island and noting submerged reefs between it and the mainland, Volkersen lowered a boat which sailed to and fro along the shore. The following day they saw fires 'burning fiercely . . . [and] smoke rising in many places', which must have encouraged them to believe that they had been seen by survivors.[16] A party was sent ashore, and because of bad weather, could not return to the ship for two days. But when it did, Volkersen heard news he could not have expected so soon. The beach was littered with wreckage from the *Vergulde Draeck,*

> but no footpaths nor any place where people had lived, although they [the search party] had gone far and wide, both inland and along the beach. The remains of [*Vergulde Draeck* were] . . . a heavy beam, a piece of oak planking, a piece of the outer planking, a small keg, buckets, thwarts of the boat, pieces of chests, staves and similar rubbish.

But also signs that survivors had been there: 'a number of pieces of planking had been put up in a circle with their ends upwards'.[17]

Volkersen sailed north, presumably looking for signs of survivors, but to no avail. The weather was unusually bad for that time of the year; he lost an anchor and the barge he was towing. On seeing fires on land, and assuming that these had been lit by inhabitants 'as a signal', he sent a boat to investigate but 'tremendous surf and fast-increasing wind' prevented it from landing. That evening (February 27)

Emeloort was sighted, having sailed northwards along the coast from near Bunbury where she first sighted the Southland. There is no record of contact having been made by the two skippers, only a terse entry by Volkersen in his journal for March 2 that during the night *Emeloort* 'drifted away from us; wind blew strongly in heavy gusts'. Bad weather continued for fifteen days during which they kept well out to sea. On their return, *Waeckende Boey* anchored at the north-east corner of Rottnest Island. A boat was sent ashore and on its return the helmsman reported that he had found it difficult to land because 'all around, close to the shore, there were stone reefs'. The island was well wooded and they had seen two seals, a 'wild cat' and 'much rubbish from below the sea', information which did not encourage Volkersen to explore the island again.

From March 20 we have the diary of Abraham Leeman (the uppersteersman who had survived the wreck, sailed a boat to Batavia for help, and now was back to assist with rescue operations) to compare with Volkersen's rather terse daily journal.[18] Beginning with information that he had already been ashore four or five times, and that he was about to go again, Leeman then reported finding more wreckage. Believing that the circle of upturned planks on the beach might mark the resting-place of bodies or perhaps some of the coins from *Vergulde Draeck*, he ordered his sailors to dig a trench one or two metres deep inside the circle and then thrust their cutlasses as deep as they could into the sand. Nothing was discovered.

The following day, after further searching, a slight breeze arose from the south-south-west and, as the sea began to rise, Leeman decided to return to *Waeckende Boey*. Apparently three weeks earlier they had almost lost the boat when they tried to return to the ship in heavy seas, an experience which gained him Volkersen's severe criticism. On returning to the ship, Volkersen disputed with Leeman the impending storm and, according to Leeman, ordered him back to shore despite his request to come aboard:

> If I do get bad weather ashores [pleaded Leeman], where shall I find shelter, for there are neither islands nor coves; if I am washed ashore, I shall be killed, and I shall not be able to beat out to sea; also the water is dangerous, being full of rocks.

Volkersen was unmoved. Leeman pleaded again, this time to the secretary, but to no avail. It was a tough and ominous decision. In view of what later transpired, Volkersen's journal entry could well have been written *after* March 22.

> The boat arrived [with wreckage of small value] . . . and as it was nice, lovely weather, and it did not look like changing, have sent same [the boat] after putting provisions on again, ashore, where they arrived with the sun still in the sky . . .

Leeman's foreboding was well-founded. By nightfall a storm broke and the sea rose so high that Leeman and his men, unable to land, set sail and in darkness tried to ride it out. Volkersen confirmed its ferocity and now wished he had not sent the boat ashore. Well out to sea, away from the reefs, he

shot the cannon, lit a fire in order to make it easier for the boat to find us, if this
was at all possible. Thus remained 'riding' with great anxiety for the boat and
being in great danger of drifting against the reefs, until midnight, when the rope
broke, dropped another anchor . . .

The March storm worsened the following day. Leeman sailed the little boat as best
he could around the shoals but the wind

was so terrible that we could not bear it, our rudder broke loose and the top-
most pintle was dislodged from the sternpost and the bottom gudgeons were so
loose on the rudder that·we were in great trouble; took two oars on either side
of the boat to steer with, wind and sea still rising terribly . . . so that the crew
began to groan and cry, for we were shipping a great deal of water and could
not keep going much longer, fearing to be turned over with each wave. I, seeing
no chance on earth to find the ship, was forced to run before the wind and sea
at the mercy of God, so that we looked at each other very sadly. I said: 'Come,
let us trust in God and turn to him: we must die at sometime'. Each prepared
himself, for we saw nothing but death before us; we knelt down together, I
leading in prayer, and called upon God with full hearts, so that most of the crew
had tears running from their eyes.

Pl. 3.2 Typical coast where Leeman was wrecked. Hair seal on Fisherman's Island.
[Photo by R. E. Johnstone (1977)]

At mid-afternoon, seeing a small islet with grey sand between two rocks, Leeman
decided to try and land the boat, even though the sea was surging strongly, 'an awful
sight to see'. With little control over the boat, he made for the beach; the boat began
to fill with water but his men were so terrified that they would not man the bailers.

Sweeping through the surf out of control the boat crashed on to rocks and the crew 'tumbled overboard and made for the land [where] . . . overjoyed as if they had found a new life, dried themselves well'. That night they sat down to a meal of roasted seal and young sea-gulls which they had found on the small island.

Meantime, the crew of *Waeckende Boey*, riding out the storm in relative comfort, were extremely anxious for the safety of their shipmates. Volkersen thought they could not possibly have cleared the offshore reefs, so he called a council meeting to work out 'for the benefit of the East Indian Company and for the preservation of ship and lives', the best means of getting his vessel under sail in the 'most efficient way'. For the next four days he sailed on the open sea and then returned to the mainland 'close enough to the shore to be able to distinguish a man'. Cannons were fired during the night at the very spot where the boat had left them for the shore, but there was no response. Volkersen concluded that they must have been wrecked and so, after obtaining the agreement of others on board, he decided to sail back to Batavia. However, that evening (twenty-second), they saw a fire on land, close to shore. Volkersen's response, as recorded in his journal is difficult to understand. He assumed it had been

> lit by 'Christian' folk, either from the *Dragon* [*Vergulde Draeck*] or the *Hope [Goede Hoop]*. As the like of this fire had never been seen before, we discharged the cannon, upon which immediately another fire was seen close to the first.

But having no barge on board, and assuming that Leeman's boat had been wrecked, he could not go ashore to investigate. So, finding no suitable anchoring ground, he set a little sail and 'stayed in the vicinity and waited for daybreak', by which time the vessel had drifted well north of the spot where the land fires had been seen. Though he sailed towards the shore the next morning, Volkersen does not record specifically that he reached the spot. His journal simply records that he sailed past the shore and on the way found a reef and several islands, 'sometimes getting to within 2 or 2½ miles from the shore . . .' From a bearing of 29° 45' he sailed *northwards,* then out to sea until the plumb could not reach the bottom at 275 m. Several weeks later he reached Batavia.

During the four days that *Waeckende Boey* was riding out the storm, Leeman and his crew were doing all they could to repair their damaged boat. Constantly searching the western horizon for the sail of *Waeckende Boey*, they survived by killing more seals and gulls and drinking brackish water found in the rocks. A religious man, Leeman prayed every day for help and succour and made his crew do likewise. When the weather abated, they made their way cautiously through reefs to another island, where roasted seal and 'six pints' of brackish water 'tasted like a wedding-feast'. The next day they returned to the mainland near where wreckage of *Vergulde Draeck* littered the beach. But by now all of them were worried and desperate lest they be stranded there. Leeman was undisputed leader. Indeed, he lamented that consultation was pointless for 'they would do whatever I told them, so the cares were all mine'.

On the twenty-eighth, the crucial day when *Waeckende Boey* returned to the coast, they prayed as usual that a ship would find them and, miraculously,

> in the evening at sunset, a man who was on the lookout cried suddenly, 'A sail, a sail!', then we ran up the hill together, and I saw that this was true; had a fire lit at once, and set fire to a great many bushes so that it seemed that the entire island was on fire. I was glad as if we had found a new life.

Shortly afterwards, *Waeckende Boey* reduced sail, 'as if he was going to come to anchor', and fired a gun, to which Leeman's men responded by burning 'a terribly big fire', and walking along the beach waving large pieces of burning wood so that they could be seen more easily. They would have sailed their boat to the ship immediately but the sea was 'foaming everywhere', it was dark and they were afraid of running it on one of the many surrounding reefs. Instead, they decided to wait until morning. Watches were formed to keep the fires burning all night. But when the dawn of the fateful twenty-ninth broke *Waeckende Boey* was nowhere to be seen. They sailed their boat out to sea trying to find her but to no avail.

Returning to the island, the men 'groaning, complaining, cursing and pleading', soon lost heart and by April 1, recorded Leeman, so did he. But a lost heart is not the end, at least not to a man of Abraham Leeman's calibre. There was only one solution—to sail the boat back to Batavia. Despite his crew's reluctance, for their spirits were very low, he persuaded them to cut 60 cm stanchions from available timber and fit these to the gunwales, on which were patched seal skins to make the boat more comfortable for the long voyage on the open sea. For a week they worked, roping on the stanchions, cutting and fitting the skins, drying seal meat for the voyage ahead, sewing blankets to make a storm sail—always hoping that the ship would return. Leeman became very sick and could hardly walk and his crew brought him seal's meat for they were 'anxious about me lest I fell ill and died'. His final pre-departure act was to scratch a chart on the stern of the boat, 'putting in a piece of the Southland and of the land of Java, also made two pair of compasses out of wood . . .'

On the morning of 8 April 1658, after prayers, Leeman climbed a hill to see 'what would be our best way out', and in the boat which was still leaking badly, they felt their way along crags and rocks to the open sea where, from a spot about 107 km north of present-day Fremantle, began one of the most heroic sea voyages of all time. Matching in courage and seamanship the later, and now better known, small-boat voyages of Bligh and Mary Bryant,[19] Leeman sailed the leaky craft for twenty-one days along the barren western coast and across the Timor Sea to Java. The incredible fact is that he was making it for the second time! They went ashore where they could, dug for and found water, but when their flint was lost they could not make fire and so had to eat dried sealskins with some wild 'celery' that they collected ashore. Once they reached the high-cliff coastline, it was impossible to get ashore and their conditions deteriorated rapidly. Thirst was terrible.

> When one or the other wanted to urinate, he did this in the bailer or in a shell, let it sometimes stand a while to cool down and at once somebody else was at it

and drank it, so that they would fall into an argument over it . . . . Everything
was so miserable that it is hard to describe.

On April 19 one man who had been constantly calling for water died; they all
became so weak that it needed many hands to hoist and lower the mizzen. And when
they were still 160 km from Java their compass was accidentally smashed so, wrote
Leeman, 'at night I set a course by the stars, and just sailed on in the name of God'.
Two more men died of thirst before the coast of Java was sighted on the twenty-
ninth.

Their troubles, however, were far from over. Anchoring their boat close to a
beach, five of the crew somehow swam ashore, where they immediately drank their
fill of water and coconut milk, ignoring Leeman's call to bring some back to those
still on the boat. Even when he threatened to leave them there and sail on, they
would not come. The next day, in attempting to land the boat it was wrecked and the
party became separated. Intent on reaching Batavia as soon as possible, a small
group headed by Leeman walked along the coast, living on coconuts, crabs and
oysters, but too fearful of wild animals to journey inland. They found, and tried to
sail, some Javanese proas but could not. They then met the fishermen to whom
Leeman, who could speak Malay, told his adventures and intention. By now, ten of
the original crew had died or been lost and Leeman had only three companions, one
of whom could not walk. They were taken to the natives' village, where they
recuperated, continued their journey and, after many more experiences and delays,
four months after their boat had been wrecked, they reached Japara, where 'we
came again to our people, for which Almighty God must be thanked and praised
everlastingly, Amen.' Two months later Leeman reached Batavia only to learn that
Volkersen had died as the result of an accident. Whether Volkersen was punished or
upbraided for his negligence on the Southland is unknown, but he was still skipper
of *Waeckende Boey* at the time of his death.

Volkersen's instructions for the expensive voyage to the Southland had been quite
explicit. First, he was to give special attention to the navigational hazards of d'Edels
landt. The charts which he and Jonck of *Emeloort* brought back certainly provided
a clear picture of the coast's dangers. His journal and his report[20] indicated that offshore reefs extended from about 5 km from the shore, and the sea broke on them
with 'great force'.[21] A boat could negotiate channels through the reefs but 'everywhere is a dangerous coral bottom'. He had found only one place, 43 km north of
Rottnest Island, 'that shelter is afforded for a boat, and there one can effect a landing, but the ground is everywhere rocks'. The depth of water increased rapidly as
one left the coast and the bottom outside the reefs was generally sandy, thus providing good anchorage.

Concerning his second instruction—to examine the land, and if it were inhabited
to describe carefully the natives' way of life, and especially to report on the existence
of precious metals—Volkersen had little to say:

> The southland has, on its coasts, downs covered with grass and sand so deep
> that in walking one's foot is buried ankle deep and leaves great traces behind it

.... Further from the coast there is a raised ground, tolerably level, but of dry and barren aspect, except near the island where there is some foliage.

Of the island itself, 'in nearly 32°S and nearly three leagues from the coast'—presumably Rottnest for his charts depict its familiar shape—he wrote that it contained

> some rather high mountains, covered with wood and thickets which render it difficult to pass across. It is dangerous to land there, on account of the reefs of rock along the coast; and, moreover, one sees many rocks between the continent and this island and also a smaller island [Fig. 3.1] somewhat to the south .... I assume that both fresh water and wood will be found there in abundance, though not without considerable trouble.[22]

Volkersen chose not to name the island, leaving that privilege to the governor-general in Batavia.

He saw no Aborigines, although his journal often records seeing fires, so he was unable to fulfil the long instruction concerning their 'towns and inhabited villages, the division of their kingdoms, their religions', etc. However, nine men from *Emeloort*, who went ashore at 30° 25'S on March 10 at a spot where fires had been seen, saw some. They came across three huts and five persons of tall stature and imposing appearance who made signs to them to approach, but they would not because they mistrusted the natives' intentions.[23] Instead, they moved cautiously back to their boat, followed by the natives of whom they were apparently quite terrified. Describing them as 'of stalwart frame, naked, very dark-skinned' and wearing head-dresses which formed 'a sort of crown but with no covering on the body except at the middle', the crew also reported seeing much brushwood on the shore 'and in some places crops of growing grain which they [the crew or the Aborigines?] set fire to', and portions of land 'under cultivation',[24] but no fruits and, further inland, no trees or fresh water.

Neither Volkersen nor Jonck found minerals such as gold, silver, iron, lead, copper and precious stones—and they did not seem interested in going inland, where these might have been found. Nor did they say much about the fauna—two seals and a 'wild cat' and 'certain animals' (because they had seen excreta) on Rottnest Island. Whether Volkersen, as instructed, took formal possession of all the places, lands and islands is unknown; his journal makes no mention of his having done so.

The governor-general could not have been pleased with the results. Volkersen had done little to justify the cost of the expedition. He took no initiatives in discovering minerals, fauna and flora, seemed uninterested in Aborigines and made only desultory remarks on landscape. Constantly worried about the safety of his vessel when close to the dangerous shore, he succeeded best at what he was trained for—charting the coast and identifying offshore reefs. Had he been more inquisitive about the coast south of the wreck site, he would have almost certainly discovered the entrance to the Swan River.

When Leeman finally reached Batavia and reported his experiences to the governor-general and councillors, they decided not to mount any more expeditions of search for the survivors of *Vergulde Draeck*. We assume, they declared, 'that of the poor people of the ship, the *Draeck*, no one will be present any longer'.[25] Had survivors been ashore during Volkersen's exploration they would have signalled with fire, but on more than one occasion Volkersen was confused concerning whether fires had been lit by natives or by survivors. In 1659 van Riebeck of the company's Cape station was still under the impression that he had to send light vessels bound for Batavia to the Southland at 31-32°S. One such vessel, *Immehorn*, detoured without success before orders reached van Riebeck to abandon further searches. Thus on 21 August 1660 the company declared that because 'all missions have been fruitless, we will have to give up, to our distress, the people of the *Draeck*, who had found refuge on the Southland'.[26]

III

As the purpose of Volkersen's and Jonck's voyages had been to search for a lost vessel and its survivors, so the purpose of the next major Dutch voyage to Swan River was also to search for a lost vessel, the *Ridderschap van Hollandt*. In this instance, however, the vessel's whereabouts were unknown. No survivors had reached Batavia or any other place to sound the alarm. She had left the Netherlands for Batavia on 11 July 1693 with 325 souls and cargo, reached Table Bay early in 1694, but was not heard of thereafter. It was believed that, like the *Vergulde Draeck*, she may have been wrecked on the Southland, 'or that she has made the coast for want of food or water, and as this Coast is full of shallows and rocks, she may be wrecked, as there are many examples to be found which happened previously'.[27] At first it was decided to send a search vessel from Batavia. The company later changed orders and on 3 May 1696 sent an expedition of three vessels from the Netherlands which comprised the newly built frigate, *Geelvinck,* under the commodore of the expedition, Willem de Vlamingh, the hooker *Nijptangh* (skipper, Gerrit-Collaert) and the galliot *Weseltje* (skipper, Laurens Zeeman).[28] The skippers were instructed to search the islands of St Paul and Amsterdam (see Fig. 6.1) before reaching the western coast, and also to look for 'signs of man from [other] perished ships'.[29] The expedition's main purpose gave N. C. Witsen, one of the managers of the Dutch East India Company and burgomaster of Amsterdam, the opportunity to fulfil his long-held wish that an extensive survey should be made of the Southland.[30]

The company decided to plan the expedition so that it reached the Southland in summer. Vlamingh's instructions were to study known charts and log books of predecessors to the region, in particular those who visited the Southland. He was especially instructed to find the wrecks (and survivors) of the *Ridderschap van Hollandt,* the *Vergulde Draeck* and other ships, to explore the whole coast carefully, and, as far as possible, the inland.[31]

The three vessels sighted the Southland on Christmas Eve 1696, and on the twenty-ninth, Rottnest Island, which was approached very cautiously. *Geelvinck* dropped anchor in Thomson Bay and *Nijptangh* in Porpoise Bay (see Plate 3.3a). The following day Vlamingh sent a party ashore at Thomson Bay and on their return he was told that though they had carefully surveyed the island (not really possible to achieve in one day), they had not found any animals except bush rats, some of which were shot and brought back to the ship. They also saw many trees with an 'agreeable smell', and after digging for water found some which Vlamingh tasted and declared 'very good'. It is fortunate that two diaries of the Vlamingh explorations of Swan River have survived—Vlamingh's own journal and one by Mandrop Torst, upper-surgeon on the *Nijptangh*. Thus, when Vlamingh and Torst were ashore together we have two first-hand accounts of what they did and saw. On occasions where Vlamingh stayed aboard, his diary always includes a summary of the report he received from the officer who led the party. As we shall see, Torst was a more careful observer than either Vlamingh or his officers and it is to him that we are mainly indebted for the first European view of Swan River.

The observations of Rottnest Island noted above were those of Vlamingh's assistant (Joannes Bremer). On the same day the *Nijptangh* diarist was rowed along the eastern side of the island, from Porpoise Bay. Apparently the boat did not land, probably because the crew saw so many rocks and a 'reef stretching from the shore to the nearest rock, nearly one-third of a mile from the coast'. They also sighted several bays with white sand, 'which is found round the greater part of the Island'. The following day Vlamingh himself went ashore on the island, and found the 'aromatic smelling' firewood 'like that of Rose wood', several loads of which were taken back to the *Geelvinck*. The *Nijptangh* diarist also went ashore that day and recorded:

> The ground is covered with little or no soil, chiefly white sand, and rocky, in my opinion unsuitable for cultivation. There are very few Birds here, and no Animals, only a kind of rat as big as a common cat, whose dung is found in abundance all over the Island; also very few Seals, and Fish except a sort of Sardine and grey Rock-bream. Near the centre of the Island we found several Basins of excellent salty water, as much as half an hour's distance [from the beach] and digging a Pit nearly six to seven paces further fresh water welled up, fit to drink. Returning to the shore our People found a piece of wood from our own Country, with nails still in it. It was probably from a shipwrecked Vessel; and on the mainland we observed smoke arising at different points, in about three or four [Dutch] miles from us. The land looks higher than it really is, and has a coast similar to that of Holland.

From New Year's Day until 4 January parties that went ashore on the island confirmed what had already been discovered. Vlamingh was obviously intrigued by the aromatic-smelling wood. Of his next visit ashore he recorded that the aroma of this 'finest wood in the world' could be smelt all over the island and was most agreeable. Fires were frequently seen on the mainland so on the fourth he sent a party to sound the bottom in preparation for a landing. On their return, his officers reported seeing several islands in the bight—probably Carnac and Garden islands—and also that they had landed on the mainland, where they found some strange 'gummy' sort of trees. (Willem Robert, who translated the Vlamingh and *Nijptangh* diaries, believes that they landed at a spot south of the entrance of Swan River, perhaps near

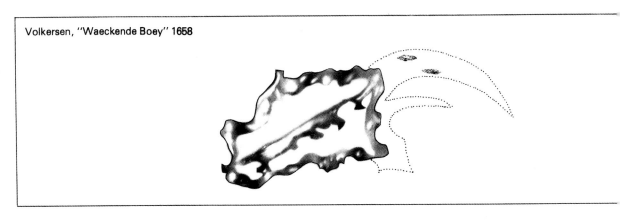

Volkersen, "Waeckende Boey" 1658

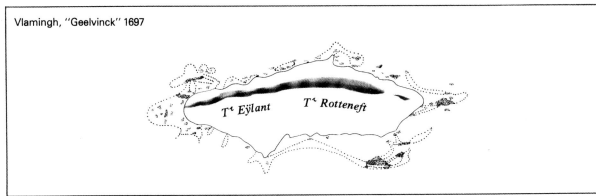

Vlamingh, "Geelvinck" 1697

T't Eÿlant   *T't Rotteneft*

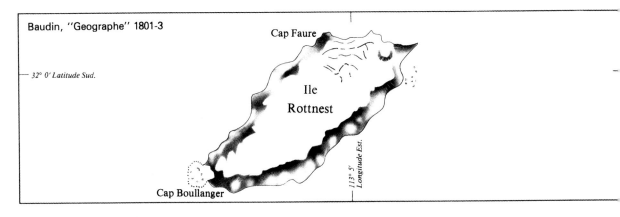

Baudin, "Geographe" 1801-3

Cap Faure

— 32° 0' *Latitude Sud.*

Ile
Rottnest

113° 5'
Longitude Est.

Cap Boullanger

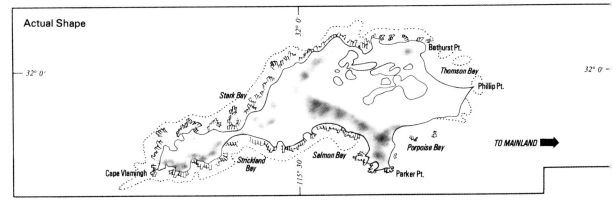

Actual Shape

32° 0'

— 32° 0'   32° 0' —

Bathurst Pt.

Thomson Bay

Phillip Pt.

Stark Bay

Porpoise Bay

TO MAINLAND ➡

Strickland Bay   *Salmon Bay*

Cape Vlamingh

115° 30'   Parker Pt.

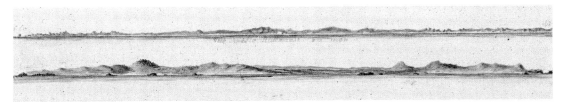

Pl. 3.3 The emerging shape of Rottnest Island as depicted by explorers: (a) see opposite page; (b), above: (1) Victor Victorsz, Plate 1 (of the Vlamingh expedition 1696) [courtesy of Maritiem Museum, Rotterdam]; and below: (2) Charles-Alexandre Lesueur (of the Baudin expedition 1803) [courtesy of Musée d'Histoire Naturelle, du Havre]

Coogee, where they would have had a clear view of the three islands.)[32] That evening a council meeting was held and a decision made to take a party of seventy or eighty soldiers and officers in the *Weseltje* to the mainland the following morning. Apparently Vlamingh did not join them, for he records that because *Geelvinck* had broken a cable he sailed her to a new anchorage while the party was ashore, and when they returned on the eighth (having been away for three days), he recorded what his delegates had seen and experienced.

On 5 January 1697 a large, well-armed party, accompanied by two 'blacks' who had been brought from the Cape, presumably to communicate with Aborigines, landed on the mainland, probably at Mosman Park near where the Vlamingh Memorial has been erected (Plate 3.1). Immediately ashore, troops were mustered, an instruction read 'to anticipate any disorder' and orders given to march eastward towards the hills. It must have been a memorable sight—eighty Dutch soldiers, prepared for anything, marching over the sandhills and limestone outcrops. Whatever their expectations, however, the *Nijptangh* diarist was clearly disappointed when, after an hour's marching in the summer heat, they discovered only a hut 'as bad as those of the Hottentots; further on was a Basin with brackish water, which we afterwards found was a river'. At that moment, Swan River had been discovered by Europeans.

Vlamingh's delegates described to him their discoveries during the remainder of the fifth:

> Went on and came to three huts which were, however, ruined, and saw near us an inland-water, we went to the beach there and came upon several footsteps, made by children and older people, but no taller in stature. Marched into the country along the river which flows inland, came to a bluff, could not walk past the beach any longer, ascended a height where we took [a rest] saw there a big tree, three fathoms [*sic*] in thickness and full of notches by which people could ascend till the top of the tree . . .

Pl. 3.4 Vlamingh expedition entering Swan River (1696).   [Engraving from F. Valentijn, *Oud en Nieuw Oost-Indiën* (1726). Courtesy of Rex Nan Kivell Collection, National Library of Australia]

After lunch, they found more huts which were also 'ruined', found pits dug by natives to obtain fresh water, and though 'smoke was rising' ahead of them they did not see any natives. That night they camped but took care to keep watch in case the natives attacked them. On the basis of these rather impressionistic entries, Robert nonetheless calculates that they had reached the river south of Freshwater Bay and by evening were still between the coast and the river near Mosman Park.

The next day (sixth), it was decided to split the party into three platoons, each taking a different direction in the hope that they could meet Aborigines. One party followed the river to where it was 'two miles wide', saw more huts and many white birds and 'blue and green [parrots] with hooked beaks'. The *Nijptangh* diarist records having been brought 'the nut of a certain Fruit, resembling the form of the Drioens, and having the taste of the Dutch great Beans . . .' He soon regretted having tasted it:

> after an interval of about three hours, I and five others who had eaten of these Fruits, began to vomit so violently that there was hardly any difference between us and death; so that it was with the greatest difficulty that I with the Crew reached the shore and thence in company of the Skipper boarded the Galliot [*Weseltje*], leaving the rest on shore.

It was an unfortunate experience—unfortunate for the diarist and for us because his diary contains no entries for three days, thus depriving us of impressions and experiences of the Swan River. On the other hand, Vlamingh's delegates provided much information. One of the parties was ordered to go along the river bank and the other to sail southwards along the coast close to the shore. After 2½ hours the coast party, having found nothing but 'part of a plank' which was very old, then discovered the mouth of the Swan River. They tried to sail into it but 'found it to be very rocky and shallow and we encountered great difficulty in reaching the river with our pinnace'. Once inside, the first Europeans to enter, they sailed up-river to the rendezvous where the other party was awaiting them. They caught black swans with a boat hook, one injured, the other not, and though there were many other kinds of birds they could not catch them.

On January 10 Vlamingh himself decided to visit the mainland and ascend the river in three sloops. Keeping *Geelvinck* well out to sea, the party of forty sailed to the river entrance in the smaller *Weseltje* where, well-armed, with two guns on every sloop, they crossed the bar in a small boat 'only . . . after many difficulties'. The *Nijptangh* diarist, who by now had recovered, joined the party and noted that there was only between 1 to 2 m of water at the river's mouth and that they ascended the river using sails and oars, from time to time being grounded on banks. They saw several fires but still no people. At 2.00 A.M., having sailed through most of the night, they dropped the drag. At daybreak, they sailed on, seeing

> many Swans (our Sloop shot down nine or ten), Brent-geese, Divers, etc., also a quantity of Fish which were frisking on the water; we also heard the song of the Nightingale. Here we thought we saw a crowd of men; but after rowing to the beach with the Sloop, we found none, but we found a Pit with fresh water, and within it, at the bottom a certain Herb, smelling like Thyme, which was evidently put into it by the Southlanders, to give the water a more agreeable taste and to take away the brackishness. All around we saw several footsteps and the impression of a hand on the sand, and marks of the thumb and fingers showing plainly that it was done not long ago. Proceeding further we found a fire which

had just been lighted, and three small Huts, one of which held a quantity of bark, of a tree known in India under the name Liplap; which, I think, was used for a sleeping-mat. Towards noon we could not go any further for want of water; and the ships being aground, we decided to return, having already ascended the River for six or seven miles (Some thought it was ten) without having seen anything of importance [*Nijptangh* diarist].

The expedition had almost certainly reached the flats just east of Perth. Vlamingh records, in words almost identical to those of Stirling and the French parties, that the river became very shallow,

> so that our men had to leave the boats to push the same, rounding a corner we found the end of the river which divides itself into many veins, [so] that we could not proceed any more.

Here, having seen many footprints, they lit fires, hoping the people would come. They sent their two 'blacks' ashore to investigate fires but no signs of life, and no natives, were observed. Vlamingh described the huts he had seen: they were 'covered on one side with wild-reed, about a foot high and the huts were 2 feet high, in which lay a lot of bark of trees which they used as beds [and] a lot of wax and gum'. He took samples of the wax and gum back to his ship.

Returning aboard, Vlamingh decided not to make any further exploration of the Swan River. On January 13 the vessels weighed anchor and sailed northwards. Though he made no contemporary appraisal of the river, his thoughts probably coincided with the *Nijptangh* diarist:

> As regards to the Country, it is sandy, and, in the place where we have been were a great number of Trees, among which were some almost three or four fathom [*sic*] thick but bearing no fruits; in short, full of prickles and thorns. Several of these Trees yielded a kind of resin nearly like wax, of a brownish red colour. All were very shy, the Men, the Birds, the Swans, the Brent-geese, the Crammed-gees, the Cockatoos, the Parakeets etc. The best of it is that no vermin are found here: but during the day one is terribly tormented by the flies.

At noon on the thirteenth the *Nijptangh* diarist recorded that they passed an opening which might have been a river, perhaps, writes Robert, the Moore River, and on the fourteenth a reef 400 m off the coast, probably the Leschenault reef. Seeing 'a great smoke' on the fifteenth, Vlamingh sent two boats ashore but his uppersteersman later reported that although they explored 2.4 km inland, they found only sand-dunes, overgrown with heather, and the footprints of birds like cassowary. The *Nijptangh* diarist, as usual, provided more information. The bottom near the shore was foul and not adapted for anchoring—this was probably a spot near Island Point (Jurien Bay)—and the land,

> dry and dunelike . . . not adapted for Animals, still less for Human-beings. We went inland nearly 1½ mile, but found neither People nor fresh water, only several footsteps of Men and prints like that of a Dog and Cassowary; further no Trees, only thistles and thorns. One of our Men said that he had seen a red

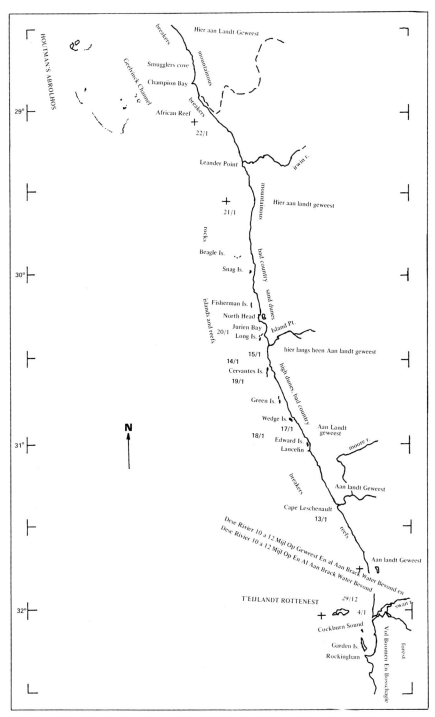

Fig. 3.4 Route taken by Vlamingh from Swan River to Champion Bay. [Copied from a chart by Robert, *Explorations*]

Snake; some others said that as soon as we reached the shore [they had seen] a yellow Dog leaping from the wild overgrowth and throwing itself into the sea as if to amuse itself with swimming. What truth there was is unknown to me; I did not see these things myself.

In the evening of the fifteenth, when they were near the site of the wrecked *Vergulde Draeck*, though they seemed not to know it, they saw several fires along the coast, 'like we have seen as long as we are here', wrote Vlamingh. The next day, Vlamingh sent his uppersteersman ashore again, and he reported finding a water-place

with fresh water with a little hut close by, which was covered with branches of trees, and had also seen several footprints of people, small ones as well as large ones but naturally also a number of footprints of beasts such as tigers; proceeded inland for about 3 miles, found many fires but no people.

On the seventeenth Vlamingh described the coast as having high dunes 'like on the Vlie'—he was known as a capable Vlieland skipper from the island off the Dutch coast[33]—and on the high land two places like small forts. Encouraged perhaps to believe that these may have been built by humans, he sent a party ashore which, as usual reported having seen only bad, treeless country for 5 km and that the 'forts', which they had thought resembled the castle at Dover, were only natural stone outcrops. Victor Victorsz, an 'artist' on the expedition, to whom we must be greatly indebted, was also impressed by the 'forts' for he made them the subject of one of his fifteen paintings done while on the western coast (see Plate 3.5).

Sailing northwards, and then southwards for two days, they found it difficult to land during the mornings because of offshore easterly winds and also because of the large number of small islets, large rocks and reefs over which the sea constantly broke. Nor did the land look to be worth exploring: 'here are dunes all over the country'. The *Nijptangh* diarist who went ashore on the twentieth found 'nothing but a great Plain, very barren', a description confirmed by the members of the same party who reported to Vlamingh that there was 'nothing but bad, desolate land, without bush'. The waters were especially treacherous (near Beagle Island), and with each report confirming the land's aridity, the *Nijptangh* diarist recorded that they had not learned 'anything new'. It is clear that their views of the coast were by this time confirmed. However, they pressed on, Vlamingh ever willing to send boats ashore if there was a chance of finding something new. Especially interested in meeting Aborigines, he must have been mildly excited on the twenty-third when the sloop returned with news that ten men, entirely naked and black, had been seen from the sloop but as there was heavy surf at the spot they had to sail on another 1½ km before landing. Though they failed to find the Aborigines, they did find a salty inland-water which was 'blood-reddish' in colour, a discovery confirmed by the *Nijptangh* diarist, who thought it was due to the bottom being red mud and sand. Perhaps, calculates Robert, they had discovered Hutt Lagoon.

The sighting of Aborigines seemed to stimulate Vlamingh into making a final, concerted effort to meet them. On January 24 a council was held and it was decided

Pl. 3.5   Coastal view of rocks which resembled forts.   [Victor Victorsz, Plate 2. Courtesy of Maritiem Museum, Rotterdam]

Pl. 3.6   Dirk Hartog Island, showing where the plate was discovered.   [Victor Victorsz, Plate 12. Courtesy of Maritiem Museum, Rotterdam]

Pl. 3.7   The coast of d'Edels landt, showing fires attributed to Aborigines.   [A painting by Lesueur. Courtesy of Musée d'Histoire Naturelle, du Havre]

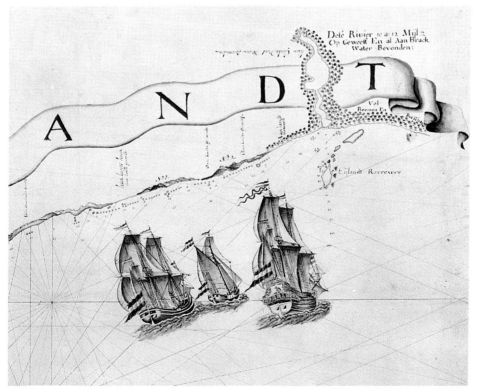

Fig. 3.5   Part of the Vlamingh map. Entrance to Swan River with three vessels.   [Courtesy of Algemeen Rijksarchief, 's-Gravenhage]

to send an expedition, comprising all the soldiers, thirty-six crew, the two 'blacks' from the Cape and equal numbers from the *Nijptangh*, into the inland with eight days' provisions. This was a huge party, similar in size and objectives to the one Vlamingh had sent ashore at Mosman beach.

The *Nijptangh* diarist provides the most informative account of their experiences:

> On reaching the shore we found many Oysters, and put ourselves immediately at a marching pace, but were obliged occasionally to rest ourselves on account of fatigue caused by the burning of the Sun and the impassability of the roads caused by Brushwood . . . . But if the road had been difficult a great trouble was yet in store of us; for finding no fresh water we thought we would be parched with thirst. We could see our Ships easily, and wished a thousand times over that we were on board again.

But another party had found fresh water, and also a little hut and footprints nearby, so they made their way towards this place, and camped the night, having posted soldiers as sentries. Though several parties traversed the land none had seen 'Men nor Cattle, nothing but wild Brushwood'. On the twenty-seventh, having been ashore only three days when they had provisions for eight, they returned to their vessels, the crew complaining greatly of sore eyes.

Due to these disappointing results, Vlamingh decided to sail on. A few days later they sailed past the Zuytdorp Cliffs south of Shark Bay, 'high steep land very sheer rising', as Vlamingh described it, 'very high and bare everywhere without anything green on top . . . as if it were chopped off with axes, without a beach [but] with heavy breakers . . .' (Plate 3.8). In a rare moment, Vlamingh showed some excitement; to a mariner's eye it was 'marvellous to see!' They arrived at Dirk Hartog Island on January 30, where they stayed for twelve days replenishing food supplies with fish and turtles which, at night, were easily caught, and also took 'as many turtle eggs as you want'. The land was still a variation on the aridity theme: 'very barren and sandy without trees'. Vlamingh went on a five-day expedition in the bay but, as Robert shows, it is difficult to recreate the journey from his journal although it appears that he reached the southern end and discovered the mangrove swamps around Useless Loop. The *Nijptangh* diarist described the land where his vessel touched as 'steep, and red-sanded and stony land, barren and poor'. The crew dug pits for fresh water but none was found. Strong winds, so characteristic of the bay in summer, not only impeded their explorations but caused the death of a carpenter when the galliot capsized. On the fourth the party from *Geelvinck* reported to Vlamingh that while on the outermost end of Dirk Hartog Island, climbing a mountain to see if they could spot the remains of any vessels, they found a pole 'with a tin plate lying near it' which they brought back. They had, in fact, discovered the plate left by Dirck Hartog, the Dutch discoverer of the western coast, in 1616. Vlamingh was obviously impressed by their discovery and promptly arranged for another plate to be made on which was embossed both the contents of the Dirck Hartog plate and its discovery by his crew (Plate 3.6).

Following a council meeting on February 12 they left Shark Bay and sailed along the coast to near Carnarvon, then westward to Dorre Island and back to Shark Bay.

Pl. 3.8 The Zuytdorp Cliffs. [Photo by Alex George]

82	THE BEGINNING

Thereafter they sailed north past North West Cape and on the twenty-first, after another council meeting, Vlamingh 'signalled to set sail and leave the Southland and to advance in the name of our Lord on our voyage to Batavia', having, as instructed, 'surveyed the S.land, inside and out, as it was humanly possible . . .' The *Nijptangh* diarist made a succinct but more telling entry. On hearing the five-shot signal from *Geelvinck, Nijptangh* returned three shots 'as a signal of farewell to the miserable South-land'.

The vessels reached Batavia on March 17 whereupon Vlamingh's charts and the specimens he had collected were sent back to Amsterdam, including the discs of scented wood which Vlamingh had collected on Rottnest Island. Though officials at Batavia could not identify the wood, they extracted the oil from several pieces and sent this back to Amsterdam in a bottle,[34] together with a 'box containing shells, fruits, plants, etc., gathered on the beach'. It was a miserable collection by an expedition which had been on the coast for nearly two months and the governor-general was not impressed. The whole, he wrote in his covering letter, is of little value and 'such are to be found in a better condition elsewhere in India'. Indeed, the governor-general's judgement on the value of the voyage to the company is worth quoting at length:

> nothing has been discovered but a barren, arid and wild land, both near the shore and so far as they have been inland. Without meeting any human beings, only now and then some fires, and if they fancy to have seen a number of black, naked men from afar on two or three occasions, they have never been able to come near to, or to speak to them; nor have they found there any remarkable animals or birds, except especially in the Swan River, a sort of black swans, three of which they have brought to us alive, which we would have been glad to send over to Your Worships, had they not died one by one shortly after their arrival here. Neither so far as we know, have any traces been discovered of the lost ship *Ridderschap van Holland* or any other vessels. . . . So that nothing of any importance has been discovered in this exploratory voyage.

In the summer of 1698 Nicolaas Witsen, one of the managers of the company in Holland who had strongly supported the mounting of the expedition, reached similar conclusions. On the basis of the journals kept and reports made he reiterated the governor-general's conclusions and also criticized Vlamingh for not being more interested in making 'deeper' inland explorations. Accusing him of being 'too much addicted to drink' and having spent too much time at the Cape on his outward voyage indulging in 'feasts and frolics'—criticism based, perhaps, on conversations he had with some of Vlamingh's crew when they returned to Holland—Witsen nonetheless acknowledged the value of Vlamingh's charts.[35] Even so, he wrote on 3 October 1698, the expedition had discovered nothing which 'can be anyway serviceable to the Company': the soil of the country

> hath been found very barren, and as a Desert; no Fresh-water Rivers have been found, but some Salt-water Rivers, as also no Fourfooted Beasts, except one as great as a Dog, with long Ears, living in the water as well as on the land.

The natives seen were

> all as black as Pitch, and stark naked, so terrified, that it was impossible to bring them to conversation . . . they lodge themselves as the Hottentots, in Pavilions of small Branches of Trees.

Soon after Witsen had received the reports, he edited and published extracts in his *Noord en Oost Tartarije* (1705), thus providing the public with their first knowledge of the land and people at Swan River. Witsen actually claimed that Vlamingh had named the Swan River the Witsen River after him and that he had in his possession charts drawn on the spot to prove it. More important than whether Swan River had been named Witsen River, however, is Witsen's published speculations concerning what lay behind the barren sandhills and ranges seen by Vlamingh. Tasman had recently discovered the southern tip of Van Diemen's Land (see Fig. 1.8). Witsen therefore concluded that what Vlamingh had seen was the western extremity of a land that 'extends to Van Diemens Land'. The soil, fruit and trees as described by both explorers were similar, whereas in New Zealand the people, fruits and vegetation were different. The primitive native huts Vlamingh had seen on the western coast, conjectured Witsen, may be only beach houses which they use when visiting the coast to catch fish; their permanent dwellings may be further inland. Or, perhaps the coast is inhabited only by 'wild, naked men' and the 'more civilised persons are inland'. However, these conjectures could not be tested until Christians had visited the hinterland. Vlamingh had the opportunity to find out, claimed Witsen, but according to some of the crew whom Witsen interviewed, he had been too timid to proceed further than the 'flats' (Heirisson Island) at Swan River even though they had seen smoke at the foot of the ranges. In the comfort and protection of Amsterdam many months later, the crew told Witsen that *they* would have gone further inland but Vlamingh had refused on grounds that his vessel was not at a safe anchorage and he was anxious to return to it, and that he was afraid of being surrounded by a large number of natives. As a result, wrote Witsen, all that is known of the natives aside from descriptions of their huts is that they know nothing of shipbuilding (not a single native boat was seen on the western coast), that they are easily frightened and 'hide themselves in the woods', and that according to the crew their excreta is 'like that of animals, so it seems that they are eating grass, fruit and leaves'.

Witsen's published conjectures were important for they confirmed the emerging 'image' of the western coast and kept explorers at bay for more than a century. The Dutch government showed little further interest in the Swan River area, Vlamingh's report, concludes Robert, having provided the 'final condemnation'.[36] His main contribution, like Volkersen's, was a journal full of *nautical* data and charts whose accuracy, once minor adjustments are made to latitude readings, has astounded marine archaeologists in Western Australia who have retraced his voyage.[37] One puzzling thing, which may say much about Vlamingh, is that he systematically refused to name islands, bays, hills etc., which is why Dutch names are conspicuously absent from maps of the western coast.[38] He was, concluded Robert, 'an honest, unimaginative person who only told what he saw, and indeed [to him] nothing inter-

esting could be seen on this coast'. His superb chart of the western coast from the
Swan River to North West Cape was kept secret for over sixty years when Van
Keulen used it for his printed map of Western Australia (1753). What a gift to posterity were the landscape paintings of Victor Victorsz, who had been instructed to
'produce paintings and maps of any coastline which came into view during the
voyage'. Almost certainly the first water-colours ever done of the Australian mainland, one can only lament that he did not fulfil his commission to the letter, especially that he did not paint anything of Swan River and the Aboriginal huts discovered
there. We can only be grateful, however, that his fifteen water-colours of the coast
were discovered in 1970, nearly 270 years after they were painted, when presented
privately to the Prins Hendrik Maritiem Museum and identified by Günter Schilder
as coinciding with the numbers 1 to 15 written at various places on the Vlamingh
map (Fig. 3.5).[39]

IV

Throughout the eighteenth century European interest in the western side of New
Holland was very slight. Bruny D'Entrecasteaux, on his voyage in search of La
Pérouse, the great French explorer of the Pacific, touched the southern coast east of
Cape Leeuwin and sailed eastward for 1450 km, fulfilling instructions to survey the
coast as if he were discovering it for the first time. Fifteen months earlier George
Vancouver, on his way to explore the north-western coast of America, explored a
much shorter distance of the same Australian coast though, unlike D'Entrecasteaux,
he was favoured by better weather which allowed him to enter, name and carefully
explore King George Sound. However, the Swan River area remained unvisited by
Europeans during the eighteenth century, with the exception of St Allouarn, who
was with Kerguelen when he discovered the island of the same name far to the south-
east of Africa. He then sailed to Cape Leeuwin, where, as already noted, he tried to
go ashore (possibly at the mouth of the Blackwood River) but failed, sailed north
and by-passed Swan River (although he probably saw Garden Island), then sailed on
to Shark Bay where he claimed the land to the north-west of his anchorage for
France.

Vlamingh's report had effectively discouraged any European government from
mounting an expedition to the western coast of the Southland during the eighteenth
century. Swan River therefore remained untouched and unchanged. Its Aboriginal
people lived as their forebears had lived for centuries, passing down from generation
to generation stories of the brief visits by strange white men and probably anxious
that others might again disturb their tranquillity. By contrast, the eighteenth century
was a period of constant turmoil in Europe, where bloody wars and revolution raged
and philosophical issues of the greatest divisive significance were vigorously
debated. In France, after the death of Louis XIV, the monarchy was progressively
undermined as French intellectuals led Europe into a new radicalism known as the
Age of Enlightenment. Its watchwords were rationality not tradition; happiness in
this life, not salvation in the next.[40] Philosophers such as Rousseau and Montes-
quieu were leaders in a movement seeking a fresh approach to accepted beliefs.[41]

Rousseau's *Discours* claimed that man, having emerged from his natural state into an artificial and intricate society, had been depraved by the false environment in which he was compelled to spend his days.[42] Man, he argued, 'springs from the hand of nature unspoilt, virtuous and noble'. France had been relatively inward looking during this period, concerned mainly with internal problems and continental wars. However, her explorations into the Pacific focused attention directly on the idea, not new, of the 'noble savage'. While the voyages of Cook and Bougainville had revealed the idyllic life-style of Tahitian natives, Diderot then took up Rousseau's view that colonial ventures to these perfect societies were harmful, thus providing a new and important emphasis to the philosophical debate. Towards the end of the eighteenth century, the concept as enunciated by philosophers was challenged by Christians who considered that belief in the natural virtue of pagan savages was repugnant.[43] But as Europeans became aware of the physical and social differences between races, scientific method which investigated both nature and man became more acceptable. Thus, La Pérouse's instructions were to study the Pacific peoples with objectivity.

By 1777 the journals published by Pacific explorers had revealed a disparity between philosophical laws and the physical forces of nature. The idea that climate was a factor in differential racial characteristics was debated; and as incidents occurred involving the death of navigators, writers and artists at the hands of these 'noble savages', so attitudes changed and the idea of the 'ignoble savage' emerged.[44] A scientific approach to native peoples was therefore encouraged; e.g. La Pérouse's artists were instructed to depict native peoples in great detail. Republican writers continued to champion the idea of hard primitivism, endowing savages with those virtues to which they themselves aspired—simple in needs and desires, self-disciplined, courageous, and with a great capacity for endurance—views graphically portrayed by Labilliardière of the D'Entrecasteaux expedition.[45]

The Baudin expedition to Australia of 1801-04 was mounted at a time when these ideas were still being strongly debated in France. It was, without doubt, the best-equipped scientific expedition ever to leave Europe for the Southland. Strongly supported by the French government and national scientific bodies, it was lavishly provided for and the crews carefully chosen.[46] As already noted, the motives of the French in mounting the expedition, though avowedly scientific, were nonetheless unclear at the time, mainly because France and England were still at war and therefore unlikely to reveal their real reasons for such expeditions. The British government of the day, however, appeared not to be unduly concerned about the intentions of the Baudin expedition, for it issued passports to the commanders of the two French vessels, *Géographe* and *Naturaliste*, granting them immunity from attack and capture by British warships, and allowing them to pass free and unmolested during 'their present intended voyage'.[47] Even so, neither at the time, nor subsequently, was there unanimity concerning French intentions. Aside from Baudin's own comment at the time that the voyage would be 'most interesting for the sciences as well as for politics' and that there was also 'talk of Commerce and Settlement', and that he had been specifically instructed to find out whether the British had established a settlement at Van Diemen's Land, and to explore Bass Strait carefully, doubts nonetheless lingered. When the expedition, having spent several months at Port Jackson, then sailed for Van Diemen's Land, Governor King of New South Wales, suspicious of Baudin's intentions, hastily sent a vessel to 'cover' the French ships. On reaching *Géographe*, the master of *Cumberland* delivered a letter from King which intimated that he had heard only after Baudin left Port Jackson that it was Baudin's intention to establish a French settlement at Frederik Hendrik Bay. 'It is also said', wrote King, 'that these are your orders from the French Republic.' Baudin was not unduly concerned by the event. In his journal he expressed doubts concerning the legitimacy of Britain's claim to Van Diemen's Land, believing that it was based 'merely on Captain Phillip's Proclamation'.[48] King's suspicion of Baudin's intentions was restated in a letter to the Duke of Portland. In reporting the movements of Baudin's vessels he said that they had discovered and anchored in a very spacious bay between Swan River and Cape Leeuwin. The remainder of their voyage, declared King, was a secret.

Then, during April 1814, a decade after Baudin's vessels had returned to France, Governor Macquarie of New South Wales wrote Lord Bathurst of his belief that the purposes of the French expedition had not been purely scientific and that they had been sent out with the idea of choosing a French colony in the South Seas. Furthermore, he wrote, if Bonaparte had not been preoccupied in Europe, he would have conquered the British settlement and established a French colony.[49] Even as recently as 1974 Jean-Paul Faivre, in his foreword to an English translation of Baudin's journal, declared that 'in spite of the almost total absence of documents I still persist in believing in the political character of the Baudin expedition'.[50]

Already possessing knowledge of surveys conducted in other parts of the continent by English navigators, and by their own D'Entrecasteaux in the southern coast and in Van Diemen's Land, the French government expected that information collected by Baudin and the scientists would complete their knowledge of the 'entire coastline of this great southland'.[51] It was incomprehensible, implied the French government, that although the Southland was not far from countries in Asia where, for three centuries, Europeans had been forming settlements, it 'has seemed until recently to be condemned to a sort of oblivion'.[52] The Baudin voyage, more than any other to leave Europe, was better equipped in both manpower and supplies to reveal the Southland's secrets. *Géographe* and *Naturaliste* were impressive craft and the inventory of supplies placed aboard them at Le Havre, whence they sailed, and which may be seen in the Maritime Archives at Paris, still boggles the mind with its size and coverage of even the most inconsequential need. Scientists from all the recognized professions were carefully selected for the voyage. Aboard *Géographe*, commanded by Nicolas Baudin, were an astronomer, engineer-geographer, botanist, mineralogist and three zoologists, including François Péron. *Naturaliste,* commanded by Felix Hamelin, also had a team of scientists—astronomer, geographer, botanist, mineralogist, two zoologists and their assistants. Although most of the scientists kept notes and made reports on their observations (and these are available in Paris, having hardly been sighted since they were delivered to the Archives), two of them—Péron (together with Lesueur, his artist), and Freycinet, the sub-lieutenant aboard *Naturaliste*, who later commanded a third vessel, the *Casuarina*, which Baudin had purchased in Port Jackson—published selected parts of their diaries some years after the expedition returned to France.

The Baudin had been instructed to explore all parts of the continent, but his attention was especially drawn to the land between Rottnest Island and Cape Leeuwin which 'has not yet been examined; and it is one of the parts of this coast, starting from Zwaan [Swan] River, which demands to be investigated'.[53] Péron, for his part, interpreted this instruction to mean that he was to reconnoitre the coast and, because of the imperfect navigation of the first explorers, 'to go up the river of Swans as far as it was practicable, to take a particular chart of isle Rottness and part of the neighbouring coast'.[54] Shark Bay also merited 'examination in some detail, at least with respect to the anchorage, because it is the only bay in this area which appears to offer some shelter for ships'.[55] The reputation given to the entire west coast by the Dutch was well known to Baudin and the scientists. Péron declared (in his journal) that every expedition to that part of the world had been 'marked with misfortune or very fruitless attempts'. To strengthen this point, Péron added that Vlamingh had written that the remains of wrecks 'covered' Rottnest which, to say the least, is not an accurate or scientific interpretation of what Vlamingh actually wrote. Péron accepted the superiority of the British as discoverers in the sciences, but at the same time he was determined to do all he could for the honour of France.[56]

The vessels *Géographe* and *Naturaliste* sailed from Le Havre on 18 October 1800, called at the Ile de France (Mauritius) and then, on 25 April 1801, sailed westward across the Indian Ocean (Plate 3.9). Baudin's instruction was to proceed from the Ile de France to Van Diemen's Land, and then sail westward along the south coast of the Southland. It was expected that he would reach Cape Leeuwin in mid-July, then sail north to the northern point of Eendracht Land by the beginning of August, a journey which should take no longer than fifteen to twenty days at the outside.[57] For some reason, which Baudin himself does not explain, he led the expedition to Cape Leeuwin, reaching it on 27 May 1801, where he then decided to sail *north* along the western coast. Though he makes no mention of the change of plans in his journal, in a letter to the ministre de la Marine, dated 5 October 1801, Baudin explained that bad weather had prevented him from going south to Van Diemen's Land as his government had instructed, so he made for Cape Leeuwin.[58] The month of May, like the time suggested by the French government (mid-July), was the worst time to be sailing along the western coast of New Holland, so it would appear that the French had not heeded the lessons learnt by the Dutch. St Allouarn's charts from Leeuwin northwards were fairly primitive, a point frequently made by Baudin, and as the vessels moved steadily north from Cape Leeuwin, Baudin entered in his journal comments varying only in emphasis for the entire journey along the western coast: 'All the land that we have explored has looked arid to us . . . . Sometimes we made out a few plateaux with trees of a rather lovely green, all of which only served to make looking at the parts that lacked them more disagreeable . . . saw *no* ravine which seemed to be an outlet for water flowing into the sea'.[59]

Pl. 3.9 *Naturaliste* and *Géographe* at sea.   [A charcoal drawing by Lesueur. Courtesy of Musée d'Histoire Naturelle, du Havre]

About 110 km from Cape Leeuwin, Baudin reached another cape, which he named Naturaliste, around which he sailed into a bay he named Geographe, where the scientists aboard both vessels were elated by the opportunity of beginning their research after so many months at sea. Though Baudin had been told that the sole aim of the expedition was the perfecting of the sciences,[60] and that he must do everything to facilitate the scientists' objectives, he was also instructed to keep to the sailing schedule which had been drawn up in Paris by the ministre de la Marine. On no account was he to ignore difficult weather, and at all times he must be firm, never allowing the scientists to get the upper hand.[61] Baudin interpreted the latter instruction almost to the letter. Péron's journal reveals that even on the voyage out relations between himself and Baudin were far from conducive to facilitating these objectives. By the time the vessels reached the Southland relationships had greatly deteriorated, the journals of each revealing animosity and dislike to the extent that effective liaison was impossible. Péron was clearly critical and disrespectful of the non-scientific, self-taught Baudin. Baudin, for his part, saw Péron as an unsympathetic, other-worldly scientist who had no understanding whatever of the practical problems involved in keeping two vessels together during a long voyage and also keeping them safe on a notoriously dangerous coast. His journal is spiced both with gleeful asides when Péron returned to the vessel worn out or injured, and with harsh criticism of his thoughtlessness in staying ashore too long.[62] Finally, Baudin became so exasperated that he would not allow Péron ashore unless he himself accompanied him.[63]

Geographe Bay was the young French scientist's introduction to the Southland. His journal simply exudes enthusiasm when, with his faithful artist Lesueur, he finally landed on the continent he had come thousands of kilometres to research and on which he would spend almost three years:

> As soon as we landed on the beach I ran towards the interior in search of the natives, with whom I had a strong desire to be acquainted. In vain I explored the forests, following the print of their footsteps, of which I saw here and there the recent traces.[64]

Others who had landed in another part of Geographe Bay came across an old Aboriginal entirely naked except for a kangaroo skin over his shoulders. At first he seemed unperturbed by the Frenchmen's presence, but quickly became very agitated, pointing often to the vessels and seeming to tell the scientists to go back. He was interested in the necklace that they gave him but would not come close to them and soon ran off into the bush. This report seemed only to increase Péron's determination to meet the Aborigines. On his next excursion ashore, he found ceremonial grounds which he described in some detail in his journal.[65] What stance Péron took concerning 'the noble savage' is unclear, but the sight of the ceremonial grounds led him for 'a few moments to the reflections . . . [that it] naturally inspired'. He conjectured that the river and adjoining marshes were the source of food for what might be a new race of Egyptians who, like the ancient inhabitants of the Nile, had consecrated by their gratitude the stream which supplied their wants. He recollected the runic characters of northern Europe, the hieroglyphics used by Mexicans to convey their ideas, and the Bosjesmans of Africa . . . Péron was certainly turned on! On a more practical note, he then observed that none of the trees or shrubs bore fruit, and though there were signs (burnt trees and extinguished fires) that Aborigines inhabited the area, he found none. Making his way back to the shore, Péron was perturbed that the boat and crew were not waiting for him. However, Lesueur and Ronsard soon appeared and told him of an extraordinary interview with a female savage. She was initially accompanied by other Aborigines, who ran away when Lesueur approached them. This woman stayed on the beach simply because she was pregnant and therefore unable to run with the others. As Lesueur described her, Péron's views of Aborigines were instantly conditioned: she was entirely naked, had a small bag made from the skin of a kangaroo tied around her neck and a kind of string made of rushes on her back. The colour of her skin, the nature of her hair and the proportion of the body of this woman, reported Lesueur, perfectly resembled other savages in New Holland. By the time Péron published his book, he had seen many Aborigines, but he went to some lengths to describe the first one seen by Lesueur:

> In other respects she was horribly ugly and disgusting. She was uncommonly lean and scraggy, her breasts hung down almost to her thighs. The most ex-

Pl. 3.10   Aboriginal huts at Geographe Bay.   [Engraving from a sketch by Lesueur]

treme dirtiness added to her natural deformity, and was enough to disgust the most depraved among our sailors. After viewing this miserable child of nature with all the interest such an object naturally inspired, our friends offered her numerous presents: . . . . But she continued her position on her heels, and indeed the poor creature seemed totally stupefied, and it was impossible to make her accept any of their presents: when they left her these were left also on the spot near her.[66]

Although this experience, admittedly related by his friend, obviously affected Péron's attitude to Aborigines for the remainder of his stay at Geographe Bay, he was kept busy noting Aboriginal artefacts and houses, fauna and flora, all of which were faithfully recorded by the artist, Lesueur. Péron seemed reluctant to leave Geographe Bay. It had been a bitter-sweet experience: on the one hand he was clearly excited to be investigating the natural characteristics of the Southland; on the other he had clearly been adversely affected by what he had heard about its Aborigines.

Mariners in the expedition saw Geographe Bay through different eyes. Freycinet reported to Baudin that the country seemed 'to offer no other resource than that of firewood',[67] and the soil was too sandy to be fertile. Clearly influenced by descriptions and information given to him by mariners and scientists, Baudin reported to the ministre de la Marine, in a letter dated 5 October 1801, that while a few hills were covered with trees of small height, others had only dreary bushes. A most extraordinary feature, he added, was that creek-beds in streams showed no effects of drainage, and so concluded that rainfall infiltrated the sandy hills. He also noted that land- and sea-birds were scarcer on the coast than in mid-ocean, and concluded that the land must therefore be quite sterile and unable to provide sea-birds with food. Elsewhere in his report Baudin wrote that the ground appeared to have none of the products belonging to 'the realm of God', and that sand dominated the entire area. He also reported what his 'first gardener' had said about the products of the soil—that all were of a new variety to him; that the land on which he walked was very dear to him because he was becoming acquainted with new species all the time; and that almost all of these were unknown to Europeans, but could probably be transplanted to the south of France where they would grow well. However, the cultivator could only regret having come to a land which had none of the signs of advantageous culture. From the shore to the summit of gentle, high mountains, there was only white, arid sand—not a single tree which could claim attention by its vegetation or as a thing of beauty. The highest tree did not reach 8 m, obvious proof of the sterility of the ground. In all the places he had seen, reported the gardener, the trees had been burnt by fire, but he did not know whether these had been started by the natives or whether they had been caused by natural accident following drought. There were, he concluded, no grasslands on which cattle could feed.[68]

Baudin kept a daily journal throughout most of his voyage on the coast of New Holland, but it was read by only a handful of Frenchmen after the expedition returned to France. Indeed, the journal has only recently been published, and in English. Baudin's letter to the ministre de la Marine is therefore of great signifi-

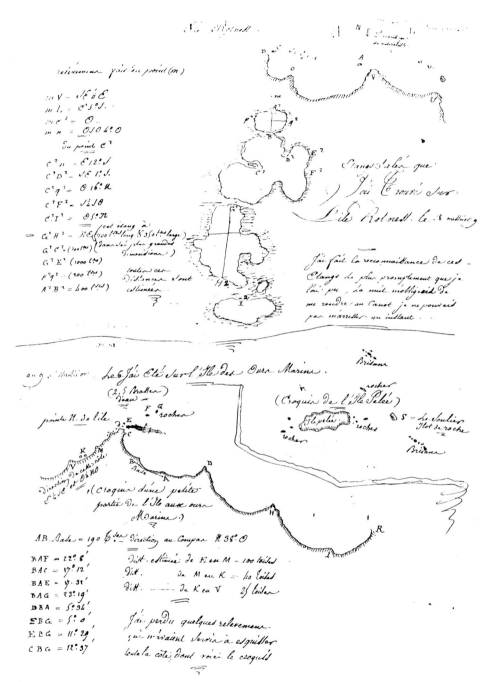

Fig. 3.6 A page of Freycinet's workbook—Rottnest Island. [Courtesy of Archives Nationales (Marine), Paris]

cance. Being his first report from the south-western coast of New Holland, it would have greatly influenced initial French opinion concerning the prospects of establishing a settlement there.

North-west winds blew hard for much of the expedition's stay at Geographe Bay and prevented the parties from moving at will between ship and shore; valuable equipment was lost when boats foundered in the surf; and when one boat tried to reach the ship on its last journey, the unfortunate Vasse was lost overboard.[69] Finally, when the two vessels left Geographe Bay, strong north-to-north-west winds caused them to part company. This was the expedition's first taste of the western coast's winter storms; until then they had been sailing in 'the finest weather imaginable'. 'It was', wrote Baudin, 'the worst weather we had had since leaving France', and made Geographe Bay 'an extremely dangerous place'.[70] Outside the Bay the weather worsened, and for two days *Géographe* made little headway; indeed she was driven 96 km to the south. Finally Baudin reached the approaches to Rottnest Island, the next rendezvous, only to experience even stronger winds. On the nights of 18 and 19 June there was, he wrote, 'A howling gale' with rain, thunder and lightning, and it 'seemed as though the elements were convulsed'.[71] Meantime, *Naturaliste*, buffeted by the same winds, did reach Rottnest and dropped anchor in the lee. But Baudin clearly had had enough. Although *Géographe* approached Rottnest, and was actually seen by sailors aboard *Naturaliste* at anchor, Baudin kept her well away from the dangerous reefs and set course to the north where he expected to find more hospitable weather.[72]

Naturaliste remained at Rottnest Island for two weeks, during which the scientists made expeditions to the islands and the mainland. A record of their activities was made by Freycinet, and published by Péron as Chapters X and XI in his book.[73] It is a great pity that Baudin was unable to bring *Géographe* to join *Naturaliste* at Rottnest, for it has robbed posterity of the articulate Péron's observations and Lesueur's paintings of landscape, fauna, and Aboriginal dwellings. We therefore have an interesting, but unfortunately not very expansive, set of observations of Swan River by *Naturaliste's* scientists, none of whom had Péron's perceptive eye. Nor did any of them display artistic talent for, aside from charts of coast, islands and river made by Freycinet, no sketches were made of fauna and flora. Their enforced stay while they waited in vain for *Géographe* was not a happy experience for Captain Hamelin and the scientists, even though Hamelin made good use of the stay by sending separate expeditions to Rottnest, the islands to the south-south-east (of Rottnest) and to the Swan River. The stormy June weather which had kept *Géographe* from joining them also made these island expeditions very hazardous. Freycinet and Fauré (the geographer) were almost wrecked when they tried to land on Rottnest, and were forced to stay there for two days before a caulker from *Naturaliste* could come ashore and repair their boat. Exploring the islands on foot in the meantime, but finding the rocks on the northern side of the island too steep to climb, and the woods so thick that progress inland was slow, they soon discovered 'a delightful valley at the bottom of which were several ponds; we went down to the brink of one of them; a prodigious number of bivalve shells of one single species, formed a sort of beach

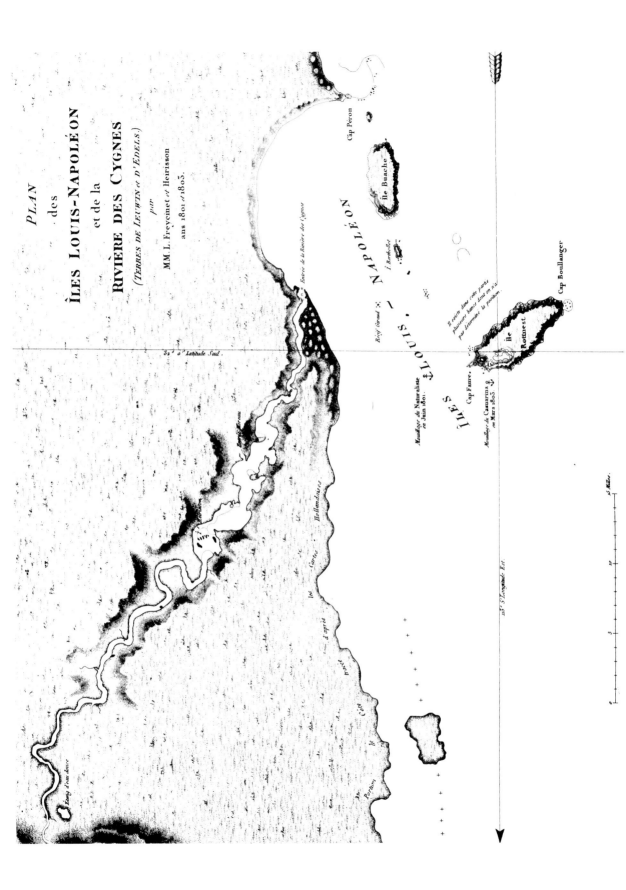

PLAN
des
ÎLES LOUIS-NAPOLÉON
et de la
RIVIÈRE DES CYGNES
(TERRES DE LEUWIN et D'EDELS.)
par
MM. L. Freycinet et Heirisson
ans 1801 et 1803.

32° o' Latitude Sud.

Entrée de la Rivière des Cygnes

Récif (étang)

ÎLES LOUIS-NAPOLÉON.

Cap Peron

Île Buache

Î. Bertholet

Il existe dans cette partie
plusieurs bancs dont on n'a
pas déterminé la position.

Île Nordouest

Cap Boullanger

Cap Fauve.

Mouillage du Naturaliste
en Juin 1801.

Mouillage du Casuarina
en Mars 1803.

Hollandaises

Côtes

les

Côte

d'après

Portland

Étang d'eau douce

115° 5' Longitude Est.

0   5   10   15 Milles.

around it about the breadth of 15 feet. The water of these ponds is salt and brackish'.[74]

Finding on the seashore a piece of wood—'a crosspiece of bits belonging to a vessel of 300 to 350 tons burthen'—and certain that it was from a recent shipwreck, their anxiety for the fate of their *Naturaliste* was 'much increased', for she was at anchor near dangerous reefs. Heavy rain, impetuous squalls and thunder which reverberated with great violence added to their anxiety. They spread their sail to catch rainwater and killed seals for food. The following day (19 June) they sighted their vessel again, and immediately lit a large fire to let the crew know where they were.

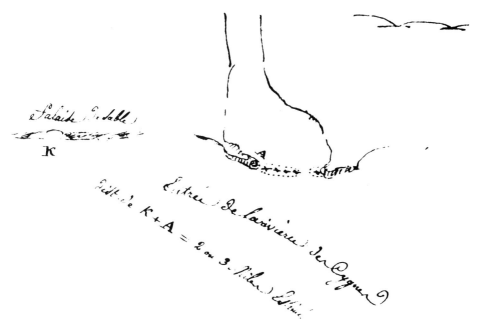

Fig. 3.8 Entrance of Swan River. A sketch by Colas, pharmacist with the Baudin expedition (1801). [Courtesy of Leslie Marchant]

On reaching *Naturaliste*, Freycinet learned that the party which had been sent to the islands to the south-south-east of Rottnest, had fared little better. Headed by Lieutenant-Commander Millias and Levillain, the zoologist, they had sailed their chaloupe cautiously along a long bed of rocks and had drawn near to a small island which they named Berthelot (Carnac).[75] Freycinet's chapters in Péron's book make no reference to landing on Berthelot, but a separate report on the expedition by Levillain to Captain Hamelin of *Naturaliste* shows that they did. Levillain's spelling is atrocious, and the report (in French) now held in the Battye Library[76] is therefore difficult to translate, but it appears that they saw many seals on the island and some very large birds, like eagles, and very big crows. Though the island was very sandy, it produced a large number of trees and plants with red and yellow flowers. Before leaving they left a bottle with a note inside reporting their stay, and that they had named the island Berthelot, or Island of the Seals, five of which they killed for food.

South of Berthelot another island as large as Rottnest was discovered, which they named Ile Buache (Garden Island). The same storm that had almost wrecked Freycinet's boat on Rottnest also caught Millias's party, which spent an anxious night at sea, the waves beating against their chaloupe with so much force that it took three men all their time to keep it baled out. Dropping a grappling, they weathered the storm until morning; but then, while trying to make *Naturaliste*, their mast was broken and the boat, out of control, was driven by waves onto rocks, where it was dashed to pieces. The men were thankful that none had been drowned. Levillain appears to have lost his personal belongings and 'good French money' in this episode. While waiting to be rescued they too lit a large fire to show their whereabouts and, like the Dutch in Vlamingh's expedition before them, roasted what they thought were almonds, and with similar consequences. Soon they were suffering terrible stomach pains and 'dreadful vomiting'. For my part, reported Levillain to Freycinet,

> I was extremely ill; after bringing up the small quantity of food which I had on my stomach, I continued to strain and retch till I brought up two large glasses of blood. . . . What a dreadful alternative for navigators. In such situations they are reduced to the necessity of either suffering all the pangs of famine, or being obliged to eat such food as may be poisonous and destructive.[77]

While the two parties were exploring the islands, *Géographe* was sighted from the masthead of *Naturaliste*, making sail to the north under her topsails at a distance of about 40 km. The crew were at a loss, wrote Freycinet, to know why she did not 'come thither to meet us'. There is no doubt that she was seen. The date and time is confirmed by two other diarists: Ensign Victor Couture and an anonymous crew member.[78] A flag had also been flown from Rottnest Island to attract *Géographe* but, as already noted, Baudin was simply not prepared to risk his vessel in such stormy seas and so sailed on.

The third party led by Sub-Lieutenant Heirisson, and including Joseph Bailly, the mineralogist, went on an expedition to the Swan River, which they reached on 17 June. They returned to *Naturaliste* on the twenty-second. Only Bailly's report (as given to Freycinet) appears in Péron's book, although this can now be supplemented with separate reports by Bailly (which includes additional material), Heirisson and Colas, a pharmacist who accompanied the party. Collectively, these represent a disappointing account of this important expedition: Bailly's interests are almost entirely geological and Heirisson confined his report to navigation hazards. Colas's report is short, although interesting, and he actually drew a map of the entrance to the Swan River (Fig. 3.8).

The party entered the mouth of the river where a bar of rocks almost denied them passage, and had to make three attempts before finally getting through. As drawn by Colas, the passage into the river was on the starboard side.[79] The entrance, according to Bailly's separate report, is by calcareous rocks full of excavations made by water erosion, and the surrounding land is covered by a thick layer of sand. As he proceeded up-river, the water depth increased rapidly and he noted that an abrupt cliff of calcareous rocks seemed always to be on one side of the river.[80] When this disappeared on one side of the valley, it suddenly appeared on the other side. It bore horizontal marks which, he concluded, proved that the sea was once there. Shells and other bodies continually formed in the sea constituted the base of the cliff. Trees, roots and fibres were still visible as well as other vegetable bodies encrusted in this calcium stone, forming the main part of the cliff. All these elements were very well conserved, so he concluded that the whole area had been under water not long ago. Some rocks, he noted, had very interesting formations, and looked like walls falling apart, or European castles which 'symbolised the picture of slavery'.

Proceeding up-river they reached Melville Water, where the country was flat, but once again they found steepness on the left shore (Mount Eliza?). It was in this basin that they found 'a sort of branch or creek which seemed to open another communication with the sea', and named it Moreau Entrance, after a midshipman in the party. This was the entrance to the Canning River. Before camping ashore for the night (beneath Mount Eliza) they ascended the cliff behind them, and

> were charmed with a beautiful prospect. On one side we discovered the upper course of the river, which went up towards a range of flat mountains in the distance, and on the other we could follow its course down to the seashore. The banks of the river appeared almost everywhere covered with beautiful forests which extended a considerable way into the interior of the country.[81]

Though their description was not unlike Stirling's, the latter's objectives, as we have written, were quite different from those of the French.

At the flats they, like the Dutch before them, were grounded, and got off only after much labour. Describing the river there as almost closed by a string of small, low, wet islands, they named these Heirisson Islands in honour of the officer commanding their party. Moving up-river, Bailly described the land as low and almost under water, with a bed of coarse sand covered with a bank of thick, reddish and sticky clay. In his other (independent) report, Bailly added that their journey up-river was hampered by trees which grew along the banks, some so old that they had fallen apart and lodged in the river, thus slowing it down. He observed that these trees were then quickly covered by sand and alluvial soil, and concluded that coal might be found underneath. Colas, the pharmacist, made a similar observation on the flora: trees were 15 to 18 m high, and their circumferences were between 3 and 5 m. The next day they sailed towards the hills but did not leave the boats and journey overland to the base, as was their intention, because provisions were running short. They therefore turned about and descended the river to the flats where they again ran aground. By making a raft and unloading the heaviest provisions from the boats and 'pushing with all their strength' they got off the bank, only to get stuck again, this time getting off with the assistance of a brisk afternoon sea breeze. Thirteen hours of hard labour in mud up to their waists found them 'sinking with faintness and fatigue'. Provisions were by now very low, and realizing they would be unable to reach the boat within twenty-four hours, they decided to land, dry themselves and rest,

> when all at once we heard a terrible noise which filled us with terror; it was something like the roaring of a bull but much louder, and seemed to proceed from the reeds which were very near us. At this formidable sound we lost all desire to go on shore; and, though benumbed with cold, we preferred passing the night on the water, without food, or being able to close our eyes, and suffering the whole time from the rain and the weather.[82]

The next day they sailed down the river to the bar where on the northern side they saw the tricolor flying and, on investigation, found nearby a bottle containing a letter from Millias who had apparently been blown ashore on the mainland while trying to sail from the islands back to *Naturaliste*. By nightfall the party reached *Naturaliste*, 'cruelly harassed with fatigue, and almost famished'.

It had been neither a fruitful nor pleasant expedition. Bailly's observation on soils along the upper reaches of the river was at best indefinite, although Colas, the pharmacist, thought that the land became more fertile the further inland they went. One variety of plant (unspecified) was very abundant and seemed to Colas to have been put there by 'human hands' (in a huge, wide field in which he detected signs of cultivation, i.e. furrows). Aside from finding the prints of a man's foot, of an extraordinary size, while making a short excursion from their campsite on 18 June, they found no sign of Aborigines and certainly did not see any, although Levillain, on his unscheduled visit to the mainland, reported seeing, in addition to kangaroos, green birds with red bellies, an enormous bird's nest in a tree, and 'two Indian houses newly built but not inhabited' by the banks of the river. They left two knives and two pieces of blue material in the houses. In his private (unpublished) report, Bailly speculated that the Swan River's source might be a chain of mountains running from east to west, 'directed towards the centre of new Holland and I believe it constitutes the skeleton of the country'. (A similar conjecture was made many years later by John Barrow of the British Admiralty in his article for the *Quarterly Review*.)[83] The party brought back to *Naturaliste* a bottle of water from the upper Swan, and those on board who tasted it agreed that it was fresh.

On the day before *Naturaliste* sailed from Swan River, Bailly made a visit to Rottnest Island where, like Freycinet, he discovered the salt lakes, noting that the tide was 'sensibly observed' in these ponds owing probably to the fact that the soil was so soft that the levels moved in concert with the sea. Impending departure gave Freycinet the opportunity to summarize the findings of mariners and scientists. Rottnest Island, he wrote, though rocky and sandy on its shores, was well wooded inland and the aspect very beautiful, *but* it did not appear to have any fresh water. It contained a small species of kangaroo which Péron later concluded belonged 'to a new and remarkable species'. A large number of seals were found, the fat of which was very good to eat, and they often made use of it to fry their fish. The fur of these animals, concluded Freycinet, was mostly fine and thick, and would be a valuable commodity because a rich cargo could easily be procured.[84] Large reptiles, between 1 and 1½ m long and the colour of unpolished steel, and an extraordinary species of lizard, were observed; fish were plentiful around the islands, though on some days none could be caught. Sharks were both plentiful and enormous; they caught one nearly 4 m long, and weighing nearly 600 kg but actually saw some twice that size. Bertholet was entirely barren and Ile Buache (Garden Island), though surrounded with shelves thus making it difficult to land on, was very woody in the interior. 'Partridges and ravens', of a smaller kind than those in Europe, were killed and had a delicious flavour. Of Swan River and the mainland Freycinet had only one comment: it could not be a proper place to supply water necessary for a ship because it was difficult to enter and one had to travel a great distance up river before finding fresh water.

On their leaving Rottnest Island, unfavourable winds forced them to sail well out to sea, but on several occasions they came close enough to the coast to distinguish the general constitution of its soil, and to confirm what had already been written of the area by the Dutch:

> And on all this part of Edel's Land we saw the same melancholy appearance as that on the shores of Leuwin's [sic] Land.[85]

Using Dutch charts, which Freycinet thought erroneous in many respects, they reached the Abrolhos islands, where contrary winds prevented them from making detailed navigation. By 16 July they had reached Dirk Hartog Island and Shark Bay where they again waited in vain for Baudin in *Géographe*, 'doomed to waste our time on these desolate shores'.[86] They found Vlamingh's plate 'half covered with sand, near the remains of a post of oakwood', but did not take it, preferring instead to leave their own plate.

Géographe and *Naturaliste* did not rejoin company until they reached Timor. After taking on provisions, both vessels sailed along the western coast of the Southland, but well out to sea, turned east around Cape Leeuwin and made for Van Diemen's Land, then sailed along the south-east coast of the continent to Port Jackson for well-earned and much-needed recuperation. On the journey back to France, *Géographe* called at both King George Sound and the Swan River area, the latter having been by-passed by Baudin on the outward voyage. Even fine mid-March weather could not entice Baudin to stay. Unexpectedly finding *Casuarina*, a small vessel he had acquired at Port Jackson, and which had become separated from *Géographe* on the westward passage, waiting for him at Rottnest Island, Baudin decided to 'go on, for the place, already explored by the *Naturaliste,* was not worth the trouble of stopping there'.[87]

Baudin had been officially instructed to give special attention to the relatively unknown coast between Leeuwin and Swan River. While his reports and those of others on the expedition provided detailed information of the coast and two parts of the mainland (Geographe Bay and Swan River), these could not have encouraged the expedition's sponsors, who were interested in finding safe anchorages and soils that could be cultivated. 'All that can be said of Swan River and its environs', wrote

Baudin, 'judging by the report of Captain Hamelin and his officers who stayed there quite a long time, is that the anchorage is very bad, insecure and open to the winds from south-west to north-west, and that at such times as they are blowing, the sea is very heavy there. The Swan River, which was explored for 18 to 20 leagues, offers *no resources at all* [our emphasis]. Here and there some fresh water was found in the streams that enter it, but they are very small.'[88] Baudin presumably wrote these words when he returned to Swan River in 1803 so it would appear that neither Hamelin nor Freycinet of *Naturaliste* had changed his mind about the place by the time they rejoined and reported to him in Timor. Even though Baudin's second visit along the coast from Leeuwin to Swan River was made in more favourable weather, it only reaffirmed the view he expressed on his first visit. It did not have 'a single place that can offer shelter against winds from north-east through west to south-west'. Even Geographe Bay was safe only in summer months when the winds were north-east to south-west, and Swan River/Rottnest Island was no better able to shelter a ship in bad weather. These places, he declared, offered nothing more than a temporary anchorage in fine weather during summer months.

Baudin had also been instructed to examine Shark Bay in some detail, at least in respect to the anchorage. This he did on his way back to France in 1803 and con-sidered it the only part of the western coast worth settling, primarily because it offered considerable commercial potential as a whaling-station which, he alleged, was why the Dutch had not provided accurate charts of the bay; further, the bay possessed 'an infinite number of places offering havens (as secure as they are roomy) for medium-sized trading vessels drawing no more than 12 feet of water'.[89]

The unfortunate Baudin never reached France. He died on the homeward voyage at Ile de France after a long illness probably caused by a disease he had contracted in Timor. Had he first explored the south-western coast during summer months his, and the others', reports may have been more enthusiastic. Yet the fact remains, no safe winter anchorages had been discovered, the coastline near Swan River was demonstrably dangerous, the river was difficult to enter and even harder to navi-gate, and the soil seemed to offer little prospect for agriculture. Swan River had been classified not worthy of further interest, a status which discouraged explora-tion for a further twenty-three years.

The French vessels returned to Le Havre in 1804. Péron's journal of the voyage was published in English in 1807 and a second volume posthumously in 1817, Péron having died in 1810. British reviewers of the French volumes in the influential *Quarterly Review* roundly criticized both the purpose of the French voyage and the ability of Baudin and his officers. They also took the opportunity to censure the French government for incarcerating Flinders at the Ile de France on his way back to England.[90] The first reviewer, writing while France and England were still at war (1810), claimed that the British government, in granting the French vessels passports of immunity from attack on grounds that they were undertaking a round-the-world scientific expedition, had been grossly misled. Baudin's negligence in not controlling dysentery and scurvy had led to appalling death rates, which Péron himself con-firmed, for of the twenty-three scientists who left on the voyage only three returned—a point made with almost malicious satisfaction. Flinders's accusation that he had been imprisoned in Mauritius for seven years in order to provide the French sufficient time to publish ahead of him the results of the Baudin expedition, was reiterated and note taken that this treatment compared shabbily with the generous hospitality accorded French crews and scientists during their long stay at Port Jackson. Indeed, the French crews were too weak even to sail their vessels into Sydney harbour and had to be assisted by British crews. The reviewer was especially disappointed that not a single chart or sketch of the Australian coast appeared in the atlas accompanying Péron's volume, and even the five or six views of the Southland looked like 'so many strips of coloured riband'.

The same points were emphasized again in the *Quarterly Review* critique of the second volume, which had been partly edited by Péron before his death, completed by Freycinet and published in 1817. Charts in the small atlas accompanying the volume were, wrote the reviewer, '*very like those of Captain Flinders* only very inferior in point of execution' (the reviewer's emphasis). However, Péron's and the other naturalists' scientific work was acknowledged, despite the disadvantages under which they had been placed by the 'harsh and unfeeling' Baudin. The reviewers' disappointment with the contents of these volumes, especially the information provided by Freycinet, Bailly and others on the Swan River area, would have only confirmed official opinion in England concerning the impressions already provided by Dutch explorers.

V

European visitors to Swan River between 1619 and 1803 were unanimous in one impression: the danger that numerous off-shore reefs posed to their cumbersome vessels. Each skipper quickly and rightly assessed that the shallow waters between Rottnest Island and the coast contained geological structures inimical to the safety of their sailing-vessels, although once outside the reefs the same skippers were heartened when the water's depth increased with remarkable regularity. Even between the reefs the soft, sandy bottom provided good holding-ground (see Fig. 3.1).

The coastal plain along much of the south-western coast has been formed during millions of years of erosion at the fringes of the Great Western pre-Cambrian Shield (see page 2), a process which geologists argue has caused the shield 'to retreat' several kilometres eastwards.[91] During this long process, the area west of the present coastline to the continental shelf (which lies west of Rottnest Island) underwent periods of being submerged and then exposed.[92] The melting of massive glaciers after the Pleistocene Ice Age (2½ million or so years ago) which greatly increased sea levels around the Australian coast (see page 2), also left their mark on the Swan coastal plain. The most recent exposure of land, extending as far as eight or more kilometres west of Rottnest, occurred only 20 000 years ago, Rottnest and Garden islands being joined to the mainland as recently as 7000 years ago (Fig. 3.9).

A major legacy of this process has been the formation of coastal limestone outcrops which form in parallel ridges of dunes extending in a north-south direction

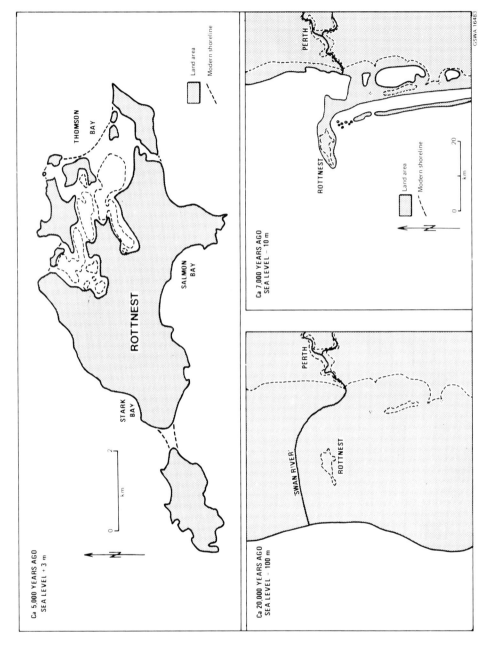

Fig. 3.9 Palaeogeographic maps of the Rottnest-Perth area illustrating shorelines approximately 20 000, 7000 and 5000 years ago. [From *Geological Survey of Western Australia*, Report No. 6, 1977, article by Phillip E. Playford & R. E. J. Leach. Reproduced with permission of the Director, Geological Survey, Department of Mines, Western Australia]

from Rottnest Island to Mount Eliza.[93] Seddon identifies eight or nine of these north-south 'systems', the first of which comprises Rottnest and the outer reefs; the second Carnac, the Stragglers, Point Peron and Garden Island; and the third, Fremantle. Assumed to have been formed at various stages since the late Pleistocene, the subterranean reefs protrude from the soft-sand sea-floor, posing the navigation hazards feared by all mariners mentioned in this chapter. Though there are passages between the reefs, these were not charted until after first settlement.

Having carefully negotiated offshore reefs, however, mariners then more carefully noticed the composition and nature of the landscape. The same causes which resulted in the marine geology discussed above applied equally to the coast. On first acquaintance, the land appeared to be only an exposed variation of the sea bottom—exposed limestone outcrops and sandhills. Rottnest Island, generally visited first because of its location, set a theme which hardly altered. Leeman and Vlamingh's men, having explored Rottnest and later having walked a few kilometres inland on the mainland from Jurien Bay and places further north, recorded observations which varied only in emphasis—sandy, barren and extremely difficult and uncomfortable to walk over. The coastal plain in the entire Swan River basin is made up of various sand-dune systems, and inland as far as Mount Eliza from the coast, these are interspersed with limestone outcrops. Explorers who traversed inland complained of thorny, prickly bushes, and with justification, for, as Seddon shows, in a Mediterranean-type climate where rainfall is very sparse in summer months, the vegetation *is* hard-leaved, and the leaves tend to hang downwards so as to reduce exposure to the sun's rays. The leaves, too, are invariably grey in colour to aid reflection of the sun's heat, they are covered with a fine felting of hair-like threads to reduce water-loss, and may also be covered with a waxy surface and have oil glands.[94]

Rainfall on the Swan coastal plain is substantial (876 mm per annum), but most of it falls during a few winter months (June-August) when westerly winds move northwards from high latitudes and, typically, in a regular series of low-pressure fronts, bring soaking showers to the coast. North-westerly winds herald a typical two to three day period of heavy rain, followed by strong west to south-west winds of near equal velocity. Once the front has passed to the east, winds may be quite gentle until the next front appears. During summer, wind patterns are typically diverse—morning easterlies which gradually weaken and are replaced during the afternoons by sea breezes, which can reach high velocities. Thus, gale-force north-west to west winds in winter, persistent easterlies on summer mornings, and south westerlies during summer afternoons, in an ocean containing many limestone reefs between Rottnest Island and the coast, is the main reason why the mariners whose experiences are recorded in this chapter were so uniformly apprehensive about being at anchor there during *any* period of the year, and why, at the first sign of worsening weather, they quickly weighed anchor and made for the open sea. The especially boisterous *winter* storms is the reason why, after short experience, the Dutch East India Company declined to send vessels of search and/or recovery to Swan River during that season.

Behind the arid sand dunes, however, lay a river which, though sandy and rocky along its shores, impressed men of the Vlamingh and French expeditions who sailed on its waters. The limestone cliffs (which represent the other five or six north-south dune systems identified by Seddon) gave this old, serpentine, shallow river a beauty and tranquillity in its lower reaches which men of both science and the sea readily appreciated, even though the terrain there was still sandy, varying only in colour, and the vegetation prickly. Both expeditions were there during the summer (or late summer) when the Swan estuary was still saline, not yet washed by run-off from the scarp, and fish, crabs, jellyfish and the unique birdlife (black swans, pelicans, herons, etc.) were to be seen in abundance. The upper reaches beyond the flats were seen only by Heirisson's party, and although he was impressed by the large trees which grew on rich alluvial flats, spreading their branches across the banks, Heirisson made no mention of the area's agricultural potential. His party was not comfortable on the Swan River. They unfortunately expended much energy pushing their boats off sand- and mud-banks, and seemed constantly concerned lest they should be attacked by natives, who remained unseen, but whose presence through newly made huts and fresh footprints was obvious.

The absence of contact with Aborigines by any European explorer to the Swan River area between 1619 and 1803 (save the few met by sailors from *Emeloort* on the coast near Jurien Bay), when there was so much evidence of their presence, is one of the salient characteristics of European contact with Swan River. As the *Nijptangh* diarist wrote, 'all were very shy' and unwilling to reveal themselves, but they were almost certainly watching with great apprehension the progress of strangers who miraculously moved across water on the backs of huge 'birds' and could instantly kill a black swan merely by pointing a stick at it and making a loud noise. Ronald Berndt believes the Aborigines thought that white Europeans were the spirits of the returned dead, and if this is so, it is no wonder they were apprehensive and unwilling to meet the strangers.

It is now almost impossible to calculate how many Aborigines lived around Swan River, or where and how they lived, but pioneer archaeological work by Sylvia Hallam on the Swan estuary is increasingly revealing more information than it was hitherto thought possible to obtain. Though commendably cautious in her conclusions, Mrs Hallam, on the basis of her own archaeological work and the reports of first European settlers after 1829, calculates that the area centring on Guildford to the north and south for 96 km, eastward to the hills, and westward to the coast (i.e. 4650-5200 km^2), contained at the time of the first European settlement a minimum of 420 Aborigines, or about one person per 10 km^2.[95] On the basis of numbers of sites discovered, the population density of Aborigines increased eastward of the flats. Aborigines apparently returned to a complex of sites, where grinding materials indicate that they were frequently used. The Swan coastal plain, writes Hallam, offered the most basic requirements for Aborigines—fresh water in the lakes and swamps of the sand plain, with frogs, turtles, crustaceans and roots as a standby even at the leanest time of the year.[96] Perceptive first European settlers such as Francis Armstrong and Robert Lyon listed several 'tribes' in the area,[97] apparently comprising about 120 persons each. Little is known of their European pre-settlement way of life, although first settlers noted that they congregated around the estuaries and lagoons in the summer (the season when Vlamingh and the French expeditions were there) and 'dispersed in winter through a wider hinterland which included sites large and small at the foot of the scarp and into the hills'.[98] Governor Stirling was greatly impressed by their 'truly wonderful' skill in spearing fish. We have already noted their peculiar form of animal husbandry—fire-stick farming— which apparently was widely practised and probably may explain why some European explorers thought that the land had been cultivated, with grasses growing strongly between sparsely scattered trees.

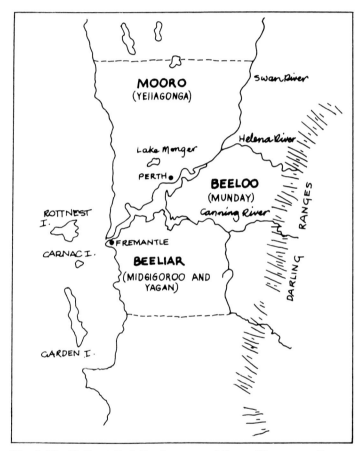

Fig. 3.10 Native tribal districts around Swan River according to the researches of Robert Lyon in 1832. [From George Seddon, *A Sense of Place*]

But by and large, the European visitors mentioned in this chapter knew nothing more of the Aborigines than that they lived in the most primitive huts imaginable— the Vlamingh party's reference to these being worse than the Hottentots is an extremely derisive analogy—and that they were probably responsible for the frequent fires, and the evidence of earlier fires, seen along the coast. One Dutch explorer noted that their excreta looked similar to that of animals, and therefore concluded that, like herbivores, they must also eat grass. Men like Volkersen had been instructed to make contact with their chiefs, to make treaties which placed the Aborigines under Dutch protection, to explore their kingdoms, and to note their manufactures and their fisheries—expectations which had been clearly conditioned by the instructor's knowledge and experience of the Javanese milieu. Dutch mariners understandably tended to bring with them their Dutch experiences. To Vlamingh the coast looked like Holland; birds that looked like Brent geese were so named; they heard the song of a 'nightingale'; and trees that they had known in India seemed to grow also on this continent. Vlamingh also brought blacks from the Cape to communicate with natives. The apprehension felt by these European mariners seemed to increase as they found themselves unable to make contact with the Aborigines, and whenever they went ashore, they were usually well armed in case they should encounter, or be attacked by, Aborigines. Shipwrecked sailors like Leeman could readily survive by killing and eating sea-gulls and seals, but when other mariners tried to emulate the natives by roasting what they thought were European chestnuts (actually zamia palm nuts), they became violently ill, because they did not know, as the Aborigines knew, that the nuts had to be leached of their poison before being consumed.

4

Decision and Preparations

With these few and general instructions for your guidance, assisted by the oral and written communications which have taken place between yourself and this Dept., you will, I trust, be able to surmount the difficulties to which you may be exposed at the outset . . .

SIR GEORGE MURRAY TO JAMES STIRLING
30 DECEMBER 1828

Before James Stirling left Port Jackson for northern Australia to complete the job he had been sent to do—disestablish the settlement at Melville Island—he joined exploring parties into the interior,[1] an experience which would have increased his meagre knowledge of the Australian bush and possibly provided the opportunity to hear from pioneer settlers the problems they faced in trying to bring virgin country into production. There seems little doubt that he also discussed the opportunities for pastoral activity with merchants in Sydney, for this was a time when the quantity and value of the wool clip had reached new heights.[2] Indeed, before leaving Australia Stirling purchased 3890 ha of land in New South Wales which, in addition to 1040 ha granted him by Governor Darling for his services to the colony, led Darling to conclude that he intended employing his capital there—a view supported by Somerville, who contended that Stirling's decision was the result of his being 'deeply infected with the boom in sheep and wool'.[3] *Success* reached Melville Island during mid-June 1827, having been grounded on a sandbank during the voyage, and Stirling then chose Raffles Bay as the alternative site. Other vessels with troops and stores were waiting to be unloaded, so the annexation ceremony was carried out the next day (18 June 1827) and the new settlement named 'Fort Wellington'. During Stirling's six weeks' stay, when he attempted to fulfil Governor Darling's instructions to get the settlement established, he experienced considerable trouble with natives, and, according to Uren, seemed anxious to get away from the place, 'itching to get to London to further his plans for the occupation of the Swan River—with himself at the head, of course'.[4] Soon after arriving at the East India station and reporting, as instructed, to the commanding admiral, Stirling became very ill and, at his own request, was again placed on half-pay and returned to England, which he reached during May or June 1828.[5]

Though pleased to be back in England, where he could actively promote the cause of Swan River, Stirling must have been bitterly disappointed to learn that the

Colonial Office had decided against establishing a settlement there and therefore had declined his offer to be its leader.[6] But Stirling's recommendations had not been dismissed out of hand.[7] His report had been sent for comment to one of the most knowledgeable and influential public servants on colonial affairs—John Barrow, secretary of the Admiralty.[8] Barrow had been one of the strongest supporters of the plan to establish a settlement in northern Australia, having been greatly influenced by King's report and by discussions with that officer later in England. In fact, Barrow was 'furious' when he learned that Stirling had been given permission to postpone his mission and sail off in what he called a 'Quixotic' expedition to Swan River in direct contradiction of original orders, 'and, in utter ignorance of what he has proposed', and expected to hear that *Success* had been wrecked on that notorious western coast.[9] Thus when he was asked by the Colonial Office to comment on Stirling's report on Swan River, he gave it more than usual attention. On the basis of what Stirling and Fraser had written, Barrow acknowledged that the area contained all the physical elements required for a settlement—anchorage, hinterland, vegetation, building materials, water, etc.—but there, he wrote, its advantages ended. He seriously questioned the application of Stirling's professional observation to wider economic and political issues (see Chapter 2, p. 44). Anticipations of commercial intercourse with India and Malaya, a key condition for the success of a settlement at Swan River, were, he wrote, 'quite fallacious'. The Malays and Chinese do not 'trust themselves Southward of Torres Strait', and therefore would not trade with Swan River. Nor had Stirling provided sufficient information to allay long-held fears about the western coast. 'The whole range of the Western Coast', wrote Barrow, 'even that part of it in question, is full of danger, and ships bound to India will *avoid* rather than *seek* it' (our italics). He also seriously questioned the viability of the proposal to establish a convalescent station, mainly because Stirling, in his letter of 14 December 1826 to Governor Darling seeking permission to visit Swan River, had suggested, almost as an aside, that the China traders, in addition to bringing stores from England to Swan River, could alternatively bring 'Prisoners, if it were thought proper to make it a Prison Settlement'. The suggestion (though not repeated in Stirling's report after he had been to Swan River) was anathema to Barrow: 'our Indian Gentlemen would [never] think of repairing to a penal Settlement on the Western coast of New Holland . . . as Capt. Stirling has vainly imagined'.[10]

On balance, however, Barrow was undecided whether or not to support the establishment of a settlement at Swan River. But if one were established, it would have to be independently governed for it was as much separated from New South Wales as from England, and all the difficulties Governor Darling had experienced in servicing King George Sound would be replicated if Swan River were placed under his control. On the other hand, he argued, if King George Sound were to be continued, he would support another establishment at Swan River because, on the basis of Stirling's report, the land between each was probably good and settlement would naturally spread from one port to the other. Finally, however, he expressed doubts concerning the advisability of continuing any settlement on the western side when so

many millions of acres remained unoccupied on the eastern side of the continent—
land which improved 'in beauty and fertility as we advance to the Northward'. The
only justification for a new settlement, he concluded, was political: to prevent the
French or Americans from getting a foothold on the continent. But even in that
event it would be 'a long series of years, before they could give our other Colonies
much annoyance'. He was obviously not impressed by Stirling's and Lockyer's
arguments that enemy powers on the western side could intercept and annoy British
vessels using the southern route. Nor was he impressed with Stirling's proposals for
a 'naval and military station on a grand scale' at Swan River to protect the India
station, or for the detour of China traders resulting in full cargoes for their entire
voyages. Neither 'advantage' was even mentioned by Barrow in his report to the
Colonial Office.

Pl. 4.1 John Barrow of the Admiralty. [Courtesy of the National Portrait Gallery,
London]

Although Barrow had not unequivocally refused support for Swan River, his
views were sufficiently negative for the Colonial Office to take no action. In their

letters of January 1828 to Governor Darling, the Colonial Office used all Barrow's arguments, and many of his exact sentences, to conclude that it would be 'inexpedient, on the score of expense' and *unnecessary, with a view to any urgent Interest to attempt a new settlement at Swan River*' (our italics).[11] The only action the government intended taking was to inform the East India Company of Stirling's discoveries in case they might be inclined to establish a settlement there.[12] For the same reasons, the settlement at King George Sound would probably be withdrawn, but this would not be decided until the East India Company's intentions were known. Meantime, Darling was instructed to retain and service the outpost.[13]

These letters to Darling were written about four months before Stirling returned to England, by which time (May/June 1828) the East India Company, despite the 'benevolent energies of India merchants such as Prinsep, and doubtless Mangles, Stirling's father-in-law', had declined to become formally involved with Swan River.[14] But the determined James Stirling, still recuperating from illness, was in no mood to see his plan lapse for want of support from either the government or the East India Company. And it was his determination and conviction, together with fortuitous political changes which brought two of his friends to positions of power in the Colonial Office, that paved the way for a reversal of decision by the government.

Lord Bathurst, a high Tory, was secretary of state for war and the colonies from 1812 to April 1827. In a difficult post-war period, when he laid the foundations of the Colonial Office, Bathurst showed special interest in New South Wales, partly because his government was determined to reform the treatment of convicts, and partly because it recognized the colony's considerable economic potential.[15] Lord Goderich succeeded Lord Bathurst for only five months (April 1827 to September 1827) before becoming prime minister for an equally short period. In the period of relative political upheaval which followed,[16] the Duke of Wellington became prime minister and chose Sir George Murray, his old quartermaster-general and chief of staff, for the Colonial Office portfolio and Horace Twiss as political under-secretary. Though both were friends of James Stirling, and were appointed during the very month he returned to England (May 1828), neither was a good choice for office. Sir George Murray had a reputation for inefficiency and for being 'totally incapable of grasping administrative detail or keeping the department in order', and Twiss was said to be indecisive, and so occupied with detail that he became incapable of reaching a conclusion.[17] In these circumstances, the permanent under-secretary of the department, Robert Hay, a man with a reputation for going 'straight to a decision', was the essential link for unity of action and continuity of policy.[18]

Despite his friendship with the politicians Murray and Twiss, Stirling was astute enough to realize that the administrators Hay and Barrow were the key men to convince and, accordingly, within weeks of returning to England he saw each separately. This was good tactics. Hay and Barrow were close personal friends, Hay having appointed Barrow's son as his private secretary.[19] Stirling reiterated to Hay all the favourable features of Swan River: Cockburn Sound 'may easily be converted into one of the finest harbours in the world', and as a place for settlement, Swan

River was 'not inferior in any natural essential quality to the Plain of Lombardy'.[20] To convince the doubtful Hay, he had already taken considerable steps beyond the position taken in his 1827 report. He also put forward a plan which would facilitate settlement by placing the colony under naval discipline. Such arrangements would be 'cheap and simple' (the government had rejected his 1827 proposal because it would be too expensive) and would not require parliamentary enactments. He also pointed out that, failing support for this scheme, Swan River should be considered as the location of a penal settlement, being closer to England than was New South Wales. Though Hay's reaction to Stirling's proposals is not known, Barrow is on record as having been greatly persuaded by Stirling's information about Swan River. His doubts of October 1827 were soon resolved: Stirling's report on soil had been confirmed by 'a person fully competent to judge' (Fraser), and the discovery of a fine anchorage, entirely overlooked by French navigators, would induce both the French and Americans to 'assume possession of the only spot on the Western Coast of New Holland that is at all inviting for such a purpose'.[21] Having been won over, Barrow then recommended to Twiss that the establishment at King George Sound be *transferred* to Swan River.

Within a month of seeing both Hay and Barrow, Stirling, now heartened by the reception he had been given, put behind him the 'new' proposals for a colony under naval discipline, and a convict colony; and in association with Major Thomas Moody touted yet another 'basis' on which Swan River could be settled—through private capital raised by an association which would obtain a propriety charter similar to those adopted in the settlements at Pennsylvania and Georgia.[22] The great advantage of this scheme, they agreed, was that it would overcome one of the two objections registered by the Colonial Office—'the score of expense'. The other reason for the Colonial Office's lack of interest in Swan River was that there was now no urgent military reason for establishing a settlement, d'Urville having left Australian waters without making the territorial claims feared by Governor Darling. Hay, however, was not convinced that the French were still uninterested and wrote to his friend Stuart de Rothesay, Ambassador at Paris, asking about French aspirations. In reply, Rothesay enclosed a copy of *Le Moniteur Universel* for 22 August 1828 in which proposals for a penal settlement, perhaps in New Holland, were discussed, and also reported that the ministère de la Marine had examined the possibility of French transportation to Australia.[23] French interest was clearly still active. By October 3 Barrow had been persuaded that a settlement should be established at Swan River, expense being the only obstacle.[24] Stirling then discussed with Barrow and Twiss his proposal that private capitalists be encouraged to settle Swan River, and on 22 October 1828 assured Twiss that 'a Gentleman of Judgment and ability . . . [was] disposed to participate in the adventure', as were many of his friends. The main hurdle, he wrote, was that the government had not revealed *its* intentions and settlers could not be expected to proceed to Swan River if there was a chance that on their arrival it was already occupied by another power.[25] He urged the government to despatch at once a ship of war to Swan River with instructions to take possession of the country, to commence surveys and make arrangements for the reception of settlers. Stirling even offered to accompany the vessel and, if necessary, hire a vessel at the Cape at his own expense.

Two weeks later the Lord Commissioners of the Admiralty were requested by Sir George Murray to give immediate orders to the officer commanding H.M. forces at the Cape of Good Hope to despatch one of the ships of war under his command, without the smallest loss of time, with directions that he take formal possession of the western coast of New Holland. The place at which he would take possession was to be at, or as near as possible to, Swan River and he was to remain on the spot until he received further instructions. James Stirling had won a major battle. It had not been easy. More than once during the summer of 1828 he had been exasperated by the government's procrastination, and told his brother that officials trembled at the thought of increased expenditure.[26]

II

Charles Howe* Fremantle, born on 1 June 1800, was the son of an illustrious father who, by his deeds at Trafalgar, had become one of the national heroes of that great naval battle. Though only five years old when his father fought at Trafalgar, Charles would have heard the deeds recounted many times during his childhood. How his father's ship *Neptune*, second in battle line to Nelson's *Victory*, encountered *Santissima Trinidad*, a towering, four-decked Spanish ship much larger than any vessel in the English fleet; how, unable to match the foe in size and cannon power, Fremantle used a tactic he had used in earlier battles—closed in under *Santissima*'s stern and rained cannonball into her hull; and how, when the battle was finally over, *Neptune*, battle-scarred and laden with prisoners, towed *Victory* to Gibraltar with Nelson's body on board.[27] During his childhood at Swanbourne, Buckinghamshire, in the house his father had bought seven years before Trafalgar, Charles was surrounded by naval memorabilia, including the Spanish rear-admiral's sword of surrender and ornaments taken from *Santissima*'s chapel before she was sunk.

Though separated from his father by the latter's frequent voyages and tours of duty in foreign places, there was never any doubt that Charles would join the Navy at an early age. Even so, it is remarkable that at age eleven he had joined his father at Palermo, and when he had to be sent back to England because of sickness, his father made certain that his name was retained on the ship's books so that he 'would not lose any of that indispensable commodity—time served'.[28] He was nineteen when his father arranged for him to serve in a sloop in the Adriatic where, wrote his father, if he were disposed to learn he would never have a better opportunity, for his mentor would be Charles Smith, the renowned astronomer, surveyor and draftsman. The skills young Fremantle learned from Smith would be used in a lifetime of naval service. A few months later his father asked Lord Melville, First Lord of the Admiralty, to make Charles a lieutenant. Patronage of this kind was neither uncommon nor irregular in the Navy at that time. (James Stirling had similarly been sup-

* He was given this name because he was born on the day of Lord Howe's victory over the French.

Pl. 4.2 Charles Howe Fremantle as a young man. [Painted by Christopher Fremantle from a miniature in the possession of Lord Cottesloe]

Pl. 4.3 H.M.S. *Challenger*. [By Lieut. Dashwood of *Challenger*. Courtesy of the Battye Library]

ported by his uncle, Rear-Admiral Charles Stirling, during his early years in the Navy.)[29] But both young men had to match the favours by passing their examinations. Charles Fremantle also distinguished himself by swimming through heavy surf to save life aboard a shipwrecked Spanish brig, for which he was awarded the Royal National Lifeboat Institution's gold medal for gallantry. At age twenty-four he received his first command, the sloop *Jasper*, employed mainly in fisheries protection off the south coast of England. It was towards the end of his second year there that his naval career almost ended when he was accused of raping a maid-servant in his lodgings at Portsmouth. Incarcerated pending the hearing at the Winchester assizes, Charles was rescued by influential friends, who 'rallied around, witnesses were persuaded not to offer any evidence, and the prosecution was withdrawn'— action which led to unfavourable comment in local newspapers.[30]

Charles Fremantle also had influential friends in other places. His Uncle William (his father's youngest brother), to whom he was very attached and wrote frequently, was (in 1826) a member of parliament, a privy councillor, a commissioner for the India Board and treasurer of the household. Immediately after the charge at Winchester had been withdrawn, Uncle William renewed family lobbying with Lord Melville for Charles's further promotion. Accordingly, on 4 August 1826 he was promoted to the rank of captain and, although he had to wait two years before receiving a command, what he got was worth the wait. *Challenger,* launched at Portsmouth on 14 November 1826, was a frigate of 615 tonnes, 38 m in length and had a crew of 160.[31] Though armed with twenty 32-pounder cannonades on the upper deck, six 18-pounders on the quarter-deck and two 9-pounders on the foc'sle, she was by no means an impressive ship-of-war, having once been described by Fremantle's nephew as of the class which some said could neither fight nor run away.[32] But the young Fremantle did not see it that way. Believing that the decision was due once again to the benevolent support of Uncle William, his letter of thanks expressed the sentiment that *Challenger* was the very ship he would have selected himself (see Plate 4.3).[33] He could hardly wait for her return from Canadian waters and her refitting for what then was unknown service.

The day Fremantle received word of his command (1 September 1828), James Stirling was in London anxiously awaiting the government's decision on Swan River. On 5 November Sir George Murray requested the Admiralty to send a ship from the Cape of Good Hope to Swan River to take formal possession of the western coast of New Holland. This was only a few days after *Challenger* had returned from Quebec, later than expected by the impatient Charles, who, two weeks before, had told his Uncle William that he had been 'hourly expecting her, and as the Wind has been fair some days, I cannot understand why she is not arrived'.[34] As requested by Sir George, the Admiralty acted 'without the smallest loss of time', for only a week after the request was made Fremantle received orders to fit *Challenger* for foreign service with the utmost despatch.[35] Though he had no idea where he was to take the ship, four days later he heard from a friend that he would be ordered to relieve the vessel *Tweed*, stationed at the Cape, because that vessel is 'to go immediately to pave the way for establishing the Settlement on the West Coast of Australia'.[36] The purpose of this latest letter to his influential uncle was not to inform him of the pending decision but to beg him to do everything in his power to have the orders changed. There is no doubt whatever that Charles Fremantle did not want to be stationed at the Cape. His objections to it were 'manifest; there is not the slightest possibility of distinguishing oneself or of receiving the slightest benefit in any way . . . . It is the only station (with the exception of Halifax) I do not wish to go to.' Instead, his aspirations were for the important India station, which offered much better opportunities, and higher pay. Clearly agitated, he wrote again to his uncle expressing confidence that intervention with Cockburn would have the desired effect, adding that he also intended writing to Cockburn himself requesting that *Challenger* be assigned to the India station.[37] He also asked his mother to write to Vice-Admiral William Hotham, presumedly a family friend, who might lend support to his cause.

Uncle William's influence with the Admiralty was again decisive. On 2 December John Barrow wrote Commander Schomberg at the Cape, changing the order of November 7.[38] The following day Fremantle was told to proceed immediately to the Cape and deliver to Schomberg despatches instructing him to keep *Tweed* at the Cape and send *Challenger* to Swan River in her stead. Should Schomberg be absent from the Cape station, Fremantle was to open the instructions himself, 'and proceed to *New Holland* and be guided by the Orders therein contained', and should he meet Lord John Churchill in the *Tweed* (at sea), he was to order him back to the Cape.[39] Though not entirely happy with the change of plans because they did not assure him that the India station would be his final destination, Fremantle was nonetheless relieved that his stay at the Cape would be so short. 'There is no doubt', he wrote to Uncle William, 'but that I am quit of the Cape and that my ultimate destination will be India . . . I like the prospect . . . it gives me such a good opportunity of seeing a new Country.'[40] Charles Howe Fremantle was destined to see a great deal more than one new country during the expected four years' voyage which began with *Challenger*'s departure from Portsmouth on 14 December 1828.[41] Preparations had to be made with unusual haste; especially significant, as it transpired, was the 'high speed' with which John Septimus Roe, the young hydrographer who had accompanied King on his Australian maritime explorations, was ordered by the Admiralty to copy Stirling's chart of Swan River.[42]

From the beginning, Fremantle was delighted with *Challenger*'s performance; she sailed fast and repeatedly beat *Pallas,* which accompanied her to Tangier.[43] But the young captain soon had cause to reflect on the responsibilities, loneliness and occasionally the rewards of command—reflections which he expressed in very personal letters to his mother. He confessed to being seasick and lamented that his servants, like hers, were always quarrelling but, unlike her, he would give them 'a good flogging to make them agree'. He longed to be home, and was 'bored to death . . . sometimes in the Evening having nobody to talk to, as you are aware that a Captain is not very intimate with his Officers'.[44] He quickly established a reputation for firm leadership on a voyage which was fairly uneventful save that a sailor was lost in stormy seas off Falmouth, that *Challenger* was becalmed for a week in the tropics, and that poor James Green was 'flogged for theft . . . 3 dozen'.[45]

When he reached Simon's Bay (the Cape) ten weeks out of Portsmouth, Charles's worst fears about the station were confirmed: 'You cannot conceive a more wretched doghole of a place than this Town', he wrote his mother, 'indeed it does not deserve such an appellation as there are not more than half a dozen houses and a Dockyard establishment'.[46] Though he liked Cape Town—39 km distant along a road which part of the way ran along sands up to a horse's knee—he thought this might be because after such a long confinement on board ship anything would appear to be paradise. Neither in his diary, nor in his letters to Uncle William and his mother, did Charles mention, let alone make comment on, the significance of the fact that *Tweed* was still at the Cape when he arrived, and that he would therefore be proceeding to Swan River. Indeed, he was surprisingly reluctant to record views on significant and important issues. For example, he made no reference to attitudes at the Cape concerning the proposed new settlement, even though he spent most of his time ashore, stayed with Schomberg and the governor, who, with other residents, must have been concerned whether the French, as some expected, had already claimed the western coast. One of his own crew recorded hearing that the French had already decided to establish a convict settlement at Shark Bay.[47] Yet he was not reluctant to record (in his diary) his hostility on learning that First-Lieutenant Mouat had expressed a wish to exchange places with any officer at the Cape station. Fremantle saw this as an adverse reflection on his leadership and told Mouat that he did not think much of him as an officer and recommended that he leave the ship immediately. Chastised by the confrontation, Mouat protested to the over-sensitive commander that the rumours were false and he never wished to leave *Challenger*. Mouat stayed, but Fremantle would not forget: '*So it ends at present*' (his italics), he recorded in his diary.

To his mother, Fremantle expressed concern about the indefinite nature of his proposed stay at Swan River, where he would employ his ship's company in erecting huts and dwelling-places for the troops which would follow. He thought he might be forgotten and 'remain unnoticed till I have devoured all my provisions'. Even worse, he might be 'attached' to Swan River, employed in conveying stock and provisions to the settlers, and therefore 'banished for three years'. He was apprehensive about the natives, whom he understood were 'troublesome, rather warlike and savage to the utmost extent', and so spent all his ready cash on presents which he hoped would make them friendly. He wished another vessel was accompanying *Challenger*, 'for it's lonely going by oneself to such an out of the way place without a person in the world to talk to but my own people'.[48] Despite these apprehensions, he was also confident that the expedition would have its rewards: 'I take with me', he wrote to his mother, 'a bull and two cows and some English sheep that I have left to commence stocking my estate, so there will after all be a Fremantle villa, as I intend taking a grant, indeed I shall help myself, and build a house ready to lett to the Governor, Captain Stirling (our old friend in the *Brazen*).'[49]

With 168 days' provisions aboard, *Challenger* sailed from the Cape on 20 March 1829.[50] To his mother, the young captain could not conceal his disgust that the ship of which be was so proud should now be so laden with provisions that he had nowhere to stow anything. A Robinson Crusoe voyage, he called it, which had converted his ship of war into 'a deep laden Collier full of everything in the world'. Though he expected the voyage to take only six weeks, there was no chance of writing home for a long time, but when his work at Swan River was done he expected to go to Port Jackson, where 'communication is frequent to England' and then to India—the ultimate destination.[51] Strong winds off the Cape increased to gale force, 'whipping up the most tremendous seas in all directions. Two seas would meet in the opposite directions and end up like a pyramid and break.' If *Challenger* had been a smaller vessel, the situation would have been dangerous; as it was, one wave smashed his cabin window, saturated the fittings and defaced his books. The storm soon passed and on prevailing westerlies they headed for the mid-Indian Ocean island of St Paul, but he did not land, being anxious to reach the Swan as soon as possible. Fremantle was not a superstitious man, because he tried without success to shoot an albatross with his new rifle. Discipline remained strict: a marine was flogged for insolence and drunkenness ('3 dozen'), and a lad who fell overboard from the mizzen chains, though saved immediately, was 'given a good rowing for carelessness'.[52]

Challenger took only five weeks to reach the western coast of New Holland. Cape Leschenault was sighted on 24 April 1829; on the following day the anchor was dropped just west of Garden Island and preparations made to enter the passage between Garden and Carnac islands discovered two years earlier by James Stirling.[53] Even before he dropped anchor, Fremantle was concerned by both the appearance of the anchorage, noting that if there was no nearer secure mooring for merchant ships it would be 'inconvenient for establishing a Colony', and by the irregular soundings. He therefore decided to send his master in a boat through the passage marked on Stirling's chart—which was just as well, because the markings on the chart were incorrect, the passage being 'rocky but possible to enter'. The master was therefore the first of many who would dispute the accuracy of information provided by Stirling on his 1827 visit to Swan River. The following day Fremantle himself went in a gig to look at the passage and found it 'difficult at the Entrance, being rocky between the reefs . . .' He then decided to survey it before taking *Challenger* through, and sent the master, second master and a mate in three boats to mark a passage with buoys. This completed, they were to hoist a flag and Fremantle would weigh anchor and proceed towards a passage. On seeing the flag, and weighing the anchor, Fremantle waited at the entrance for the boats. What should have then been a simple exercise in navigation between markers almost ended in tragedy. Fremantle asked the master which side of the first buoy he should sail *Challenger*, and the master answered 'starboard'. As soon as the vessel reached this point it struck reefs, the master 'having mistaken the buoy on the rock for the one in the fairway and consequently ran the ship immediately on the top of it'. She hung there for about five minutes, striking three or four times, but then moved off, still floating, as they prepared to lower the boats. Fremantle then ignored the remaining buoys and took *Challenger* through on the basis of his own observations earlier that day, but keeping the three boats close ahead sounding the way until he reached a safe anchorage 2.4 km east of Carnac Island and inside all the reefs.

Fremantle was understandably furious at the master's incompetence. 'Never since I have been at Sea', wrote the twenty-eight-year old captain on his maiden voyage overseas, 'have I ever witnessed anything to equal the carelessness and stupidity of the Master.' Underscoring his diary entry in a manner matched only by his entry concerning Lieutenant Mouat's rumoured wish to leave *Challenger* at the Cape, Fremantle fumed that the master actually '*placed a buoy on a rock and then steered for the buoy and ran the ship immediately on it.* It was a thousand chances that we escaped being knocked to pieces, which must have been the case had it not been beautiful weather. *The Master deserves to be hanged immediately.* Unless I attend to everything myself ever so trifling, something invariably goes wrong; so much for the assistance a Captain derives from his Officers.' The near disaster did not, however, deter Fremantle from naming the passage after his vessel—an appropriate designation, for it proved to be quite a challenge for mariners who later tried to bring their vessels through it.

After carefully sounding the waters between his anchorage and Garden Island, he shifted *Challenger* to Cockburn Sound and anchored on good holding-ground in 22 m of water, fully protected from north-west gales which blew the following day. Parties which explored the island discovered that fresh water could be obtained by digging about 2 m; they also caught fish, killed seals and tried unsuccessfully to shoot kangaroos. While all this was 'great fun', Fremantle was troubled by the unknown damage to *Challenger*. She was making nearly 8 cm of water more than usual, but to his relief an inspection revealed that, though the hull had been extensively rubbed, it was not badly damaged. On May 1, having spent much time on the island replenishing their stock of water, they took a boat across the Sound to the river's entrance but found it 'impossible to enter from the excessive sea on the reef or bar extending from point to point'. May 2 was a fine day so they returned to the bar with two boats, fourteen men and enough provisions to explore the river for three days. As the French had discovered, the best passage through the bar was on the south side (by Arthur Head), which they negotiated only by taking everything out of the boats. Even then, the gig was 'caught by a sea and driven against the shore' but not damaged. Stirling's charts, which identified shoals to be avoided, were used for the journey up-river to Pt Heathcote, where they spent the night.

Fremantle's seeming lack of interest in important and formal occasions was revealed again by the absence of any reference in his diary to the fact that on that day (2 May 1829) he took formal possession for the Crown of the entire western coast of New Holland, the main reason for his being sent from England with great haste. Only in a letter to the Admiralty from Trincomalee five months later did he report the event, but gave no details about the time, exact place and who attended: a clause in that letter simply states that on May 2 'formal possession was taken of the whole of the West Coast of New Holland in the name of His Britannic Majesty and the Union Jack was hoisted on the South head of the River'.[54] If he did write letters home describing the event, which is unlikely for he had already told his mother that there was no way of communicating until he reached Port Jackson, none have survived. His diary suggests that he was more interested in recording progress with the mainland campsite for first settlers, and his exploration of the islands and the river. He was especially interested in the Aborigines who, he had told his mother, were reputed to be 'troublesome, rather warlike and savage to the utmost extent'. These apprehensions might have been formed by reading Stirling's report on his 1827 visit, for Péron's journal of the French visit in 1801 (written by Bailly) makes no reference to human life at Swan River, save that while exploring near Heirisson Island they

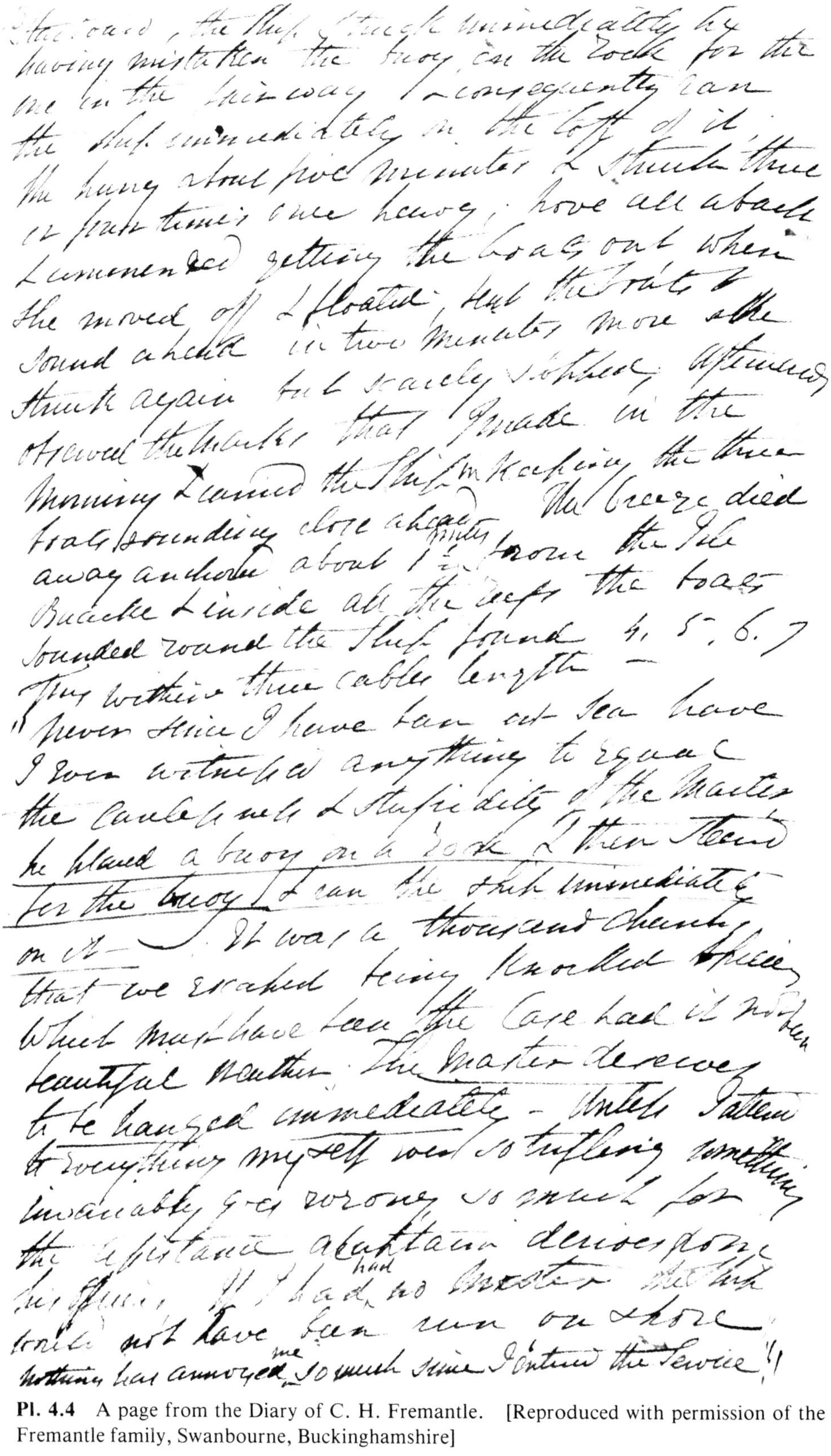

aboard, the Ship Struck immediately by
having mistaken the Buoy on the Rock for the
one in the Fairway & consequently ran
the Ship immediately on the top of it,
She hung about five minutes & Struck three
or four times once heavy; hove all aback
& commenced getting the boats out when
she moved off & floated, but the Rocks
found ahead in two minutes more she
Struck again but scarcely rubbed, afterwards
observed the Marks that she made in the
Morning & carried the Ship in Keeping the three
boats sounding close ahead. The breeze died
away & anchored about 1 ½ miles from the Isle
Buache & inside all the reefs the boats
Sounded round the Ship found 4. 5. 6. 7
Fms within three cables length —
Never since I have been at Sea have
I ever witnessed anything to equal
the Carelessness & Stupidity of the Master
he placed a buoy on a Rock & then steered
for the buoy & ran the Ship immediately
on it — It was a thousand chances
that we escaped being Knocked to pieces,
which must have been the case had it not been
beautiful weather. The Master deserves
to be hanged immediately — Unless I attend
to everything myself all so trifling something
invariably goes wrong so much for
the assistance about ten deserves more
his officers, If I had had no Master the Ship
would not have been run on shore,
nothing has annoyed me so much since I entered the Service"/

Pl. 4.4 A page from the Diary of C. H. Fremantle. [Reproduced with permission of the
Fremantle family, Swanbourne, Buckinghamshire]

were 'surprized at the appearance of the print of a man's foot, of an extraordinary size'.[55]

III

Fremantle's expedition was the third seen by Swan River Aborigines in twenty-eight years. Coming so soon after Stirling's visit, the appearance of other white men would probably not have been quite so astonishing. Though the Aborigines did not know it, Fremantle's party was the vanguard of occupation; his camp at the river entrance marked the beginning of an era in which land that for centuries had been their abode and source of sustenance would be taken from them and cultivated. It is easy to see why Fremantle, forewarned by Stirling's experiences, brought gifts to gain their friendship and why he was apprehensive about their potential hostility. His response to the first contact was similar to Stirling's: ignore them. On leaving the bar the party rowed a considerable distance before seeing Aborigines on both sides of the river 'who halloa'd to us very loud and appeared to cry "Warra, Warra," which I supposed to be "go away". I took no notice . . .' His main purpose was to find water, and in recording that all sources were underground and therefore required digging to reach, he wondered how the natives, lacking tools (shovels), managed to obtain it. His second contact was made within 3 km from the river entrance when he heard shouts and saw some Aborigines running along the hills and towards the river bank. Assuming that they were friendly, he rowed to the shore,

> one came to the boat and I gave him a biscuit which he eat [sic] immediately and he made signs for my hat, which being *very* old I gave him and he gave me in return a bit of string with which his hair was bound round, as I wish'd to shew him that it was our intention to be friendly; another one came to the Gig, and the boat's crew gave them some old frocks, stockings, and other cloaths, which we put on them. Three or four came down afterwards and one a very noisy fellow singing and dancing; he looked like a chief as he was marked down his stomach with three stripes of white and had in his head two bunches of feathers dyed red. I gave him a fishing line and hook but could not make him understand the use of it, and I was afraid every moment that he would have hooked himself. They were perfectly naked, with only a string tied about three turns (made I should think from the bark of trees) round the head and another round the lower part of the body; they were very anxious to get everything out of the boats, and in return for what we gave them, handed us a kind of spear or rather stick about 8 feet long with the end hardened in the fire and a barb to it. We saw no other kind of spears, but I am inclined to believe that they have much better ones, and what we saw were only intended for spearing fish. They were very quiet and friendly, but as I saw there was no satisfying their demands (altho' I had given my hat) I thought it advisable to shove the boats off, but two of them clung on and tried to pull the oars out and prevent them leaving the shore. They made a great noise, and the same two ran along the side in the water with astonishing agility; altho' the water was above their knees they jumped quite out every step and went much faster than the boats could row, and tried where the water shoaled to regain the boats, but I sheered off into deeper water, and they remained behind on my firing my gun at a diver in the water. . . . They appeared to be in the greatest state of savage ignorance and had no idea of the use

of a Musket, their limbs were disproportionably slender, their heads did not appear so large (at any rate my hat fitted one, therefore I must be very *big headed* also); the teeth quite white, and hair long and straight, quite black; one old man came down to us, I should think nearly sixty years of age; he was very quiet and the most respectable of the party; he had a large wound in the side and I made signs to him to know if done with the Spear and he appear[ed] to say 'Yes'. They talked very fast, but to understand a word was impossible.

Fremantle's apprehensions were allayed by this enjoyable experience, although that night the party made a blazing fire round which they sat singing and 'making quite noise enough to keep off all the Natives in New Holland'. A watch was kept all night because Fremantle was still uncertain of the Aborigines' intentions, an attitude which was vindicated the following day while exploring the southern side of the river entrance (probably the site of present-day Fremantle port):

> I had not proceeded far before I heard the yelling of the black fellows (as Jack calls them) and we gained the top of the hill where we saw a Native with a firebrand in one hand and two spears in the other, shouting 'Warra' 'Warra' and pointing to the shore where the boat was, desiring us to go away. I proceeded on when he became furious and stood on a Rock about thirty yards off and pointed his spear at me, holding one in one hand across which he placed the other, evidently with the intention of throwing it. As I should have been sorry to have commenced hostilities, which must have followed had the spear been thrown, I moved off to the right taking care not to turn my back on the savage. When he saw we did not persevere in going forward he left us, and I make no doubt that the occasion of his irritation was in consequence of our getting near their Women and Children, as we heard many voices under the Hill. I cannot conceive they could have been our friends of the preceeding [*sic*] night; if so our old cloaths and good fellowship does not appear to have conciliated them much.[56]

After crossing the bar on their return to *Challenger*, Fremantle's party landed at 'a little bay just round Arthur's Head, which looked clean and grassy and appeared a good place for making our first encampment'. Being outside the river entrance, boats could service this spot without having to cross the bar, and the little bay provided them with shelter. Fremantle had no idea where Stirling would establish a town when he arrived, but he reckoned that the encampment was an ideal place for settlers to go 'on landing first'. As these settlers would also wish to maintain friendly contact with the Aborigines, he ordered the crew he had designated to erect the camp to behave always in a manner which would maintain the good relations he had established. Two days later he sent a party of twenty-five, led by Lieutenant Henry, to establish on that spot the first permanent European outpost on the western side of New Holland. They built sheds (one measured 4.8 m by 2.4 m and was 3 m high), erected a 'respectable flag staff' and dug a protective ditch 2.5 m deep, 3.4 m wide and about 50 m long from bank to bank in a semi-circle which he hoped would 'puzzle the natives to get over it'.[57]

During the following month, Fremantle and his crew were kept busy maintaining *Challenger*, digging wells, buoying the channel between Garden and Carnac islands

Pl. 4.5 'A View in Western Australia from the left Bank of the Swan River'. The flagpole erected by Fremantle's sailors can be seen in the clearing left of centre. [Lithograph from a painting by Lieut. R. Dale. Courtesy of Art Gallery of W.A.]

(the original buoys having been washed away during a storm at the end of May) and erecting the mainland camp. They caught fish and birds for food, and seals for oil in such numbers that the population soon dwindled. Sharks were a problem. Some actually swam within a few metres of the beach: 'they are most numerous and voracious, which renders it very disagreeable, as to bathe even from the beach is hazardous'. Vines brought from the Cape were planted on the mainland, as were seeds, but Fremantle did not expect them to survive. Some of the men, like those in the earlier Vlamingh and Stirling expeditions, ate some nuts which they found near a native camp, and became 'exceedingly unwell'. Despite this warning, some midshipmen later did the same, with the same consequences, which led Fremantle to conclude that one had to treat the men 'exactly as children'. Discipline was relaxed a little, and some crew were allowed ashore to fish ('anything to amuse them'); but when, without permission, a group stayed overnight, they pushed their captain's generosity a bit too far. 'If they had not passed a most unpleasant night I should have flogged them', wrote Fremantle. Other miscreants were not so fortunate: Locke was punished for insolence, Palmer for disobedience, Green for desertion and Lee, Windfield and Graham for drunkenness.[58]

In several visits to the mainland camp, Fremantle consolidated his good relations with the Aborigines. On May 14, two he had met before ('recognised as our friends') visited the camp and were given handkerchiefs and biscuits. They returned the following day,

> were very friendly, and brought us fire, some spears and knives of a very rude construction, a piece of flintstone fastened on the end of [a] stick about a foot long with gum which comes from the trees about and adheres very strongly when put on hot. They were as before quite naked, but two of them by way of ornament had a piece of bone about the size of a little finger and six inches long struck through the septum of the Nose; they gave them to us, and also some dressed fish which they brought folded up in the bark of [a] tree; some of the people tasted it and it appeared to have been thrown on the fire and taken off when done, as it was full of sand. I gave them two knives, some mutton, tongue, biscuit, and some fish which we had caught, and they left us making signs by the Sun pointing to the West that they would return at sunset. They did not express a wish to go near the Tents, and the only thing which appeared to surprise them was the Bull,[59] as they were continually pointing to him and talking to one another. I went afterwards up the river to the Mineral Spring[60] to taste a pool of fresh water which we had found and to try and get a wild duck, and on discharging my gun found the three Natives just over my head, which shews that they watch us about very narrowly and followed us all the way which must have exceeded four miles. As I had only a youngster and Mr Henry with me I did not like going further from the Tents, as I do not esteem my naked friends well enough yet to trust myself unless superior to them in force. They have no knowledge of the musket, and I want an opportunity of killing a bird before them; the noise does not alarm them much.

The natives did not return to the camp for ten days, their absence being explained by Fremantle as due to their having gone inland for food. On May 25 his friends returned and were '*very pleased to see us*' (his emphasis), but he would not allow them to enter the encampment whose perimeter had by then been clearly delineated by the ditch. When a party of about ten returned the following day, Fremantle gave them all the birds he had shot and tried to explain that the gun had killed them. He then

> shewed them a looking glass at which they shouted and were perfectly delighted, all except the Old men; but I was determined that they should see their old worn out Countenances, but one look satisfied them, whilst the Younger ones of the party were continually pushing forward to look at themselves and did not appear displeased with their appearances. I made some of our men strip and shew their Arms, the Size of which astonished them very much and they could not refrain from feeling them and in fact were not satisfied without seeing all the parties', then our legs which excited more surprise than our Arms; and well they might as I think the limbs of some of our people would make three of some of theirs. I have a couple of good looking young lads in my Gig, whose chins happened to be particularly smooth, and they evidently believed them to be women, also the Youngsters with me, and I do not think that they would be brought to believe the contrary. They wanted the men to take off their trowsers after the shirts, but Jack had too much decency to think of satisfying their curiousity in that particular . . . . No traces of their Women or Children and I do not think they mean to introduce us into

their society, but I make no doubt but they were close to, from the noise we heard in the morning, somewhere in the Neighbourhood of the Mineral Spring.

Fremantle must have been greatly heartened by the way relations between the two races developed during the first month. Since first contact, when he avoided blood-shed only by retreating from an armed native, he could now report that they came to the encampment and exchanged their spears for knives, biscuits and other European goods. His observations were those of a 'civilised' man meeting 'savages' for the first time. He expressed understandable pleasure at their naïvety. He called them his friends, but it was a calculated friendship. Ever willing to provide gifts, he was also ever alert to the possibility that they might attack, and to dissuade this he was keen to show them, for their own good, the superiority of a musket over a spear. He chose the site of the mainland encampment because it was clear of trees and there-fore did not provide cover for attackers. He knew that whenever his men left the camp they were watched. Though he did not write it, there is implied acknowledge-ment in his diary that he understood, and even appreciated, their position and view-point, and why they had no intention of introducing their women and children to his crew. But there is incontravertible acknowledgement in the same document that he was cultivating, indeed exploiting, their friendliness to make the path easier for im-pending European settlers. During the first month at the mainland camp of the original British settlement on the western coast 'in the Neighbourhood of the Mineral Spring', there was no blood shed and much communication between the races. For that, Charles Howe Fremantle deserves much of the credit.

On June 1, his birthday, Fremantle sent a boat to the mainland camp with 200 stakes, gathered on Garden Island, for the ditch. On its return officers rushed the news to Fremantle that, on their way back, they had sighted a ship outside Rottnest Island, standing in. The purser, who had been catching seals on the southern end of Garden Island, had also seen the ship; it was *Parmelia*, with James Stirling and the first settlers.

IV

Barely three months separated the dates when Sir George Murray asked the Admiralty to send a vessel to annex the west coast of New Holland (5 November 1828) and when *Parmelia*, accompanied by *Sulphur*, sailed from England with the first settlers for Swan River (8 February 1829). These vessels took a further four months to reach their destination. The great haste with which the government com-pleted the necessary political arrangements, devised a land-grant system, appointed officials and arranged for vessels to take them to the colony, has been identified as one of the main reasons why the first settlers experienced unusually difficult prob-lems of resettlement. Some of these difficulties, it is claimed, could have been alleviated by careful planning, closer scrutiny of Stirling's and Fraser's 1827 reports and possibly by sending a pilot expedition to prepare shelter and complete land and marine surveys before the first settlers arrived. While these procedures would have been appropriate, the pressures on the British government to establish the colony quickly were many and considerable: fear that the French were about to establish a convict settlement in the area; difficulty in stemming the tide of interest in Swan River once Stirling's report had been publicized by the press; the influence exerted on the government by a settlement syndicate led by a cousin of Robert Peel, the home secretary; and the British Treasury's parsimonious attitude towards providing even basic services for the colony.

One week after Sir George Murray's letter to the Admiralty, official moves were made to assemble the expedition that Fremantle had been told would follow him to Swan River, and which he was ordered to assist as much as possible when it arrived. Murray suggested that a navy vessel of the 'bomb' type would be appropriate to take out troops, officials and provisions,[61] and on the same day Twiss of the Colonial Office informed Barrow of the Admiralty that the vessel would have to carry between 100 and 150 adults and provisions, as well as a quantity of machinery, implements and materials necessary to establish the party ashore for one year. The expense of the expedition, wrote Twiss, would be defrayed by the Colonial Office.[62] Three days later, Barrow replied that the bomb *Sulphur* would be fitted out at Chatham and Stirling was informed that he would command the vessel on its voyage to Swan River.[63] Four days later the commander-in-chief of the British Army, Lord Hill, was asked to hold sixty-eight rank and file in readiness for embarkation to the western coast of New Holland. Two weeks later Lord Hill replied that a detachment of the 63rd Regiment would go, and three weeks later reported that the personnel, 100 in all, had been selected and would be commanded by Captain F. C. Irwin.[64] The detachment was preparing to sail in *Sulphur*.

Both the Admiralty and the Army had responded with commendable haste to the Colonial Office's request. The Colonial Office itself was equally prompt in selecting the colony's civilian officials. Swan River, after all, was to be a civilian settlement. By December 31 Hay had informed Stirling that the following senior officials had been appointed:[65]

Secretary:	Mr P. Brown	salary £400 p.a.
Storekeeper:	Mr J. Morgan	,, £200 p.a.
Surveyor:	Mr J. S. Roe	,, £300 p.a.
Ass't Surveyor:	Mr Sutherland	,, £200 p.a.
Surgeon:	Mr Simmons	,, 15/- per diem
Harbour-master:	Captain Currie, R.N.	No salary at present
Naturalist:	Mr Drummond	,, ,, ,, ,,

The first three were young men who represented diversity of experience and talent. Peter Broun, thirty-one years of age, had been born in the Channel Islands, son of Sir William Broun, sixth baronet. His early working life was spent in Scotland as a gentleman clerk. Married for only three years, he had been recommended for the position by Sir George Murray 'and other influential patrons'. John Morgan was about thirty-six years of age, and had served as a commissioned marines officer in America during the war of 1812 before serving in Canada—

Pl. 4.6   John Septimus Roe.   [Courtesy of the Battye Library]

significant experience because it was there that he developed many ideas on colonization, which were published in 1824 as *The Emigrants' Note Book and Guide.* In it
he showed Canada's advantages as a place of settlement and, when appointed storekeeper of the Swan River settlement, he was actually the agent in Wales for the
Canada Land Company. John Septimus Roe (Plate 4.6), thirty-one years of age,
was appointed even before Stirling.[66] A hydrographer with the Admiralty, he had
already spent many months in Australia with Phillip Parker King on his important
voyages of discovery. The son of a clergyman, Roe was a midshipman at age fifteen
when he saw service in the French wars followed by eighteen months' service in the
Far East. At age twenty he passed examinations in mathematics and navigation and
was sent to the Surveying Service in New South Wales. With King, he sailed on three
very significant coastal surveys: in *Mermaid*'s circumnavigation of Australia; on a
detailed survey of the northern coast which had not been explored since Cook's
examination; and on another voyage along the northern coastline. He then joined
Bathurst and surveyed the western coast of New Holland as far as Roebuck Bay,
provisioned at Mauritius, and returned to survey the coast between Cape Leeuwin
and Cape Leveque, though he did not land at Swan River. Returning to England in
1823 he was soon sent back to Australia in *Tamar* and at Port Essington on 20
September 1824 he established a settlement and took possession of the northern

coast of Australia for the King (see p. 107). On his way back to England he saw action in the Burma wars and in 1827 was allocated the post of hydrographer in the Admiralty to prepare important charts on Australian and other southern waters. The Admiralty was reluctant to let this talented young surveyor go to Swan River; he was therefore granted leave for only two years. Roe was an ideal choice for what was a crucial appointment in the relatively unknown colony.

Sulphur was nowhere near large or suitable enough to convey the detachment of the 63rd Regiment, civilian officials, their families and provisions to Swan River, though when Stirling received instructions to command *Sulphur* to the colony, he did not object immediately to what he must have seen as an absurd proposal. In his own time and way he prepared a carefully costed case showing that it would be financially prudent to send the detachment of the 63rd in *Sulphur* and hire another vessel to take the civilian part of the establishment. The Treasury concurred, albeit reluctantly, and by the year's end his suggestion that the barque *Parmelia* be hired for the voyage was accepted.[67] On 28 December Stirling also wrote to Hay asking that three important questions concerning his association with Swan River be re-solved: first, that unless he, Currie and Morgan had been offered and had accepted civilian appointments by 31 December they would be deprived of their half-pay; second, that his title 'civilian superintendent' by changed to 'governor', a change which he argued would increase his influence with those around him at the new colony, and for which there was a precedent—Governor Phillip, the foundation leader of the colony of New South Wales; and third, that Swan River not be made a dependency of New South Wales. Doubting that the charter for New South Wales could be 'acted upon for the trial of cases occurring beyond the limits of that ter-ritory', he also brought to bear arguments similar to those he had put forward in his 1827 report to justify separation:

1. The dissimilarity of population and commercial position;
2. the great distance from each station, which meant that communication would be slow and uncertain, and mutual protection out of the question;
3. the advantages it offered to potential settlers because of its being indepen-dent and therefore unconnected with the convict colony of New South Wales;
4. being so isolated, it would assist local government if it was responsible only to the British Minister for the Colonies.

The response from the Colonial Office was both quick and positive. Two days later Stirling was appointed commander of the expedition and accorded the title 'lieu-tenant-governor'.[68] He was also informed that, until appropriate provision could be made for a legal system at Swan River, difficulties of a legislative, judicial and financial matter would have to be combatted by his 'own firmness and discretion'. He was also instructed to establish a court of arbitration for such questions as civil rights arising between settlers. On 12 January 1829 Murray informed Governor Darling in New South Wales of Stirling's appointment and stated that, because of the difficulties of keeping regular communication between Sydney and the new settlement, the government had decided not to make Swan River a dependency of New South Wales nor to place Stirling under his orders. 'He will look to the Cape for the necessary Supplies of the Colony', added Murray.[69]

When the government agreed to hire *Parmelia* to take civilians and provisions to Swan River and to retain *Sulphur* for a detachment of the 63rd Regiment, Captain William Townsend Dance was appointed commander of *Sulphur*.[70] He was instructed to accompany, and not part company with, *Parmelia* on the voyage to Cockburn Sound 'or at such other Anchorage in that neighbourhood as may be deemed most advisable', where he should provide 'aid and protection to a Settlement of British subjects about to be established there, or until Captain Stirling . . . shall inform you that he no longer requires your presence'. He was to 'attend to the suggestions, and meet the wishes' of Stirling, although he would be under the command of Rear-Admiral Gage of the East India station.[71]

Thus, by the year's end Stirling had all the authority and support seemingly necessary to establish the colony: the status of lieutenant-governor in a settlement independent from New South Wales; the assistance of qualified civilian officials; and the protection of a detachment of troops instructed to provide all the assistance he sought. Just as January 1829 was a month of feverish activity for Stirling, so it was also a month of feverish negotiation for a group of important men who had been encouraged to play a major role in the colony's economic viability. When Stirling was trying to persuade officials that Swan River should be settled (June-October 1828), the most favourable response came when he suggested that private capitalists should be encouraged to settle there, and then assured Twiss (on 22 October 1828) that a gentleman of judgement and ability was 'disposed to participate in the adventure'. It was therefore no coincidence that, two days after the Colonial Office asked the Admiralty to provide a vessel to take troops and civilians to Swan River, four men—Thomas Peel, Sir Francis Vincent, E. W. H. Schenley and T. Potter Macqueen—put forward an imaginative plan for a settlement there.[72] In commending the 'splendid design' of Swan River, they offered to transport 10 000 emigrants (with provisions and 'every other necessity usually allowed to Emigrants') and 1000 head of cattle and to provide three small vessels for trading between the colony and Sydney. Estimating that the venture would cost £30 per head, they requested the government to grant them land at the colony at a valuation of '1/6d. per acre' as 'a Payment in the Value of their Trouble.'[73] The basis of the syndicate's enthusiasm is worth quoting:

> It is well known that the soil of Swan River, from its moist state, is better adapted to the cultivation of tobacco and cotton than any other part of Australia. Both of these articles are intended to be cultivated upon a large scale; as also sugar and flax . . .

By sending back to Britain goods for which she now relied upon 'powers which it would be their policy to suppress', the syndicate would have 'effected a national good which neither time nor circumstances can erase from the annals of British history'.

Their grazing operations will go very extensively into the rearing of horses for the East India Trade, with the most important establishment of large herds of cattle and swine, *for the purpose of supplying His Majesty's* or other shipping *with salt provisions*, as the proximity of salt mines, of the best description, holds out a great inducement towards its success [their emphasis].

Two weeks later, Thomas Peel wrote again to Twiss whom he had apparently seen, and revealed his confidence that the government's decision would be in the syndicate's favour by reporting that they had already purchased the vessel *Lady Nugent* and were preparing her with every possible speed to take 400 persons, plus horses and cattle, 'Agricultural Implements of every description for the Use of each Settler', a steam-engine for sawing wood and grinding corn and enough provisions for one year.[74] It was proposed that the same vessel would be used, with others, to take out the 10 000 settlers and goods at agreed intervals during four years. Meantime, the government had been devising terms for disposing of land to settlers who were independent of Peel's syndicate and who left for the new colony before the end of 1829. Their procrastination in replying to Peel seemed deliberate; the conditions finally devised should not give the syndicate advantages over other settlers. A document on proposed terms for disposing of land—a document which Twiss had shown Peel during their early discussions—was therefore quickly altered, and altered so radically that it was quite unacceptable to Peel, especially when, as Peel alleged, Twiss had told him that 'everything asked would be granted'.[75] The official reply of 6 December 1828 to Peel and his associates supported their proposal in principle but reduced the land to be granted from 1.62 million ha (four million acres) to a maximum of 405 000 ha. The government was not prepared to support the experiment on a very large scale in the first instance, in case failure of the syndicate's objectives led to extensive distress. The conditions offered Peel turned out to be similar to those available to other settlers,[76] which the syndicate found unacceptable even though they would have been offered the right to choose 81 000 ha of their grant *before* their settlers left England, a right not accorded other settlers. Three syndicate members then withdrew, leaving Peel to carry the project alone. The very day he asked the government that he be recognized as sole leader, the government agreed; Stirling was informed of the change the following day.[77]

James Stirling must have been perturbed at this turn of events only days before *Parmelia* and *Sulphur* were due to sail. On the other hand, he must have been heartened by the consolidation of his own position as undisputed leader and by the government's decision to grant him 40 500 ha of land in the new colony in recognition of his services.[78] Told that he could choose the land whenever he wished, Stirling responded within a week with a request for all of Garden Island ('and any stock which may be found on it, the Produce of that which I left there in 1827') and the remainder of the grant land 'situated nearest Cape Naturalist in Geographe Bay'.[79] He was also granted £600 towards the cost of transporting himself and his entourage to Swan River.[80] But he wanted more concessions. On 16 January 1829 he reminded Twiss that he had agreed to undertake the enterprise without salary, 'earnest as I was from public as well as private motives, that it should not be abandoned', and added that he still would not ask for remuneration 'until Sir George Murray in whose Liberality I entirely confide, shall think fit to remember that I am an unpaid Governor'. The grant of £600 to cover travel expenses, he wrote, was barely adequate, and the grant of land was 'a complimentary acknowledgement' of his services so far, having 'neither reference nor value as a recompence for future exertions'. It was held on the same conditions applying to 'ordinary Settlers', which meant that it had to be improved over a given period,[81] a point which he raised again with Twiss a week later when he asked whether he would be fully entitled to the grant when it was improved and whether the period for improvement was still twenty-one years. In reply Twiss assured him of entitlement and confirmed the period of improvement, implying that this was a concession because the period for all subsequent settlers had been reduced from twenty-one to ten years.[82]

Meantime, the two vessels were making preparations for departure with all haste. On January 9 *Sulphur* attempted to reach Portsmouth from the Thames, but gales carried her on to Plymouth Sound, where Captain Dance wrote to Hay of the difficulties of getting to sea, for which he blamed the overcrowding of the ship.[83] Hay was not sympathetic and Dance construed his reply as an accusation of neglect. Even so, Surgeon Collie had complained to Dance of crammed conditions:[84] soldiers and their wives were very uncomfortable, and the women were 'benumbed from wet and exposure, some affected with febrile symptoms with faintings and with Hysterical paroxysms from being crammed up in their births [*sic*] and from want of ventilation'. This view was supported by Captain Parker of *Warspite*, who recommended to the government that goods be restowed, and some luggage and passengers (including pregnant women and children) be removed.[85] Parker's suggestions were put into effect.[86] Stirling had also seen the vessel and agreed that some bricks stowed on deck should also be put ashore.

Preparations for *Parmelia*'s departure went more smoothly. Passengers, cargo and provisions were taken aboard, and also plants and seeds from the Horticultural Society;[87] and within days of sailing Stirling received a letter from Hay, who told him that on the advice of a Captain Harris who thought flax could be grown successfully at Swan River, he should add a few plants and strongly encourage settlers to 'the cultivation of this valuable article'.[88] It will be recalled that the Peel syndicate expected to cultivate flax in Western Australia. Stirling, however, seemed more interested in seeing that the military contingent comprised artificers who would be indispensable in advising on building procedures. (Governor Phillip had sought similar assurances when he had been organizing the first fleet for New South Wales.)[89] Though Hay agreed with Stirling's proposal, Dance told the Navy Office that the troops had already been selected and he could not take any more because the vessel was already overcrowded 'to a distressing degree'.[90] Three days before sailing, Stirling expressed disappointment that only three artificers had been recruited and asked if seven others could follow in *Calista* (presumably also preparing to leave for the colony),[91] a proposition which Twiss would not support and rather abruptly told Stirling to 'use the labour at his disposal'. Indeed, the government was determined that Swan River would be established, and run, at the lowest possible cost. Even when it declared that French intentions had been instrumental in the decision to establish a settlement, the government wanted it done 'on the *least* expensive scale compatible with the nature and effectual accomplishment of the project in view'.[92] In correspondence with Peel, and in the regulations prepared for potential settlers, it had been emphasized in Clause 1 that 'His Majesty's Government do not intend to incur any *expense* in conveying settlers to the New Colony on the Swan River; and will not feel bound to defray the expense of supplying them with provisions, or other necessaries, after their arrival there . . .'[93] And to pay troops and cover the expenses of the colony, Stirling was granted a mere £1000 in coins, which were despatched aboard *Sulphur*.[94]

Though his position as undisputed leader of the colony had been established, and he had been granted many of the facilities necessary to run it, Stirling nonetheless carried a very indefinite set of instructions from the Colonial Office when he sailed for Swan River on 5 February 1829: 'With these few and general Instructions for your guidance, assisted by the oral and written communications which have taken place between yourself and this Department, you will, I trust, be able to surmount the difficulties to which you may be exposed at the outset, enhanced though they will be, by the want of any regular Commission for administering the Government.'[95] Because of the haste with which preparations had been made, there was apparently more than usual confusion at departure. John Septimus Roe and his new wife were 'very much crowded and cramped in our room for stowage and have not a single square inch to spare—indeed, when the fresh passengers and their voluminous luggage were pouring aboard at Spithead the scene almost defied anything like description and it was as much as each individual could do to get in his cabin'.[96] Passengers, livestock, cargo and provisions vied for limited space on this small vessel, but she was soon shipshape and the passengers were content once the inevitable seasickness was overcome. Stirling, we are told, arranged games (but strongly forbade card games) and religious services and was generally very attentive to the passengers' needs. Days were passed in that regular routine so familiar to all seafaring passengers: 'My first move in the morning', wrote one passenger, 'is to witness the sunrise, next to get under the spout of a pump when they are washing the decks; then a good walk without shoes and stockings, and nothing on but a wrapper—thus refreshed, a good breakfast; from about ten till two, reading and talking of our future plans; then a gossip or Chess with some of the ladies. Dinner at three; plenty of poultry and fresh meat, and claret (Carbornell) and ale; a lounge on deck, all hands turned out full puff; sunset, pipes and cigars, grog; and at ten, if no dancing or whist, turn in.'[97] *Sulphur* stayed in sight for part of the journey to the Cape, and sometimes sailed so close to *Parmelia* that the passengers could speak to each other. On March 9 they met the vessel *Batavia* and another vessel bound for England which provided a rare opportunity to hand over letters for home. On March 16 boats were lowered and rowed to *Sulphur* and greetings exchanged, and on March 24, what some passengers feared was a pirate vessel bearing down on them turned out to be a trader requiring provisions.[98] On April 16 *Parmelia* sailed into Table Bay, where she remained for thirteen days. *Sulphur* arrived ten days later, having been separated a second time three weeks beforehand.[99] She had not proved to be as seaworthy as expected and required caulking before proceeding to Swan River.[100] Stirling realized that if he waited at the Cape until *Sulphur* was ready for sea, then the expedition might not reach the Swan in time to plant seeds for the growing season. He therefore decided to take *Parmelia* on alone. Before leaving he reported to the Colonial Office news both good and bad: passengers were in good humour and high spirits;[101] but Dr Daly, the Medical Officer, and his daughter had been drowned during a boating mishap in Table Bay.[102]

The significance of the two vessels in Table Bay had not been lost on Cape residents. Captain Dance of *Sulphur* reported that their arrival created 'a great sensation, and many here are wishing very much to proceed with us'.[103] Stirling, on the other hand, was more interested in the fact that Cape residents were convinced that there would be considerable benefits for them from the new settlement on the Swan, although he did not entirely share their optimism, reckoning that the new settlement would obtain its stock cheaper from Java and Van Diemen's Land than from the Cape.

Parmelia sailed from the Cape on May 1, laden with stock purchased both privately and on behalf of the government. On this last leg of the long journey, Stirling worked out the final instructions which his civil officials would administer when they reached the colony. These matters had been on his mind for some time because, in a letter to his brother sent from the Cape, he wrote that he had got his 'regulations all ready and think they will give satisfaction to the applicants for land as well as be useful to the Government'. To Roe he handed a set of regulations for the Surveyor-General's Department and to Peter Broun regulations for the Colonial Secretary's Office. He constituted a Board of Counsel and Audit and appointed Currie, the harbourmaster, as its presiding officer and Roe and William Stirling (his seventeen-year-old cousin whose conduct on the voyage had impressed the governor as 'full of zeal in the cause') as his coadjutors without salary.[104] G. W. Mangles, his wife's cousin, was appointed superintendent of government stock; H. W. Reveley, who had been recruited at the Cape, was made civil engineer to the settlement; and William Stirling was appointed registrar.[105] As *Parmelia* approached the western coast, the governor's confidence in the colony's prosperous future did not wane. Of all the passengers, he alone had been to the Swan;* he knew what was ahead and the others clearly respected his knowledge, judgement and leadership. Even so, some unusual expectations had been formed on board *Parmelia*. The anonymous correspondent to the *Sunday Times,* who spent part of his typical day 'talking of future plans', had high expectations founded upon dubious information—expectations which would soon be severely tested:

> After our arrival at the land of promise we shall probably find temporary homes prepared for us by the Tweed and Challenger which have been sent there for the purpose. We expect the discovery of a large river, and a range of snow-capped mountains. If we can find the former, communications will be afforded

---

* Though Roe had been to Rottnest Island and knew the Australian coast well.

throughout the length of a fine and generally open country, as extensive almost as Europe.

The western coast was sighted on 1 June 1829. Stirling attempted to enter Cockburn Sound through the passage he had discovered in 1827 between Garden and Carnac islands, but a heavy swell made entry dangerous so *Parmelia* beat up round Rottnest Island and hove to for the night.[106]

V

At daylight on 2 June Charles Howe Fremantle, having been told the previous afternoon that a vessel was outside Rottnest, standing in, sent a sailor to ascend the high mound at the northern end of Garden Island to see if the vessel was still in sight and to hoist a flag if it was (Plate 4.7).[107] On seeing the signal at eight o'clock, Fremantle was rowed from *Challenger* to Carnac Island, where he saw *Parmelia* sailing in around the northern end of Rottnest Island. Seeing her make for Cockburn Sound, he hurriedly despatched a cutter to warn the master that there was no safe passage into the Sound. He then went on board himself. With characteristic understatement, Fremantle entered in his diary: 'Saw Captain Stirling, Governor, who had come out in a Ship called Parmelia with Settlers for the Establishment'. Nonetheless, it was a historic meeting: Fremantle, the young, efficient navy captain

Pl. 4.7 Near the high mound on Garden Island, from where *Parmelia* was sighted by a sailor from *Challenger*. [Photograph by Alex George]

Pl. 4.8   View of Cockburn Sound from Garden Island.   [A sketch by Jane Currie. Reproduced with permission of the Mitchell Library]

who had been sent to Swan River on orders not to his liking but who had obviously enjoyed the sojourn; and Stirling, the enthusiastic colonizer who had conceived the idea of establishing a settlement and for two years worked so hard to obtain official support and then appointment as its first governor. For James Stirling, this was a day of relief and triumph. When *Parmelia* rounded Rottnest and observed the British flag (on Fremantle's newly erected pole) near the entrance of Swan River, and *Challenger* lying at anchor in the lee of Garden Island in Cockburn Sound, his relief must have been very great. There was every chance that French vessels would have been anchored in Cockburn Sound and the tricolor flying from French-annexed territory.[108]

But the day of relief and triumph almost ended in disaster. Having been warned by Fremantle that there was no entrance into the Sound from the north, Stirling sent Currie ahead in a boat and he '*found a passage*' (Fremantle's emphasis) of 4.6 m which was considered sufficient water.[109] 'The ship proceeded', wrote Fremantle, 'and in five minutes she was on shore.' They tried, but without success, to force her over the bank. In deciding to try and enter the Sound in spite of Fremantle's warning, and against the suggestion of his own master, Luscombe, that they anchor,[110] Stirling was confident that he knew the passage well and that they could proceed in safety—a judgement difficult to comprehend on nautical grounds.[111] He knew that the entrance was barred by a bank, for he had plotted it on his 1827 chart and had not taken *Success* across it. But it is a judgement not difficult to comprehend on emotional grounds. In a letter to his brother Walter (part of which was published in *Hull Rockingham*), and in his report to Twiss,[112] he admitted that *Parmelia* took the

ground under his 'over-confident pilotage'. Under the circumstances, Bryan is probably correct in assuming that Stirling 'was possessed of the vanity of any ordinary
mortal' in sailing triumphantly, 'a modern Caesar, right up to the very shores of the
country he was to command'.[113]

Though Fremantle later blamed Stirling for the accident,[114] his immediate reaction was that of a well-trained naval officer—send his crew aboard *Parmelia* to
lighten her as much as possible, put a stream-anchor astern to heave the ship if and
when it was freed, and a small anchor off the starboard bow to prevent her going on
to the reef. For eighteen hours they toiled; at times the situation looked serious,
especially at midnight when she 'thumped hard'. Snatching two hours' sleep,
Fremantle returned early the following morning to see *Parmelia* come off the bank
'entirely by herself'. 'The people on board', he wrote, 'ought to be most thankful
for her delivery, as I never expected she would move again.'[115] Rudderless, the ship
was anchored just before the onset of a storm which lasted three days when 'it blew
. . . most tremendously', and though *Parmelia* weathered it without further mishap,
she looked 'deplorable' when, having lost her foreyard, rudder, windlass, spare
spars, long-boat and skiff, and making 10 cm of water an hour, she was taken to a
safe anchorage between *Challenger* and Garden Island.[116] It was a frightening experience for all, especially the passengers. Most of the women and children were
taken to Carnac Island in the charge of John Morgan, colonial storekeeper, who
later described the experience:

> Soon after the ship struck . . . (and to lighten the ship to save her from total
> wreck) I was requested by the Governor to land upon the nearest point of the
> Island of Carnac, in charge of Stores and the families of the Artificers.—I did
> so, and had twenty-eight souls on shore from the Tuesday until the following
> Saturday. Not having any communication with the Ship, we subsisted almost
> entirely upon salt beef, and biscuit,—our table service of one knife, and one
> drinking mug for the *whole* party—Mrs. Morgan, and my daughter were on
> shore, . . . altho' obliged to sleep upon the ground night, after night, exposed to
> incessant rain, together with all the extraordinary nocturnal disturbances of a
> new Country . . . . This little affair of five days, has given me the credit of being
> the first family Settler, in Western Australia.[117]

Not all the women were sent to Carnac Island; some were accorded preferential
treatment and, with Fremantle's concurrence, taken to *Challenger* to rest in his
cabin. Mrs Stirling was amongst them, but presumedly not the wives of artificers. It
was a gentlemanly gesture by Fremantle, which he later seemed to regret when, on
returning to his cabin, he found it 'full of all kinds of women and in terrible confusion' and though he turned half of them out, by the next day (June 4) the cabin was
still 'full of women and children, squalling and making a dirt'. His annoyance was
probably more the result of having yet another indignity imposed on his naval vessel
than on his unwillingness to house unfortunate passengers.

No sooner had the storm abated and preparations begun to put settlers ashore,
than *Sulphur* was seen in the offing by men from *Challenger*, who were making a
road to the high hill on Garden Island. *Sulphur*'s fast voyage from the Cape (thirty

days) was made in 'one continued gale . . . the whole way, with the most tremendous sea the oldest seaman on board ever remembered to have seen'.[118] Winds were still strong when she reached the western side of the islands, and as she was heavily laden, Captain Dance decided to run 'the hazard of the dangerous and still unknown passage between the islands' (Challenger Passage), although his chart (drawn by Stirling) had shown a clear passage of 9 m. It was a bold decision, but *Sulphur* sailed through, grazing once 'hard enough to perceive that we *did touch*' (Dance's emphasis). Fremantle, who watched her, was aghast: 'her situation was most perilous as on the bar outside there was a great sea and dangers appeared in all directions . . . . I think Dance very rash in attempting to run for the coast during such tremendous weather; we all thought he must have been wrecked.'[119] Fremantle had clearly not forgotten Dance's rashness by nightfall, for over dinner on *Parmelia* he thought the young captain 'talked much nonsense!'

Though the first three vessels to reach the colony had touched on entering, the most serious damage had been sustained by *Parmelia*. It is therefore puzzling why Luscumbe, the master of *Parmelia*, should have waited five weeks before asking Fremantle to repair the vessel.[120] At first, Fremantle was inclined not to provide assistance; Dance had brought despatches ordering him to proceed to India, his hoped-for 'final destination', and by then (July 17) he was on the point of sailing. Furthermore, by having stayed five weeks to assist settlers, his provisions had been reduced to barely enough for fifty days. But he relented, and on July 28 ordered an initial survey of *Parmelia* by the masters of *Sulphur* and *Challenger*, who reported that the vessel was not in a fit state to go to sea and would have to be hove down, a difficult and tedious procedure. It appears, however, that the vessel was not fully hove down, further examination having revealed that only the copper on her hull had been rubbed a little; the main repairs were to replace the broken yard and rudder.

In addition to repairing *Parmelia*, Fremantle's crew assisted settlers to land their goods and livestock, erected huts (including Stirling's) on Garden Island and generally 'employed as many men as could be spared from the Ship in any manner the Governor chose to occupy them'. They accompanied Stirling on his up-river explorations and Fremantle himself accompanied Dance up the Canning River, which, he wrote, was 'decidedly wrongly laid down on Captain Stirling's charts'. Stirling called them 'competent and zealous adventurers' on important exploration parties.[121] The weather was against them most of the time and it was June 21 before soldiers from *Sulphur* could cross the Sound and relieve those members of Fremantle's crew at the mainland camp. Fremantle was justly proud of his crew (which itself was a tribute to his leadership), and for performing their unusual duties so well he asked the Admiralty that they be granted extra pay.[122] Before leaving Swan River, Fremantle unloaded all the extra stores and articles, especially tools to 'enable them to continue the building of houses as well as to fit out a small Schooner which had been brought out in frame'.[123]

Fremantle's ready assistance was indispensable during the first two months of settlement, especially his saving of the stricken *Parmelia*. The settlers' high hopes and expectations were all but dashed by that nerve-wracking experience. Even Stirling expected the ship to 'go to pieces' and envisaged his own 'total ruin',[124] although in his official report he seemed to discount the seriousness of the situation.[125] The companionship, as much as the assistance, of *Challenger*'s crew must also have been greatly appreciated by the new arrivals. There was no lack of social intercourse amongst officers—Jane Currie's diary is a record of almost continuous exchange of parties and dinners.[126] Inevitably, then, Stirling wrote Fremantle a letter of appreciation:

> I cannot contemplate as the Officer entrusted with the direction of this Settlement the departure of the Challenger without being deeply sensible of the loss we shall sustain thereby, and the great advantages we have already derived from your protection and assistance while here—Your conduct in the various proceedings connected with the formation of this Colony has been governed by motives and aided by abilities which I cannot sufficiently praise, but it will afford me greatest satisfaction to convey (to the Government) my warm testimony as to the assistance I have received from you here aided by the efficient state of discipline of your ship and the abilities of the officers under your command . . . . I am not distinctly aware whether or not your views are directed to the acquisition of a Grant of Land in this Territory but I beg to acquaint you that if you desire it I shall have great pleasure in appropriating as a mark of the esteem and gratitude entertained by this Government towards you an extent of land amounting to 5000 acres subject to the confirmation of the Secretary of State for the Colonies and to the condition of being improved in the course of ten years to the extent of 1/6d. per acre.[127]

In his formal reply, Fremantle was gratified by the expression 'in such flattering terms' towards his officers and himself and was pleased to think that 'any step which I may have taken should have met with your approbation'.[128] But in his diary he wrote what he probably really felt:

> Every assistance that it was possible to render them in the power of a Ship I gave them, and generally employed the whole of my Ship's Company either in the boats or clearing grounds etc. on the Island; indeed I do not conceive that they possibly could have done anything without us, as they arrived perfectly without resources and the Sulphur is of little or no use to them, having few men and being more like a Merchant Ship than a man of war, with constant complaints and *rows* on board.[129]

Fremantle accepted Stirling's offer of a grant of land and nominated William Stirling as his agent at the Swan.[130] Other officers requested, and were granted, smaller plots of land (and nominated Morgan and Irwin as their agents),[131] an action which was not unanimously supported by colonists. J. Lyon, a leading colonist, later claimed that these 'large grants of land in the best situations to officers of Challenger, Sulphur and others', leaving inferior land to genuine settlers, was a major cause of the colony's difficulties during the first few years.[132] At the time, however, a grateful Stirling saw them simply as recompense for services rendered.[133]

Thus, on August 25, Fremantle shifted *Challenger* towards the entrance of

Challenger Passage. The sea was rough and he was unwilling to go through so he returned to the anchorage and waited until the twenty-eighth. At 9 o'clock, watched anxiously by Jane Currie from the top of Garden Island's high hill,[134] they cleared the Five Fathom Bank on the western side of the passage (see Fig. 3.1) and were 'very glad to be outside in deep water', the first vessel to go through without touching. Before Fremantle sailed, Governor Stirling announced to his settlers that henceforth the mainland encampment, and that country in the 'Neighbourhood of the Mineral Spring', would be known as Fremantle.[135]

5

Reality

*The farmer, and the botanist, it ought at all times to be remembered,—
are very different people—and in nine cases out of ten, the latter is no
more capable of giving a correct opinion upon how far a large tract of
Country, can be made available to farming purposes,—than the former
would be, to discuss the merits, and character of an extraordinary
shrub, or very beautiful flower.*

JOHN MORGAN TO R. HAY
18 MARCH 1830

Stirling's decision was appropriate. Charles Howe Fremantle had played a key role
in the colony's establishment. Not only had he annexed the whole western coast of
Australia for Great Britain and employed his crew preparing the Swan River area for
first settlers but he had also personally selected the mainland camp which Stirling
later confirmed as the first town and port of the colony.

Initially, however, officials and their families aboard *Parmelia* disembarked on
Garden Island. There were two reasons for this. First, the damaged *Parmelia* had to
be taken to a temporary anchorage in the lee (eastern side) of Garden Island where it
would be relatively safe. Second, as Stirling later wrote to Twiss, the severe winter
was too boisterous to permit constant communication with the mainland,[1] a view he
later repeated in a letter to his brother, adding that it had prevented him from making a large settlement on the mainland at a great distance from the ship.[2] The near
wreck of *Parmelia* had been a 'severe damper' to their hopes, wrote Stirling, and it
'required some management to allay people's apprehensions, but in time the hurry
of landing and the novelty of the scene had their effect'.[3] Tents, then temporary
huts, were therefore erected on the island and gardens planted to save their plants,[4]
decisions with which Fremantle disagreed. Sooner or later, he argued, the settlers
would have to move to the mainland and so anything erected on the island would
'consequently be thrown away'.[5] But once the agriculturalist, presumably Drummond, reported that soil on Garden Island was 'very good and capable of producing
anything', Stirling was determined to make his first establishment there.[6] It has been
suggested that Stirling, having already selected Garden Island as part of his own
land grant, had pecuniary motives for deciding to erect buildings there.[7] This is not a
fanciful suggestion; the reasons he gave hardly justify his decision to use precious
material brought from England aboard *Parmelia* and *Sulphur* for dwellings which,

140

from the beginning, met only a temporary expedient. The agricultural land justifying the colony's establishment was on the mainland and it was there that settlers would ultimately reside.

Though he disagreed with Stirling's decision, Fremantle did everything possible to assist the disembarkation and establishment of *Parmelia*'s passengers on the island. The crews from his vessel and *Sulphur* cleared the land, erected houses for Stirling and other officials and, as soon as a government storehouse had been erected, unloaded *Parmelia* and stacked provisions under its roof.[8] Buildings were generally a mixture of material brought from England and brushwood/timber available on the island. Captain Dance described the huts as 'made from the timber, of which there is here abundance, and thatched and closed in by small brushwood', or 'built of a few spars, the sides composed of brush-wood, and the tops made of stout canvass'.[9] Though the buildings were quite substantial, the same boisterous weather which had decided Stirling to disembark on the island and not the mainland made living conditions very uncomfortable. Some officials and their families enjoyed the relative comfort of *Parmelia* longer than others. Jane Currie, the harbourmaster's wife, recorded in her diary that she left *Parmelia* on July 8, five weeks after arriving in the colony, and while understandably relieved to be 'within our own walls' (or, in the sweetness of privacy, as Marnie Bassett puts it),[10] tending her livestock and growing vegetables, the walls were made of canvas not strong enough to withstand the fierce storms. On the other hand, John Morgan, who was destined to reside on the island longer than anyone else, landed only five days after *Parmelia* had struck, before which he was on Carnac Island looking after the wives and children of artificers. He had '*personally* [his emphasis] to prepare a shelter' for himself and family during the ensuing winter, 'the whole of the establishment being left to provide for themselves, or sleep in the bush,—as they were best able'. Though his family 'set a very good face upon the adventure', loss and destruction of property during those first winter months was 'greater by many hundred degrees, than I ever anticipated, or ever before witnessed'.[11] Stirling showed characteristic sympathy and concern for the colonists, but could do little to assist them. He well knew that many of the two to three hundred people on the island had never experienced such hardship, but his own situation was not much better than theirs; on occasions he walked about his hut with an umbrella in his hand to keep the candle burning.[12]

Having been instructed to give priority to selecting a harbour and townsite, Stirling soon visited several potential sites on the mainland. Only a week after *Parmelia*'s arrival he accompanied Charles Fremantle to Mangles Bay[13] at the southern end of Cockburn Sound and appeared to be pleased with the site, thinking that it 'might be made the Harbour and the town opposite on the Main'. It is difficult to understand why he ever seriously considered the site, its only advantage being a protected anchorage. Fremantle recorded in his diary for that day that 'a passage existed between Buacke [*sic*; Garden Island] and Cape Peron'. Perhaps Stirling thought that this would prove to be safer than Challenger Passage between Garden and Carnac islands, but a cursory inspection would soon have proved otherwise. The major disadvantage of Mangles Bay as a townsite was its distance from Swan

Pl. 5.1   Garden Island, showing huts and workshops, 1830.   [Courtesy of the Art Gallery of W.A.]

River and the upper reaches where first settlers would commence agriculture. Stirling probably realized this, for on August 12 he selected the present site of Perth as the capital. It is, he wrote to Twiss, a site of great beauty and at the same time possesses the more substantial advantages of stone, lime and clay and other building materials, and is situated at the point where the rocky soil off the sea coast gives way to the rich alluvial land on the banks of the Swan River.[14] He clearly considered it more attractive and practical than Fremantle. In a celebration described by Charles Fremantle, 'there being no stone contiguous for our purpose, to celebrate the commencement of the new Town, *Mrs Dance* cut down a tree; fired Volleys, made Speeches and gave several Cheers; named the town Perth according to the wishes of Sir George Murray'.[15] He thought the site well adapted for a town and preferable to any other he had seen: 'It communicates with the sea on one side and with the upper part of the country by the river on the other side of the Islands.' Unfortunately, communication with the upper part of the country was thwarted by the islands and flats 2 km or so up-river which Stirling in 1827, and the French before him, had experienced such difficulty in negotiating. Fremantle saw no long-term impediment, expecting that a canal would be cut through the flats, thus rendering communication easy from the upper Swan to the port.

II

One of the last entries in Fremantle's diary before he left Swan River was that the merchant ship *Calista* had reached the colony on August 5, followed by *St Leonard* the following day and the *Marquis of Anglesea* on August 23. Whereas *Parmelia* had brought the colony's officials, and *Sulphur* a detachment of the 63rd Regiment, these three merchant vessels had brought the vanguard of independent settlers— independent, that is, from those sponsored by the Peel syndicate. Settlers aboard these vessels had been drawn to the emigration threshold by publicity in England so favourable that it became dubbed 'Swan River mania'. Despite the reputation that Western Australia's coastline had acquired during the centuries of contact by European mariners (especially that part near Swan River), and which had only recently been underscored by Barrow of the Admiralty in his criticism of Stirling's report (see p. 108), public reaction in Britain to the government's offer of land grants at the new colony was swift and positive.

Despite Stirling's active campaign amongst officials and potential backers in England during the second half of 1828, the contents of his 1827 report on Swan River were not widely known to the British public. On 12 January 1829, twenty-six days before *Parmelia* and *Sulphur* sailed from England with Stirling, his officials and a detachment of the 63rd Regiment, the government, committed to establishing a settlement at the Swan, issued from Downing Street a set of 'Regulations for the Guidance of those who may propose to embark, as settlers for the New Settlement on the Western Coast of New Holland.' Potential settlers, therefore, did not have to join the Peel enterprise; they could go out as independent settlers. It was the Downing Street regulation, together with the publicity which heralded its dissemination, that was primarily responsible for Swan River mania. What exactly was being offered potential settlers? The regulation, in nine paragraphs, offered settlers who arrived at Swan River before the end of 1830 grants of land, free of quit rent, proportionate to the amount of capital they were prepared to invest in the improvement of the land. For every £3 capital value they would be granted 16.2 ha of land. Under the head of 'capital' was listed stock, implements of husbanding and other articles 'which may be applicable to the purposes of productive industry' (para. 3). In addition, settlers who took labourers to the Swan would be entitled to an additional

80.6 ha per labourer, as well as grants for women and children over ten years of age. Full title to the land granted would not be made until the settler could show that he had improved it, by cultivation or in 'solid improvements' such as buildings and works, by 1s 6d per acre. If he failed to improve one-quarter of his grant within three years, he would be liable for a payment of sixpence per acre into the public chest of the settlement; and if he had not achieved this by the end of seven years, un-cultivated land would revert to the Crown.*

Even though the government warned potential settlers that it did not intend incur-ring any '*expense*' (the government's own emphasis) in conveying settlers, that it would not feel bound to provide any 'provisions and other necessaries' once they ar-rived at the Swan, and that it would not assist their removal from the colony should they want to quit it, the generous land grant conditions were so attractive that tremendous interest, especially by landowners, was generated in the venture. Those who responded must have occasionally thought that the deal was too good to be true—land being given away solely on the basis of value of selected capital goods taken to the colony, and requirements for improvement by no means onerous or unachievable. How did they find out about opportunities and conditions at Swan River? In his detailed study of Swan River mania, James Cameron identifies three main agencies responsible for disseminating information:[16] the Colonial Office (which played a passive role, acting simply as a clearing-house for information); the press; and speculators (who were the main generators of 'mania'). Press publicity was based primarily on an article prepared by John Barrow for the *Quarterly Review*, considered the major middle class journal of the period.[17] An acknow-ledged expert on the southern hemisphere, his contribution to the *Quarterly Review* was a 'semi-official statement', and would have been seen by many readers as an im-peccable and objective source of information. The reputation was misplaced. Bar-row's excessive enthusiasm for Swan River led him to alter, emphasize and interpret Stirling's 1827 report to an extent which made it appear an even more attractive place for British farmers than Stirling had made it out to be. Other English journals of the day based their articles on Barrow's contribution to the *Quarterly Review*, ad-justing content according to readership.

Attracted by the land-grant conditions, potential settlers then learned from Bar-row's article that Swan River was nothing less than paradise on earth. First, there was plenty of good land for everyone. The coastal plain from north of the river to King George Sound contained 'an estimated five to six millions of acres, the greater part of which from the general appearance of the two extreme portions (the only ones yet examined,) may be considered as land fit for the plough, and, therefore, fully capable of giving support to a million of souls'. Of the Swan and Canning areas, the potential settler read, 'about five miles to the eastward of the river [there

---

* Conditions regarding land grants for children taken to the colony were later altered so that smaller amounts were granted to younger children. Regarding improvements, the government added a clause that at any time within ten years it might resume, without compensation, 'any land not then actually cultivated or improved as before mentioned, which may be required for roads, canals, or quays, or for the site of public buildings' *(Quarterly Review* article, 1829).

are] . . . extensive plains of the richest description, consisting of an alluvial deposit, equalling in fertility those of the banks of the river Hawkesbury in New South Wales, and covered with the most luxuriant brome grass'. Of the river land itself, 'the higher the river is ascended, the more extended the flats become, and the better the quality of the soil'. Fraser's list of advantages which the land held out to settlers was quoted in full: superiority of soil; not thickly wooded and could thus be brought into 'immediate culture'; abundance of springs and permanent humidity of soil; and a navigable river providing 'water carriage to his door'. Barrow anticipated that the Vasse and Leschenault areas would soon be settled, for the surrounding hills are 'bold and divided by beautiful meandering valleys formed of the richest soil possible'. Even Garden Island, as Fraser reported, contained a 'light sort of sand and loam' and was well suited for 'any description of light garden crops'. On the basis of Stirling's observations concerning temperature differentials between the sea and the hills, Barrow then speculated that, in addition to the 2 430 000 ha of land on the plain which was 'fit for the plough', there were probably also fertile plains beyond the hills, 'intersected by streams of water flowing from the mountains to the eastward or northward'.

Second, on the basis of the report by Captain Stirling, 'the intelligent officer who explored the country', and Fraser, 'an excellent botanist, who accompanied him, and who was well acquainted with the soil and products of New South Wales', the March climate at Swan River appeared to be delightful. 'The alternate land and sea breezes create a moisture in the afternoon which renders the climate cool and agreeable . . . . Such a climate, it is almost unnecessary to say, must be highly favourable to vegetation, which was accordingly observed to be most luxuriant.' Stirling's description of the vegetation generally was also quoted in full: 'The verdant appearance, and almost innumerable variety of grasses, herbaceous plants, shrubs, and trees, show that there is no deficiency in the three great sources of their sustenance, soil, heat, and moisture.' A potential settler should not be discouraged as were Stirling's predecessors at the Swan, especially the French, by the limestone ridge and sandhills seen along the coast from Geographe Bay to Swan River, for these are only 'from one to five miles' wide.

Third, fresh water, the commodity which others had failed to find in sufficient quantities, was there in abundance, brought across the plain from the mountains by numerous streams. Furthermore, the whole coast 'is a perfect source of active springs, discharging themselves (from rocks of the limestone ridge) on the beach in rapid rills of considerable extent, every six or seven yards'.

Fourth, Stirling's discovery of safe anchorages outside the river mouth, and his enthusiasm for Melville Water as a potential river anchorage, was quoted at length. Once a colony was established, it would have 'an incalculable advantage over New South Wales', being nearer to the civilized world and also in a position to trade with Indian Ocean countries. Barrow anticipated that the colony would grow rapidly and foresaw it supplying the products of a temperate climate to European establishments in Hindustan, and being of 'as much importance as the productions of the North American colonies were to the West Indies'. He also predicted Swan River becoming a Singapore of the antipodes with Chinese and Malay merchants, agriculturalists, mechanics or fishermen flocking there 'in any number that might be required'.

Finally, however, a word of advice to 'the multitudes who we understand are preparing to take their flight to this new land of Goshen': they must have a knowledge of agriculture and recognize that for the first year the country will afford them nothing. Half-pay officers of the Army and Navy were warned to beware, for Barrow was at a loss to conceive what many of them could do there. The colony's strength would be provided by English and Scottish farmers; 'these cannot fail', he wrote. There would also be a place for artificers, teachers and other skilled workers, but 'the unproductive class, or idlers, had better wait a few years before they embark for a country where, as yet, there is neither hut nor hovel'.

Shipowners and their agents, dedicated to obtaining as much of the potential business as possible, also disseminated and embellished the favourable press reports and, concludes Cameron, extended descriptions of Swan River to the ultimate limits of credibility.[18] This was probably best exemplified by the shipping agent, H. C. Semphill, in his quest for passengers and cargo to Swan River aboard the *Lady Campbell*. The way his brochure read, *Lady Campbell* was the only vessel worth travelling on to this paradise on earth. Having one of the 'finest climates in the universe', and only three months' sail from England, Swan River was highly suited to the production of cotton, silk, tallow, linseed, hemp, flax, corn and vines, its excellent soil was beautifully but not too much wooded, its coast and rivers 'literally teem with fish', and its proximity to the Cape, Mauritius, Timor, India and New South Wales 'must open a door for commercial enterprise of vast magnitude'. Once there, settlers would not have to pay for their lands nor even pay rent, because it would be granted in fee simple and therefore descend to their heirs forever. The land itself was ideal for agriculture and the emigrant would 'not have to wage hopeless and ruinous war with interminable forests and impenetrable jungle, as he will find prepared by the hand of nature extensive plains ready for the ploughshare. He will not be frightened from his purpose by beasts of prey and loathsome reptiles. He will not be scorched by tropical heat nor chilled by the rigours of a Canadian winter', and he will not have to 'mingle with, and employ those bearing the brand of crime and punishment'.[19]

It is therefore not difficult to see why, during early 1829, 'a very considerable sensation' took place throughout the kingdom so that when *Parmelia* and *Sulphur* sailed, no less than six other vessels were already posted at Lloyds as sailing for the same destination.[20] Who responded to the challenge? Where did they come from and what did they expect of the new colony? Though these important questions may well seem unanswerable 150 years later, painstaking research by James Cameron and Pamela Statham provide us with some general answers.[21] The Swan River Colony, writes Cameron, was the first major British colonizing venture following the Napoleonic wars. The dislocation caused by that long conflict, and ongoing changes in industry and agriculture, had created conditions favourable to emigration. The decline of agricultural prices caused widespread unemployment in that sector, so the prospect of land ownership at Swan River was especially attractive to farmers living in the predominantly arable counties in eastern and southern England which had been hardest hit by the post-war depression. As a group, the settlers arriving at Swan River during the first seven months were very young: three-quarters were under thirty years of age and a third were under fourteen years; males predominated and only one-fifth of total arrivals were adult females.[22] They were of predominantly urban origin, over 70 per cent coming from major urban centres in the south-east of England, and one-quarter from London itself, the remainder coming from the arable counties noted above. As Pamela Statham shows, their occupations and skills were diverse, reflecting their predominantly urban origins: 'Many settlers came from civil and defence service backgrounds and few of the labourers hired specifically for agricultural work had had previous experience of that kind in England. Some eventually proved to have come from parish poorhouses and to have lacked any specific skill.'[23] The majority of initial settlers intended becoming arable farmers, which is understandable in view of the description of Swan River conveyed in the *Quarterly Review*, especially passages concerning the extent and fertility of soil 'fit for the plough'. Contrary to popular belief, concludes Cameron, 'the majority of agricultural proprietors [going to Swan River] were neither large estate owners, nor had they come to the Colony to commence pastoral operations. . . . The overall impression is of men of limited means who saw in Swan River colony an opportunity to acquire a larger property or a way to maximise returns from a modest investment.'[24] As the statistics reveal, however, agricultural proprietors were a minority group. Though they would face serious problems of re-adjustment, and long, uncompromising toil in bringing virgin land into production, even greater problems would face those with no farming experience. But none, whatever their skills, had any idea of what lay ahead.

Swan River mania reached fever pitch during early 1829. By June, when *Caroline*, the fifth vessel to leave for the Swan since February, was preparing to depart, it was noted that eleven more vessels were advertised to proceed without delay. 'Judging from the state which the great body of agriculturalists are now in', declared an editorial in the *Sussex Advertiser*, 'and the interest excited in the public mind by the great advantages held out to the settlers in this new Settlement, we have no doubt that emigration to this quarter will continue to be carried on in a rapid and universal manner.'[25] Interest did not wane in the second half of the year, for on October 16 the *Leicester Journal*, noting *Warrior*'s departure, declared that from the 'desire manifested by persons to emigrate to the New Colony, there is no doubt but that it will soon increase. About twenty ships are now in Dock fitting out for the Swan River and Cockburn Sound.'[26]

Under the best of circumstances, shipside farewells to emigrants are emotional, heart-rending occasions. Despite the 'great advantages held out to the settlers', those who left England in 1829 for Swan River were probably no less apprehensive than others who had left England's shores for the new world. All but the hardest heart would have responded to the poignancy of departure. For most it was, in all probability, the last time that they would see their closest relatives in this world, declared a local newspaper recording the departure of Hardey's Methodists from Yorkshire.

It must have been a moving occasion. Four thousand persons came to see *Tranby*
sail and hear a stirring sermon preached, 'so great was the interest excited' by the
event.[27] Similarly, when Henty's party finally sailed in *Caroline*, a large party of
friends bade them farewell and 'in the warmest manner evinced the high interest they
felt for the enterprising settlers'.[28] *Warrior* left 'amid considerable bustle, flags flying and all on board in high spirits'.[29]

But high spirits are transitory and farming people who had never moved far
beyond their villages, let alone outside their country, soon experienced the discomfort of seasickness which few could have envisaged. Alfred Stone, a passenger on
Caroline, caught up in the excitement of departure, described the latter part of the
voyage to Swan River as 'exceedingly rough and unpleasant, and although I consider
myself a bit of a sailor, even to me it was most terrific and appalling . . . some of our
party were half dead with fear—and we were so thumped and knocked about by the
tremendous seas we were constantly shipping, that we were completely worn out'.[30]
Stock losses during these voyages were especially severe,[31] although, as is so often
the case, some vessels had smooth seas for the entire voyage. When *Atwick* landed
all her stock in good condition, a passenger, P. H. Dod, attributed it as much to the
master's skill as the good weather.[32] Arrival at the Cape provided opportunity to
spend a week or more ashore and diarists concur that it was a welcome relief from
shipboard routine and discomfort. The articulate Eliza Shaw probably spoke for all
passengers when she wrote that 'the sight of land, and that so near, filled every
bosom with joy'.

III

Though the long journey from the Cape across the Indian Ocean was invariably
rough and uncomfortable, passengers were assuaged by the knowledge that it was
the *last* stage and every day brought them closer to the paradise that pre-emigration
publicity had led them to believe was Swan River. August 5, 1829, was the last day
for forty-seven privately sponsored immigrants aboard *Calista*. On August 6 *St
Leonard*, whose master was to play a key role in the reporting of first news from
settlers at Swan River to anxious relatives in England, arrived, as did the ill-fated
Marquis of Anglesea seventeen days later. Stirling knew that *Calista* would be one of
the first vessels to reach the colony—she was preparing to leave when *Parmelia*
sailed from England—but he was nonetheless completely taken off-guard by her arrival so soon after *Parmelia*, and also by the arrival of the two other vessels in quick
succession.[33] Officials and their families were still camped on Garden Island and no
substantial arrangements had been made to receive the first settlers. As there was no
point in landing them on the island, they were landed on the mainland. Stirling then
hurriedly arranged to move his officials from the island to the Fremantle camp.
John Septimus Roe, the surveyor-general, who had been surveying Cockburn Sound
for safe anchorages and passages, was ordered to commence surveying the mainland, beginning with the laying out of Perth, which had been selected as the capital
city of the colony on August 12. He then laid out Fremantle. By September 18 no

rural land had been examined, let alone alienated, and no accurate plan of the region had been drawn up.[34]

Given that there was a serious lack of adequate preparation and pre-planning, that officials and the military had utilized scarce materials (and labour) in establishing a temporary camp at Garden Island, that the weather had been very wet and windy,[35] and that Roe simply had to give top priority to surveying anchorages and dangerous channels, it was inevitable that settlers aboard the three vessels, and aboard those which followed during the next few months, would face chaotic conditions. At their first glimpse of Swan River, the hearts of many settlers sank. The coastal sandhills, covered by a thin layer of stunted vegetation tough enough to endure the strong prevailing winds, were not an impressive sight even for expectant settlers who had sailed for months across the 'bleak and windy desert of the seas'. At the mainland camp behind Arthur Head, erosion had been exacerbated by the arrival of hundreds of new settlers within a few months. Thus, the first visual and physical experience of paradise was sand, which, wrote Marnie Bassett, became a byword.[36] It was the reason why so many settlers expressed disappointment, and occasionally disbelief, at their first sight of the shore and why those who erected temporary tents and huts complained that the sand blew everywhere. Alfred Stone described the appearance of the Fremantle camp on first landing as most forbidding, and a fortnight later he wrote that 'near the sea this country is the most barren-looking place you could possibly imagine'. Settler Dod also had his spirits damped by the sight,[37] and the captain of the brig *Dragon*, admittedly disappointed because he could not sell his cargo, made scathing remarks about the camp, describing it as a 'perfect bed of sand'.[38] Thomas Henty, who arrived early in 1830 with a large party and much equipment, said his first impressions were 'decidedly bad', and described Fremantle as a 'barren desolate looking place the Soil or rather the surface being composed entirely of Sand . . .'[39] A careful search of extant records and diaries has failed to uncover one uniformly favourable impression of the land that the colonists had come thousands of miles to settle and till.

Calista's passengers, and those who reached the colony during the ensuing weeks, were conveyed from ship to shore in small boats and, with their goods, left where the boats were beached. Some landed in the little cove behind Arthur Head; others, less fortunate, disembarked on beaches north of the river. For all, it was a harrowing experience. No preparation whatever had been made for their reception, save the tales of woe by predecessors; and the apprehensions that they felt when they first saw the continent from shipside only deepened when they set foot on it. In the following weeks they tried as best they could to restack their possessions so as to protect them (and themselves) from the late winter winds and rain. One settler, in a letter to an English newspaper, described how the boisterous weather had greatly damaged his canvas habitation, and while his tent kept out the rain, it was very much affected by the wind. 'A few nights ago', he wrote, 'one side was blown down, and I expected every moment to see the whole concern blow away . . .'[40] Another settler, critical of the lack of preparations for newcomers, described their plight as 'really lamentable',[41] and another that he needed a double-lined marquee for, like the governor when he lived on Garden Island, he too had to put up an umbrella as he wrote.[42] The governor, for his part, was much less perturbed than the settlers. Writing to his brother on 9 September 1829 he described the settlers as busily employed in landing and housing their goods, and in general as 'cheerful and confident' under all the difficulties. Their good humour, he wrote, could be attributed to no other cause than the strong hope they entertained for their future success.

Conditions were not much better for those who arrived during the first summer. Eliza Shaw, writing to an English newspaper in March 1830, described her family as living in tents 'higgledy-piggledy, up to our ankles in sand. Our cart serves four of us for a bedstead; the boys and men lie on beds on the ground, and more complete wretchedness you never beheld.'[43] Mrs Shenton, who reached the colony on 4 February 1830 in *Egyptian*, recorded that she and many other passengers were landed on the beach between North Fremantle and Cottesloe (see Fig. 3.1) where they stayed for two months 'in tents barricaded around with all the packing cases containing [their] furniture'. Many times, according to a relative, they 'thought [their] tents would be blown away as the gales were so severe'. *Esprit de corps* was maintained by playing a piano, and singing heartily to the tunes, on that wind-swept beach.[44]

Primitive conditions such as these took their toll of the health and spirits of the first settlers. The situation at Swan River was not improved by the large number of new arrivals during the first few months, or by the anti-social behaviour of many who were frustrated and bitterly disappointed by what they had discovered, or not discovered at the new colony. Between September 1829 and April 1830 thirty-six vessels carrying passengers, livestock and cargo reached the colony, increasing the population to over 1500. Though the governor and his officials were not equipped to receive and assist the new settlers in an adequate fashion, Stirling would not condone anti-social behaviour or sympathize with unreasonable complaints.

Charles Howe Fremantle had sailed for the India station. To him, Swan River was a sojourn, a commission completed with success. James Stirling had to build a colony and already there were signs that the difficulties would be greater than he envisaged. In his first report, written on 10 September 1829,[45] the governor recorded that exposure to the winds and rain of a boisterous winter had been the 'most serious evil we have encountered', and although most settlers had borne the privations with cheerfulness, a few complainers, unaccustomed to hardships and far too sanguine in their expectations of the colony, were causing him some concern. By November his attitude towards complainers had hardened. There were, he wrote, three main groups of settlers at the Swan: a small number of landowners and professional men who were capable, efficient and able to adapt to circumstances; a large group who were of no value to the colony and should not have emigrated, because they would be ruined by their own groundless expectations; and a third group who were 'outcasts of the parishes', having been allocated by irresponsible officials to unsuspecting employers bound for Swan River.[46] In other words, the efforts of a small number of adaptable landowners and professional men were being undermined by others who, expecting to find the colony a paradise ready to inhabit without effort, were found wanting in virgin country during a boisterous winter. If this was not enough, indentured workers had been poorly selected by irresponsible officials in the parishes that most of the settlers had come from. Though he did not say it, the governor pointed to the second and third groups, and probably especially the third, when he wrote of anti-social behaviour. On September 23 two Fremantle merchants, Leake and Samson, asked the governor to take action against people who got drunk and became violent and disorderly.[47] The following month, T. B. Wilson, a visitor to the colony, described Fremantle as 'a very bad place, owing to the idleness, roguery and thieving of those people brought out as servants [Stirling's third group?], and also of some others of a higher denomination [Stirling's second group?]'. It was so bad, wrote Wilson, that the governor had designated Fremantle a 'sink of iniquity', and had stated that he would take 'no measures to make it better on purpose to force people to go to their farms'.[48]

Esprit de corps at the Fremantle camp was probably at its lowest ebb during January 1830. The governor's views on the 'groundless expectations and helpless in-efficiency' of many settlers had not changed;[49] new arrivals had been stunned by the conditions and old hands readily greeted them with tales of woe; lethargy was rife and, wrote a contemporary observer, 'Melancholy appears to pervade all classes and great dread is felt lest there should be a scarcity of provisions'.[50] Summer heat had replaced winter squalls and with it came sand-fleas, flies and mosquitoes. Lack of adequate food led to scurvy; ophthalmia afflicted many and poor hygiene and crowded living conditions caused dysentery which reached epidemic proportions, its severity increasing as summer progressed.[51]

Under these circumstances, Stirling's decision not to improve conditions at the camp (and the means at his disposal to do so were limited) was harsh. Many settlers desperately wanted to leave the camp for their rural properties, but before they could do so, land had to be surveyed and allocated. With such a large number of settlers reaching the colony in so short a time, the surveyor-general and his assistants were hard-pressed to cope with the necessary procedures. As already noted, the acreage to which each colonist was entitled depended upon the value of certain goods, and the number of workers and livestock he brought to the colony. The colonist's first task, however, was to get his goods and stock ashore, which was not easy. Where he had been landed depended apparently on the whim of the ship's master. Some brought their vessels close to Arthur Head and conveyed passengers, cargo and stock to the shore near the camp in small boats; others, more cautious perhaps, kept well away from the Head and disembarked passengers and their possessions on beaches north of the river entrance. Wherever they landed, the absence of a jetty or landing-ramp made it a hazardous exercise. While some masters complained that it was inconvenient to discharge cargo on an open beach,[52] others did little or nothing to assist settlers, who had to make their own arrangements, which meant acting as wharfside labourers and storemen.[53] The open roadstead, un-protected from strong winds, caused long delays in the unloading of vessels. T. B. Wilson observed that bad weather had prevented any communication between his ship at anchor in the roadstead and the shore for several days—an experience he did

PI. 5.2 'Speciman of the society at The Swan River!' (All but the latest arrival have grown webbed

and the cold
of Angels only
us to behold
ve and lonely!"

l, I presume Sir.)

"Negroque similimus
cygno!"

The feast of Reason and the flow
of Souls.

society at
River!

ercolour by an unknown artist. Courtesy of the National Library of Australia] not expect because the *Quarterly Review* had stated that communication was 'convenient, and the access easy, as well as by night as by day'.[54] Inevitably, then, much cargo was damaged by surf breaking on a shoreline inimical to safe disembarkation in small boats. Some goods were actually washed back into the sea before owners could retrieve them.[55] Nor, as James Turner discovered, was cargo always landed in one place, which made it difficult to protect. One of his largest packages was 'pulled to pieces; the Goods taken out sent on shore and thrown on the beach'.[56] He had to watch it night and day to prevent pilfering.

Pl. 5.3 'Flourishing State of the Swan River thing'.   [From *The Looking Glass*, cartoons published in London 1830. Courtesy of Rex Nan Kivell collection in the National Library of Australia]

Once a settler collected his possessions, he then had to carry them from the beach to the Fremantle camp or to a protected place behind the sandhills. This was no easy task and those who, struggling ankle deep through fine sand, carried furniture, ploughs and even pianos really did, as one settler recalled, work like slaves, for the distance from beach to tents was 'a quarter of a mile and up hill'.[57] The unloading, tethering and corralling of animals proved especially troublesome and until temporary fences were erected, stock wandered around the camp or, even worse, into the bush and were lost. There was little grass and fresh water at the Fremantle camp at a time when stock was in special need of it after the long journey from England or the Cape.[58] James Turner was fortunate to get all his cattle ashore, although they were in a very weak condition, having been on short allowance of oatmeal, peas and biscuits since the Cape.[59]

The volume of cargo and stock landed during the first few months was enormous. Land-grant conditions had encouraged settlers to bring goods, which qualified for allocation, rather than cash, which did not.[60] Evaluation was made at a hastily established Audit Office at the Fremantle camp.[61] Settlers would submit details of goods landed and, where possible, invoices to verify same. Although assessment procedures followed guidelines approved by the Colonial Office, valuation was sometimes made on a rather arbitrary basis. Henty noted that allowance for cattle was 'liberal', but for general cargo it was below invoice value.[62]

Once he had been cleared by the Audit Office—and it is not clear how officials coped with settlers whose goods were stacked on beaches north of the river entrance—a settler then applied to the governor at Perth for a grant of land in size appropriate to the valuation. Once again the procedure did not always conform to regulations, and the governor frequently approved grants in excess of acreage justified by valuation, and on no consistent basis.[63] Allocation of specific land to settlers was then delayed, not only by the confusion at Fremantle caused by so many passengers and so much cargo being landed in so short a period but also by the inability of the surveyor-general and his two assistants to survey known agricultural land around the rivers quickly enough. Because the supply of agricultural land was nowhere near sufficient to satisfy allocations, the governor restricted the size of blocks to only a fraction of entitlement. The remainder of entitlement, he argued, would be allocated in areas yet to be explored. And because water carriage was the only medium of communication between the Fremantle camp and river farmland, Stirling also decided that, as far as practicable, each block would be long and narrow, stretching from the river banks, thus providing as many settlers as possible with river frontages on which they could erect landing ramps.[64] Having decided the principles to be adopted, the governor then personally supervised many allocations. He would take parties of settlers up-river and decide boundaries by marking trees by the water's edge.[65] The surveyor-general would then take settlers again to the marked plots and arrange 'formal possession'.[66]

Commendable though the governor's initiative may have been, it only shortened, but did not prevent, delays for settlers in commencing farming. Their stay at Fremantle was more likely to be months than days. James Birkett's experience is probably not exceptional. On 15 March 1830 he complained to the colonial secretary that, although he had made many visits to Perth to receive his land allocation, there had been no response from the authorities:

> I have used every possible exertion to effect the removal of my family from this detestable beach of Fremantle where they suffer extremely from the badness of the water, and the vigilant attentions required here for the preservation of property: besides, we are losing the season for preparing our land to receive seeds. My son, Sir, is actually so weakened by Dysentery at this moment as to render his services no longer available to us, and his mother is well-nigh exhausted by excessive anxiety.[67]

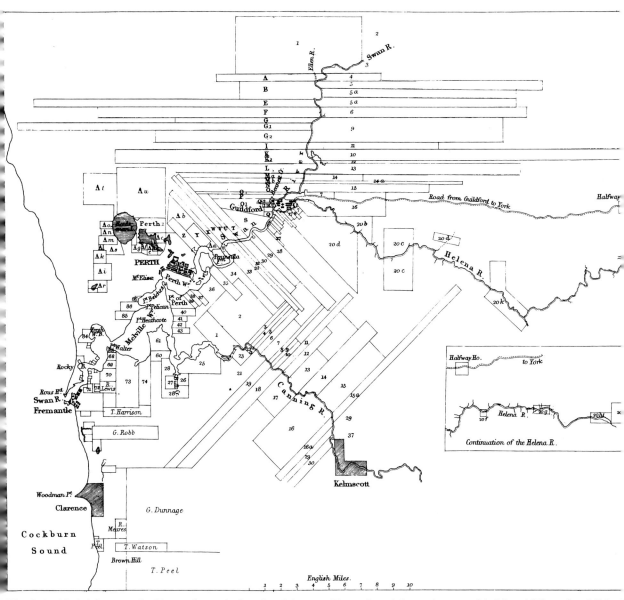

Fig. 5.1 'Strip' lots on the Upper Swan & Canning Rivers. [Reproduced from Arrowsmith Map 1839 and published
Nathaniel Ogle, *The Colony of Western Australia*]

Demand for boats and rafts to take colonists up-river was very keen. James
Turner decided to construct his own raft even though he had not been allocated
land. It was a harrowing experience, and so different from what he had expected.

we dragged [the raft] through the water often up to our waists—sometimes
through carelessness the Goods were upset, one day I had 3 tierces of beef sunk

two I recovered, the other was a serious loss. Some of my packages got so wet that even at this time [three months later] I do not know the extent of my loss in stores. One of my horses ran away into the woods and was not recovered, sheep died daily and we had great difficulty, in procuring water fit to drink.[68]

Turner finally reached the fertile land only to discover that it, and all the river frontages, had been allocated and that he would have to go a further 50 or 60 km to obtain suitable land. Indeed, all agricultural land in the Swan and Canning basins had been allocated by June 1830, and the arrival of *Lotus, Caroline* and *Atwick* increased the number of claimants astonishingly, certainly faster than the surveyor-general could survey and map.[69] The situation had been worsened, claimed Henty, by so much land having been granted naval and military officers and government clerks, often in lots of between 400 and 600 ha.[70]

Many settlers, perhaps even some in Stirling's first group, understandably complained about the hardships of life at Fremantle camp and freely criticized British government officials for not having provided basic facilities. Some were so appalled that they sailed on to other colonies.[71] But the more realistic settlers, whatever they may have uttered inside their improvised beach tents, treated their sojourn at Fremantle as an unfortunate, but only temporary, situation. Of far greater importance to farmers who had come to clear and till the land was the extent and fertility of soil at the new colony. Stirling's report, and the British journals, had led them to believe that it was there in abundance and, though many settlers must have been disappointed when they first saw the sandy coastline, they would have been reassured by information that fertile land was located well up-river towards the hills. Once they landed and stacked their goods, many settlers hired boats and sailed up-river to see the land for themselves. Hopes which had been dashed by the sandy coast and the dusty Fremantle camp were quickly rekindled by the beauty of the river and the lush vegetation along its banks. 'Swan River', wrote one observer, 'would require the language of a poet to describe it. The scenery on its banks is lovely beyond description; its course beautifully serpentine.'[72] A young man from Brighton wrote to his local newspaper that the limestone cliffs along the banks had features which at one time you would 'almost swear to be a beautiful bridge, at another it appears like an amazingly large castle with turrets and all complete'.[73] And another observer considered that beautiful Melville Water, 10 km long and six broad, merited the epithet 'Magnificent'.[74] There were navigational hazards, to be sure, but these (sandbanks and mudflats) could be easily eradicated by cutting canals at appropriate places.

Though they saw fertile land on the upper reaches of the Swan and Canning rivers, settlers quickly realized that it represented only a fraction of the land in the region. It was for this reason that Stirling restricted allocations of fertile river land to each settler. Soil on the western side of the hills was predominantly sand, and even the long, narrow blocks stretching out from the river banks contained, in their back parts, much land regarded by settlers as useless for agriculture. Thus, as sand had become a byword for Fremantle, it was soon applied to the region as a whole.

Settlers who arrived on the first vessels and were granted choice river-plots were, of course, in a better position than those who arrived later and were granted relatively inferior land or had to wait at the Fremantle camp until more fertile land was discovered over the ranges. The extent and quality of soil west of the hills was well known by early 1830, an official having clarified the situation in a letter to the *South African Commercial Advertiser*:

> Great disappointment has been occasioned among many of the latterly arrived settlers, by the very small quantity of really superior land, within the present located districts, compared with what they were led to expect from the Official Reports, published in England. The superior land consists of alluvial flats on the banks of the Swan and Canning Rivers, and is considered, even by the most experienced English farmers here, to be capable of producing anything. But it is confined to the immediate banks of these rivers in the form of a belt, not exceeding in its greatest width from the River three or at best four miles, and in general one or two, and in many places being a mere strip of about half a mile at the utmost . . . . The interior of the country . . . is . . . generally a vast plain with occasional undulations, and gently rising hills, and for the most part consists of cileceous sand, varying only in colour—pure white, grey, black (in swamps) red and yellow.[75]

The impact of this discovery on settlers who had risked a great deal by selling property in England in the expectation, based on published reports, that there was ample fertile soil, was severe, and their written comments are therefore understandably more direct than those of officials. Many settlers, wrote one, had expected that the whole of their grants would be fertile, and thus saleable; instead, 'not more than one fourth [is] good for anything'.[76] Another, who stayed at Swan River for only two months before sailing to Van Diemen's Land, claimed that during an exploration of 16 km in the interior he had 'not seen a spot that is capable of receiving a potato or cabbage; as for the fine undulated country the pamphlet speaks of . . . the soil that I have seen . . . has not sufficient moisture to support vegetation of any kind'.[77] And yet another described the bay around the plain (Cockburn Sound) like the plains further north, as chiefly a sandy soil, affording but a few spots that would reward the labour of the agriculturalist.[78] Henty, the disappointed large-scale settler, who arrived too late to secure a large part of the fertile river valley land, thought the non-river soil very unpromising and that the colony's capabilities had been 'vastly over-rated'.[79] The sad truth is that each was right because he described land the fertility of which was very inferior to that on the river flats.

Adverse comments such as these were not confined to settlers. Officials frequently wrote letters to English newspapers and (in the case of Dance, the master of *Sulphur*, and John Morgan, the colonial storekeeper, now isolated on Garden Island) to Colonial Office officials in London. While Stirling was playing down the seriousness of conditions at Swan River during the first year, and laying the blame for many difficulties at the feet of unrealistic settlers, Dance and Morgan were writing their unofficial views to Twiss or Hay, telling how it really was. Hay in particular encouraged unofficial correspondence of this kind and was criticized by other officials in London, who considered that it only led to dissension and recrimination when colonial governors like Stirling discovered that their 'private and confidential' lines to Downing Street were not exclusive.[80] Even though the practice also encouraged transmission of gossip, Twiss and Hay seemed pleased to receive the information; one suspects that they doubted the objectivity of the governor's reports. Morgan was especially grateful for the favour and the opportunity to provide superiors in London with his ideas, hopes, fears and a catalogue of criticisms. Despite his assurances to the contrary, he did not get on well with the governor and seemed especially gratified when his independent reports found favour with Hay, who encouraged him to write regularly. Morgan considered himself an expert on colonization, having lived in America and written a handbook on the subject. On the subject of soil fertility at Swan River he was especially outspoken, partly because he was also a landowner and partly because he believed his experiences of land administration in north America made his opinions worthy of consideration. Though he never stated it, there are many passages in his letters to Hay suggesting that he knew more than anyone else at the colony, including the governor, about this subject. He described to Hay his 1215 ha land grant on the Canning River as only about one-tenth good land, the rest being 'not worth even the walking over', and after three weeks of exploring in the colony, he was sorry to have to conclude that he had passed over 'more totally worthless sand—for it is a farce to call it land, than I did in three years,—in all North America'.[81] Captain Dance of *Sulphur*, whose relations with the governor were also not always amiable, was more circumspect than Morgan in his correspondence to London, although as early as 9 September 1829 he warned Twiss that much had been 'injudiciously asserted about the luxuriance of soil' and that Twiss could expect to hear very exaggerated accounts by settlers.

Settlers at Swan River needed a target at which to aim their criticism and, almost to a man, they pointed to misinformation disseminated orally in London during 1828 and early 1829, and later published in journals—information which had so influenced both their decisions to emigrate and their expectations of the new colony. In his painstaking research into this subject, James Cameron concludes that the genesis of misinformation was the imprecision of prose in Stirling's and Fraser's 1827 reports, their underlying enthusiasm for establishing a colony at Swan River, and the fact that they stayed at the site for too short a time to justify the conclusion that it had great agricultural and commercial potential.[82] Sections of their reports quoted in Chapter 2 support the first criticism. As Cameron shows, the predominance of favourable adjectives (ten to one unfavourable) was out of proportion to their assessment of the ratio of good to bad land 'and many of the adjectives were not particularly appropriate to a supposedly objective report on the prospects of an area for colonisation'.[83] They were misled into concluding that the evergreen foliage of the native forest meant that the area was well watered, which it is not. They did not appreciate that jarrah forests are restricted to poor soils and that most of the sandy soils on the coastal plain lack trace elements, a fact 'believed by the wealth of flora'. Fraser consistently overestimated soil quality, and Stirling, mainly because he was on the mainland for so short a time, did not identify all the major landscape zones. Nor did he sufficiently emphasize the *extent* of alluvial soils, an error which was the 'greatest single cause' of confusion. 'Both made erroneous conclusions as a result of assumptions implicit in their evaluation', concludes Cameron. 'Their purpose and previous experience with land evaluation, the nature of the examination and the intrinsic quality of Swan River environment emphasised these errors. In turn they were to mislead' (Fig. 5.2).[84]

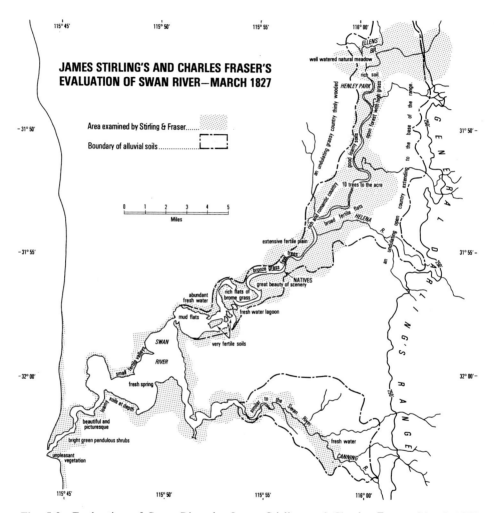

Fig. 5.2 Evaluation of Swan River by James Stirling and Charles Fraser, March 1827. [Reproduced from a map by J. M. R. Cameron, *Western Australian Readings*]

Although Stirling's report on his 1827 visit did not convince the Colonial Office that it should establish a colony at Swan River, Stirling's personal efforts in England during 1828, especially his conversion of John Barrow, led to a favourable decision.

Barrow admitted that his initial doubts on soil quality had been resolved after Stirling had shown him that Charles Fraser was a man fully competent to judge such matters. His doubts on the existence of a safe anchorage had also been resolved by personal discussions with Stirling, the experienced naval officer.

Barrow's subsequent enthusiasm for the venture, and especially his article in the influential *Quarterly Review,* were primarily responsible for the compounding of errors and misinformation. He freely admitted that the public's enthusiasm had stimulated him to write and so, concludes Cameron, 'what had been an evaluation of the potential of an area for colonisation became, in essence, a publicity brochure and a colonization manifesto. Distortion was inevitable.'[85] The salient point for potential emigrants was that their decisions had to be made almost entirely upon the information provided by Stirling and Fraser and disseminated by Barrow and the London journalists. As already shown, Swan River's reputation prior to Stirling's report had been established by explorers who were not enthusiastic about its potential. But Barrow claimed they had completely underestimated its potential. For example, Stirling's discovery of a fine anchorage had been entirely overlooked by the French who, because they were there during the winter, had left 'behind them this part of the coast unexamined; with all convenient speed'. The pity is that the 'new' information provided by Stirling and Fraser was not only questionable but it was also dispersed in a manner which distorted facts even further. For example, the map of Swan River included in the *Quarterly Review* differs significantly from the map prepared by Stirling, especially in conveying the extent of land and its possible uses (Fig. 5.3). Especially serious for potential settlers was, as Cameron shows, the way in which Stirling's statement that 'luxuriance of vegetation at Swan River indicated no deficiency in soil, heat and moisture', was extended to prove the productivity of both climate and soils. In other instances lengthy descriptions in the Stirling and Fraser reports were summarized as direct quotes, comments which could be construed as unfavourable were deleted, information provided by French and Dutch explorers was referred to only if it was favourable, and Fraser's observation that the flanks and foothills of the Darling scarp were barren and incapable of sustaining crops was deleted, his description of favourable soil up-river from the junction of the Swan and Canning rivers being applied by Barrow to the *whole* area from sea coast to hills. As Cameron's research convincingly shows, more textual changes were made in Fraser's report than Stirling's, which partly explains why he was largely blamed for misrepresentation.

Distortion of information was serious enough, but the major misrepresentations were caused by Barrow's *conjectural* expectations based on Stirling's and Fraser's observations. Though they had been on the western coast for only nineteen days and explored only small areas (see Fig. 5.2), Barrow wrote that the coastal plain extended from one or two degrees north of Swan River probably to King George Sound and might be estimated to contain 2 430 000 ha, the greater part of which was fit for the plough. Even more serious, Barrow predicted that there would probably be found fertile plains *beyond* the hills, intersected by streams of water flowing from mountains to the eastward or northward. Because Stirling had examined less than

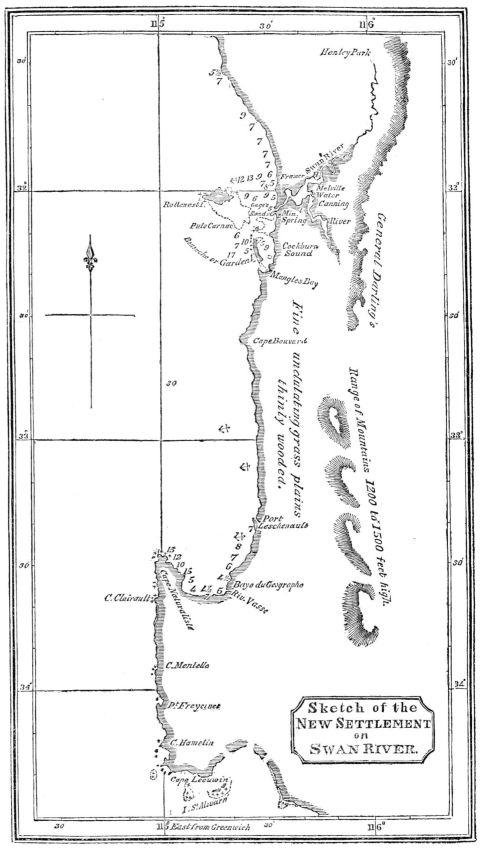

Fig. 5.3 Map of Swan River Settlement. [As it appeared in *The Quarterly Review*, January and April edition, 1829]

260 km[2], Cameron rightly concludes that Barrow's remarks were both presumptuous and over-optimistic.[86]

On the shoulders of the influential Barrow, therefore, must rest a great deal of responsibility for the settlers' plight and confusion. His excessive, even dangerous, enthusiasm was in remarkable contrast to his reaction in June 1827 on hearing that Governor Darling had given Stirling permission to visit Swan River. On that occasion he bluntly told Hay of the Colonial Office that it was a misguided decision, for it was well known that the whole of the Swan River 'is represented as a continuous succession of "sandy dunes", barren and utterly unfit for any kind of cultivation and there is no fresh water'.[87] Many of the settlers at Swan River in early 1830 would have suggested, and probably not very respectfully, that John Barrow should have stuck to this opinion!

Even so, from extant records, it appears that Barrow was not identified as the culprit. The *South African Commercial Advertiser,* in a very critical article of 7 November 1829, roundly blamed him—that 'London scribe, sitting in his elbow chair by the side of a sea-coal fire, in the Admiralty Office', writing about the '*present'* (their emphasis) prosperous progress at Swan River when the first officials, let alone the first immigrants, had not even reached the colony.[88] The settlers themselves, however, zeroed in on Fraser. Stirling was, of course, in an unenviable position, being governor of the colony and author of the original report—even though it had been seriously distorted by London journalists. At first Stirling defended what he had written, though it was a qualified defence. To his brother he wrote that what he had told him in London had been 'fully supported', although he now realized that the 'bad land is better than I then thought it to be, but the good is not quite in such great proportion',[89] a judgement he reiterated to Twiss in his first official report to the Colonial Office.[90] William Stirling, his cousin at the Swan, who wrote frequently to newspapers in London and the Cape, readily echoed the governor's views that it was not so much the absence of good soil as the 'ridiculous expectations formed in England with regard to the quality of the soil',[91] although on each occasion he omitted to explain how those ridiculous expectations had been formed. Many settlers at Swan River declined to blame anyone, preferring to await news from exploration parties seeking good land over the hills,[92] but others directly accused Fraser of providing misleading information. A naval officer at Swan River wrote that Fraser's accounts were so 'highly coloured' that anyone coming to the colony would inevitably be disappointed.[93] And John Morgan, in one of his letters to Whitehall, also pointed the finger at Fraser when he wrote that the farmer and the botanist are very different people '—and in nine cases out of ten, the latter is no more capable of giving a correct opinion upon how far a large tract of Country, can be made available to farming purposes,—than the former would be, to discuss the merits, and character of an extraordinary shrub, or very beautiful flower'.[94] Many settlers echoed Morgan's view,[95] and even as late as December 1832 Robert Lyon, another settler who also sent independent reports to Whitehall, recorded that the 'great . . . unpardonable sin of Fraser and those who first explored the country, was, their not stating fully and unequivocally' the circumference of good land.[96]

IV

In his 1827 report to Governor Darling, James Stirling claimed that he had succeeded in achieving *both* his major objectives: he had discovered sufficient soil to support a settlement at Swan River, and he had discovered a magnificent harbour. In fact, he reported finding a *complex* of safe anchorages:

(1) A 'good temporary anchorage' on the north-east side of Rottnest Island.
(2) An 'excellent roadstead for Vessels of any Size *(Gage's Roads)* which, though unprotected from nor'westerly winds, was an ideal anchorage offering at all times facilities for landing and embarking'.
(3) Cockburn Sound, which 'at all times [was] perfectly secure and available for Vessels of the greatest dimensions, as well as for any number of them,' and a passage into it of no less than 9 m. He envisaged this Sound as an ideal anchorage for naval vessels, but inconvenient for merchant ships, whose small boats would have to ferry cargo and passengers a long distance to the mainland. Such vessels would better serve the colony by sailing into the Swan River and anchoring in Melville Water.
(4) Melville Water. Though there was a rocky bar across the entrance to this protected expanse of water, Stirling expected that it could be removed 'without difficulty or expense', thus allowing vessels to sail into an expanse of water so attractive as to become 'the finest harbour in the world'. The river was 'tolerantly convenient for navigation', and when dredged at appropriate places would be sufficient for the carriage of 'products of an immense extent of country'.

Captains of the first vessels arriving at Swan River soon realized that each of the permanent anchorages listed by Stirling contained dangers to which his 1827 report did not, and could not be expected to, allude. As already noted, the first two vessels to enter Cockburn Sound through Challenger Passage using Stirling's 1827 chart narrowly escaped disaster, even though the anchorage, once reached, was as safe and commodious as Stirling had written. The passage (and the Sound) clearly required careful charting if it was to become the main entrance into the colony, and for this reason Roe spent much of the first winter buoying the channel and charting the Sound.[97] Stirling brought *Parmelia* in around Rottnest Island, thereby avoiding Challenger Passage (see Fig. 5.4) but, as already noted, inexplicably caused her to run aground on a bank across the northern entrance to Cockburn Sound, causing so much damage that many observers doubted whether she would ever sail again. It was a shattering experience for those on board and confirmed to all, settlers and passengers alike, that Cockburn Sound, safe though it might be for vessels once they were inside, was nonetheless extremely difficult to enter.

Gage Roads, wrote Stirling in 1827, was an excellent roadstead and, unlike Cockburn Sound, was close to the river entrance and offered facilities for landing and embarking. It is not clear whether the first three merchant vessels—*Calista, St Leonard* and *Marquis of Anglesea*—entered Gage Roads from around Rottnest Island. They probably did; Challenger Passage was, as Stirling recommended, the logical entry for naval vessels bound for the lee of Garden Island, whereas the

Fig. 5.4 Part of a chart of Challenger Passage drawn by J. S. Roe, 1830. [Original held by Hydrographer's Office, Taunton, Somerset]

Pl. 5.4 Part of the Jane Currie painting of Fremantle 1832. The wreck of the *Marquis of Anglesea* can be seen on the left. [Courtesy of

northern passage around Rottnest was the logical passage for merchant vessels whose passengers and cargo would be disembarked at the Fremantle camp.[98] However, at least two of the merchant vessels which had probably used the northern passage moved to Cockburn Sound. On August 25, Stirling reported that only one of the three was anchored outside the mouth of the river; the other four vessels, including *Parmelia* and *Sulphur*, were anchored in Cockburn Sound.[99] The one merchant vessel at the river's entrance was on good holding-ground, 'but the anchorage is open to winds from NNW to WNW, being protected by nothing in that direction except a bank of 5 to 6 fathoms'. She had already ridden out two gales there and seemed to be in no danger. Being a merchant ship, wrote Stirling, she preferred to remain there because of its convenience to the settlement rather than 'come around the island into the Sound'. This is an interesting remark, tending to confirm that the other two vessels had also used the northern entrance but then, exercising much more caution than had Stirling on *Parmelia*, moved into the Sound for protection. As we shall see, this became a common practice after 1830.

Stirling's obvious apprehensions about the Gage Roads anchorage were echoed by Captain Fremantle just before he sailed on August 28. The last sentence in his diary written at Swan River declared that the anchorage could not be trusted in winter. These apprehensions were confirmed a few days later when equinoxial gales of great force struck the coast.[100] As described by Captain Dance, a gale wind took the *Marquis of Anglesea*, with three anchors, and drove her onto rocks at the south of the river's entrance, where she was bilged and 'I fear can never be got off'.[101] *Calista* was repeatedly driven from her anchorage and, although she too lost three anchors, did not go aground.[102] *St Leonard* was severely buffeted, but weathered the storm without incurring severe damage. One observer wrote that each ship was hourly expected to run ashore.[103] The loss of *Marquis*, in clear sight from their beach tents of probably two hundred settlers, caused consternation to settler and sailor alike.[104] Miraculously there was no loss of life, and lesser loss of cargo than if the vessel had not already been unloaded.[105] The master of *Marquis* was understandably shaken: '*This is, without exception*', he wrote to his owners, '*the worst roadstead I ever saw. Had we gone on shore two cables' length further to the northward we must have all perished*' (his emphases).[106] Even the ever-optimistic governor was shaken by the loss. To his brother Walter he confided on September 7 that the 'badness of Gage's Roads as an anchorage' in winter (from where the *Marquis of Anglesea* had been driven the previous weekend) would have to be considered, together with the scarcity of land, as reverses for the settlers.[107]

Among the many concerns of settlers at the Fremantle camp was the effect that the loss of *Marquis* would have on insurance rates for cargo and, indeed, whether any vessels would be prepared to risk calling at the port. Swan River's long-standing reputation as a dangerous place for vessels had been allayed only by Stirling's enthusiastic and reassuring remarks in his 1827 report concerning the variety and safety of newly discovered anchorages. Lloyds of London, never an institution to be persuaded by rhetoric, had already asked to see the sections of Stirling's report 'respecting the Navigation of Swan River and particularly with regard to a bar at the entrance of that river' so that they could fix a 'proper premium for the use of insuring vessels proceeding to that intended settlement'.[108] Once news of the loss of *Marquis* reached England, settlers were certain that insurance rates would rise sharply, thus discouraging companies whose vessels provided their only links with other colonies and other countries. John Morgan told Hay that the wrecks, and others soon after, would put Swan River 'at the very bottom of Lloyds list . . .' High premiums would be exacted and therefore the interests of the infant colony would be injured.[109] William Stirling expected rates to rise as a result of 'Gage's Road's insecurity',[110] and another settler thought it would be the excuse underwriters were seeking to throw the 'roadstead and anchorage in disrepute'.[111] Settlers were no doubt very concerned about the unreliability of Challenger Passage, but Gage Roads was of greater significance because, until the bar across the river was opened, it remained the major anchorage for merchant vessels.

Higher insurance rates had, in fact, been charged before *Parmelia* reached Swan River. While at the Cape, Stirling had arranged for livestock to be sent on to the new colony (after *Parmelia* had left) in *St Leonard*, one of the three merchant vessels battered by the August storms. Captain Rutherford, the owner, insisted on charging higher rates than usual because the stock would be shipped in winter and because Swan River was as yet unknown to underwriters.[112]

But Rutherford's place in the history of Western Australia was destined to be much more significant than this. A recent, important, unpublished paper by Ian Berryman, based on years of painstaking research in London archives, shows that Rutherford, who left Swan River in *St Leonard* soon after the August storms, was not only instrumental in getting the first news of the colony's progress back to England but also himself contributed to that news in a way which had lasting deleterious consequences for the colony.

While at Cape Town, Stirling had advertised in the *South African Commercial Advertiser* (22 April 1829) for a trader to supply Swan River with a hundred head of slaughter cattle and fifty head of sheep within three months. The agent who won the contract engaged Rutherford to transport the stock in the barque *St Leonard*, 'a good staunch and strong vessel', and suggested to Stirling that the voyage could be the first of many, for the Cape was a logical place from which Swan River could draw supplies during the formative years. Rutherford also took other stock and goods for settlers and for speculation, knowing that the outward voyage would decide the extent of profit, there being little chance of getting a return cargo. *St Leonard* sailed on 9 June 1829 and took two months to reach Swan River—twice the normal period, during which probably half the stock perished. Although weather, neglect by the crew and a shortage of provisions may have contributed to these losses, and although the surviving animals recovered quickly, Stirling refused to negotiate a contract with Rutherford for a regular packet between the two ports. Rutherford intended returning to Cape Town on September 10, but a dispute with the governor over whether a passenger (owner of the stock?) named John Holland should or should not be allowed to stay at Swan River, delayed his departure until September 22. The governor won the argument, because Holland sailed from the colony on the *St Leonard*. These seeming inconsequential issues were to prove extremely important for the colony's future.

St Leonard's departure was the first opportunity for settlers and officials at Swan River to send news back home.[113] Thus, during the days leading up to September 10, the original departure date of *St Leonard*, most colonists were busy writing from their tents at Fremantle impressions of the colony's soil and its anchorages, and of their own plight, which would greatly alarm officials and relatives in England. *St Leonard* reached Mauritius about mid-October and, as Rutherford decided to stay there for some time, he handed the Swan River letters to Captain Kellock of *Dryade*, bound for England via St Helena two days later. Rutherford also gave Kellock his own critical views about conditions at the infant colony. When *Dryade* reached St Helena, she joined *Madras* (Captain Beach) and both vessels departed for England on the same day. Prior to sailing Kellock told Beach what he had been told by Rutherford. Beach told his agent—Messrs Solomon—at St Helena who promptly recorded the news in a letter to Sir Francis Freeling, chief secretary of the English Post Office. This crucial letter was taken by Beach aboard *Madras*, a faster vessel than *Dryade*, which carried the official reports and settlers' letters from Swan River. *Madras* reached Plymouth on Saturday morning, 23 January 1830, some three days before *Dryade*, and her mail (including Messrs Solomon's letters to Sir Francis) was in London the following Monday morning. The consequence of one ship sailing slightly faster than another, writes Berryman, was to have consequences regrettably too apparent. The first news from Swan River was third hand from a man whose experiences there were unlikely to be written of with either sympathy or accuracy. On receiving Solomon's letter, Freeling promptly sent it to the Chancellor of the Exchequor. The latter's reaction to what he read can be easily imagined:

> The ship St Leonard . . . reports the total failure of that [Swan River] establishment and the loss of the *Marquis of Anglesea* in a gale of Wind while riding at anchor secured by three anchors.
>
> The soil is not near so fertile as has been represented but is on the contrary of a light sandy nature, in consequence of which the heavy rains had so washed away a great part of it, and the settlers were almost in a state of starvation, but had been partly relieved by Captain Rutherford . . . who had spared them a few bullocks.

The evening papers of Monday, 25 January, broke the sensational news. The *Courier* published paragraphs almost identical with Solomon's letter; the *Globe* wrote of the 'disastrous first account', and the *British Traveller* reported that settlers at the Swan were in a state of great distress. Some Tuesday morning papers printed Solomon's letter, but *The Times*, at least, warned its readers that, because the accounts had come in a very circuitous way, they might prove to be incorrect or exaggerated. The Colonial Office was unable to answer the many questions posed by anxious relatives and financial backers until the official letters reached them. They could not even refute a piece of new information in the *Morning Chronicle* that Governor Stirling, finding it quite impracticable to carry the object of his mission into execution, had sailed for Mauritius. The *Morning Journal*, a paper strongly opposed to the government, repeated this information but stated that Stirling had gone to Van Diemen's Land, not Mauritius. These reports greatly upset relatives, officials and persons with financial interests in the colony. Chief among the latter was Solomon Levy, agent for Thomas Peel, who had already despatched two vessels *(Gilmore* and *Hooghly)* and was about to despatch *Rockingham*.

Dryade, carrying official correspondence and settlers' letters, finally reached Dover on Tuesday, 26 January, and the bags were in London the following day. A relieved Twiss, hamstrung for two days, was then able to make public a long extract from Dance's letter, which the *Courier* printed that very afternoon together with an editorial comment that it 'abundantly prove[d] the validity of doubts we felt of the accuracy of the first intelligence'. Similar relieved editorials in *British Traveller* and *Globe*, and quotes from Stirling's report to the Colonial Office of 10 September 1829 assured readers that the settlement was in a prosperous condition, the only disappointment being that the fertility of soil had been exaggerated and *Marquis of Anglesea* had been lost. These responsible accounts, wrote the editor of the *Globe*, 'throw a total discredit upon the gloomy reports which have been in circulation during the last few days'.

As Berryman shows, the political persuasion of each newspaper conditioned their interpretation of the reports. *The Times* and *Courier* fully accepted the assurances of the Colonial Office, but the *Morning Herald* and *Morning Journal* remained sceptical. The editor of the *Morning Herald* viewed Dance's letter as confirming his own doubts about the colony, especially that it was not the paradise that Barrow and Semphill had portrayed it to be:

> The prospects held out to the emigrants as respects the luxuriance of the soil, and its fitness for agricultural purposes, upon which alone they must depend, were completely delusive. It will be found, as we expected, that instead of the land about the coast being a sort of Paradise, it is, for the most part, little better than a barren waste. It seems that Paradise is yet to be discovered beyond the hills. In the official communications of Governor Stirling we understand it is admitted that the verdure and richness of the soil has been considerably exaggerated, but that it is sufficiently promising to warrant cultivation. Truly, if this is all that can be said of it, the settlers had much better have gone to Ireland and cultivated the bogs.

The settlers' letters, and especially Dance's, now partly neutralized the effect of the first reports via Rutherford. And yet, concludes Berryman, 'despite all the official assurances, the interests of the colony had undoubtedly suffered a severe blow'. Dance had written, and Stirling had all but confirmed, that the extent of fertile soil had been exaggerated and that Gage Roads was not a safe anchorage in winter. As a result of the first reports, prospective emigrants now had more substantial information than their predecessors upon which to reach their decisions, and Dance's letter certainly would not have been ignored by shipowners and mariners. Both groups became more cautious and Swan River mania quickly subsided. The owners of *Juno, Francis Freeling* and *Eliza* delayed departure by months so that the vessels would not reach Swan River during winter. And the owners of *Hercules,*

David Owen, Resource and *Persian*, advertised to sail early in 1830, never called at Swan River.

Further news from the colony reached London from the Cape in mid-February, but was not reported widely by the press. However, news from persons who had left Swan River for New South Wales or Van Diemen's Land was given much more attention in the daily papers of 6 March 1830. By and large these letters were severely critical of Fraser and Stirling, and depicted the Swan experiment, held together by 'Governor Stirling, the Autocrat of the swans and gulls, and other of his subjects . . .' as an 'entire failure, of the most perfect and unqualified description'. Another letter from Van Diemen's Land described the land as 'of a most miserable sterile quality, affording no herbage, but covered with a surface partly composed of a dwarf sort of scrub . . . there is no clay for bricks . . . [and] the want of wood and fresh water cannot fail to tend to its abandonment . . .'[114] Once again, the news-papers' political viewpoints conditioned their coverage and editorial comment on these letters. But the British public, having been taken through the whole gamut of publicity about Swan River—Barrow, Semphill, Rutherford, official letters and now further damning criticism—reacted predictably, as did the newspapers. After October 1830, the subject dropped out of public notice.

For those settlers already on the high seas and therefore unaware of the sensations reported by the English press, as for those who, despite the reports, decided to leave for Swan River, there was a trying time ahead at the Cape. Though some vessels by-passed the Cape, most made it their final victualling port before sailing on to Swan River.[115] Enthusiasm for the new colony had initially been considerable amongst Cape settlers, especially those who stood to gain financially from providing vessels and establishing an export trade. First news of the difficulties experienced by pion-eer settlers reached the Cape during November 1829 and Rutherford himself arrived there from Mauritius in January 1830. The spate of newspaper articles and pub-lished letters from settlers and officials at Swan River, together with Rutherford's opinions and those of the disgruntled John Holland, whom he had brought back, contributed to a dramatic change in Cape attitudes about the potential of the new colony. By December 1829, Cape Town was 'full of rumours and tales of dis-aster',[116] and as each Swan-bound vessel reached the port its passengers were encour-aged to go no further or at least consider going to another Australian colony. Those who had left England before the first reports from Swan River had been received were especially bewildered by what they heard; those who had left after the reports had been received were less shocked but nonetheless apprehensive. Eliza Shaw, one of the passengers who was not deterred in her objectives, wrote from the Cape that 'nothing they can say is bad enough for the new settlement' and that many Cape residents were simply jealous of the 'Government patronising the new colony'.[117] Another settler, writing from Swan River on 3 February 1831 to South Africa reported that settlers reaching the colony had said that printed placards had been ex-hibited at the Cape cautioning passengers bound for Swan River against continuing to their destination, a story that the South African newspaper vigorously denied.[118]

Nonetheless, as Berryman shows, rumours and advice at the Cape greatly depleted the numbers of those who continued on to Swan River. Of the sixty-four passengers aboard *Protector* who reached the Cape during January 1830, seventeen disembarked there; and of the ninety-nine aboard *Britannia*, sixty-two also decided to go no further. *Juno*, the vessel which delayed sailing from Liverpool because of the first reports from Swan River, reached the Cape in August 1830 with thirty-seven passengers, but her owners then decided to by-pass the new colony and head for New South Wales.[119] The effect of these losses on Swan River, especially from the point of view that they halted the immigration momentum, were greatly regretted by settlers who could do little to prevent them. George Fletcher Moore, the advocate-general at Swan River, critical of both Cape residents and of settlers who believed them, was also puzzled why they should act as though every injury they inflicted on Swan River was a positive gain to themselves.[120] Henry Camfield told his brother in England that many settlers who changed their minds at the Cape later wished they had not.[121] William Tanner was a good example: he arrived at the Cape with a party of forty-one persons and property worth £8800, but on being told that Swan River was 'almost destitute of fresh Water, [and the sand there was] so barren that nothing would vegetate so far as to be fit for Food', was persuaded by a relative to switch to the vessel *Drummoyne* bound for Sydney. But when *Drummoyne* reached Swan River, en route to New South Wales, he saw that 'it was nothing like described' by the Cape relative and so disembarked. Swan River, he later told Peter Broun, was greatly the 'reverse' of what he had heard at the Cape.[122]

The impact in England of the first news from Swan River, together with subsequent letters from New South Wales and Van Diemen's Land, not only led to the cancellation of voyages but also discouraged many potential settlers who were awaiting first-hand information before making their decisions. As a result, emigration to Swan River declined dramatically after February 1830, and was exacerbated further by rumours from the Cape. Emigrants and shipowners were now in accord: the new colony offered neither adequate soil to support a large population nor adequate anchorages to protect vessels. Loss of the *Marquis of Anglesea* had confirmed shipowners' doubts about the danger of Gage Roads, the most convenient anchorage for merchant vessels, but when news was received in England during January 1830 of the near-loss of H.M.S. *Success* while attempting to enter Cockburn Sound in November 1829, doubts were raised concerning the safety of Challenger Passage for naval vessels. Captain Jervoise, who had been master of *Success* when Stirling brought her to Swan River in 1827, used the chart he had made on that occasion to enter the passage. He was confident of the course he set, and according to one passenger's account, anticipated no danger. But no sooner had he entered at 7.00 A.M. on November 29 and trimmed his sails than *Success* struck a reef.[123] In circumstances similar to Captain Fremantle's entry in *Challenger* earlier that year, the master was in a small boat ahead of *Success* sounding the passage. He returned immediately to the ship when she struck, but unlike Captain Fremantle, was not upbraided by Jervoise for incompetence. Indeed, it was probably Jervoise's over-confidence, like Stirling's when he tried to sail *Parmelia* into Cockburn Sound from the north, which was primarily responsible for the accident.

Sails were furled and anchors dropped, but the latter were quickly lost when the cables were severed by the reef.[124] This caused the stern to be exposed to strong south-west winds, which in turn caused the ship to strike violently against the reef and to make 1.5 m of water each hour she was there. Captain Dance, aboard *Sulphur*, was told by his servant at 7.00 A.M. that a large ship was coming into the Sound through Challenger Passage. Seeing her in a dangerous position, he quickly despatched two boats into which goods from *Success* were loaded and shuttled across to Carnac Island, the same refuge for goods and passengers aboard *Parmelia* when she had struck. All hands manned the pumps and 'by an exertion of human strength, which might be supposed incredible . . . they kept pumping for eight hours, changing every ten minutes . . .' Stirling was informed of the accident and hurried to join his old ship still manned by many of his old crew. Finally, *Success* was hove off into 9 m of water, although pumping did not cease until she was safely at anchor beside *Sulphur*. According to the navigator, Jervoise's leadership and the crew's efforts left nothing to be desired. When he called for the greatest exertions, men cheered loudly, returned to the pumps, and vowed 'they would never quit her while she could swim'! And when at last *Success* was safely anchored, a divine service of thanks 'for a more omnipotent Aid than their own strength' was held, without which, it was agreed 'all would have been lost'.

Thus, within six months of Stirling's arrival with the first settlers, two of the three anchorages which in his 1827 report he had claimed were safe, had been proven by bitter experience to require abandonment in winter months (Gage Roads) or careful surveying (Challenger Passage into Cockburn Sound). In different, but nonetheless important, ways *Marquis of Anglesea* and *Success* were destined to play important roles in the colony's future. At first *Marquis*, lying high and dry on the rocks at the entrance to the Swan River, was a symbol of both mariners' and settlers' apprehensions—a salient reminder to both of Gage Roads' fickle safety. When Charles Fremantle returned to the colony in 1832 on his way back to England, he declared that the wrecks 'lying on the Beach are quite sufficient to stamp the character of this Anchorage'.[125] Even so, this symbol of failure was soon converted into a symbol of improvisation by settlers determined to make the best of very difficult conditions. *Marquis* became the colony's temporary gaol, the harbour master's office and the governor's Fremantle office until more permanent structures were erected.

In many ways, the damage to *Success* was an even greater blow to the colony's future. She too was an important symbol: the very vessel in which Stirling had 'discovered' Swan River in 1827 and from which the passage into Cockburn Sound had been found. But, more significant for the colony, the use of the unknown jarrah timber to replace broken planks was so successful that the Admiralty later placed large orders for its use in British shipyards. But what promised to be the beginning of a crucial export industry was to founder for want of capital to provide the necessary infrastructure to transport and load the timber at Fremantle. Even the timber used to repair *Success* was held at Fremantle for want of a boat large enough to transport it across the Sound to Careening Bay.[126] Correspondence between officials and Captain Jervoise show that material was seldom readily available when needed, and that almost a year passed before repairs were completed.[127] It was a massive job for a colony with very limited resources. Repairs had to be made to the whole of the main hull, and part of the stem and stern post, requiring 223 m of planking on the port side and 152 m on the starboard side. The hull also had to be sheathed with lead and then coppered, requiring at least 360 kg of lead from Morgan, the colonial storekeeper. Rigging, masts, anchors and rudder all had to be replaced and what could not be provided by the storekeeper were taken off *Sulphur*.[128] Smith, the colonial shipwright, was warmly commended by Jervoise for his 'zeal and perfect knowledge of his profession', a commendation later supported by the Admiralty;[129] and Morgan, by now the only resident on Garden Island, was thanked for looking after *Success*'s stores and for being so helpful to Jervoise and his crew.[130] Indeed, the exercise was a tribute to the diligence and skill of colonial officials and of the crew of *Success*, without which it is unlikely that the vessel would have ever been saved and almost certain that she would never have sailed again.

This, within a year, was the second major repair job that the colonists, and the crews of visiting ships, had been called to undertake on vessels that had struck while entering Cockburn Sound *(Parmelia* and *Success)*. The impact of the near-losses on settlers and Whitehall alike was considerable, and together with the loss of *Marquis of Anglesea* brought into question the viability of Swan River as a place for a settlement. One is therefore inclined to agree with Henderson that the problems encountered by shipping during these early years were not simply just one other problem for the settlement, but had a significant influence on its early decline, and that failure to remedy the problems contributed greatly to the colony's continued stagnation.[131]

6

Reassessment

*in the process of time, it will become a place of much resort for
Traders in the Eastern Seas.*

R. HAY TO JAMES STIRLING
2 JANUARY 1833

I

When John Septimus Roe moved from Perth to Fremantle during mid-August
1829 to lay out the town, it was temporarily inhabited by hundreds of settlers,
many of whom were waiting to go to their agricultural plots. Because the camp
behind Arthur Head was not a pleasant place, many settlers had moved up-river
about 2 or 3 km to a second camp where they could be 'out of the way of a hor-
rid set of thieves, who lurk about the shore, composed of sailors and others, who
have nothing to do but get drunk'.[1] Though the exact location of this second site
cannot be established, Jane Roberts, a visitor to the colony early in 1830,
described it as the best place for temporary huts.[2] Probably near the river-bank,
it was well wooded, thus providing fuel as well as supports for 'canvass hastily
thrown up.' Only settlers who owned, or who could afford to hire, wagons and
horses could shift their goods through the sand to this second site and although
they appreciated the more congenial environment, it was still a very sandy place.
Sand filled the settlers' shoes, and when mixed with ashes from camp fires outside the tents, covered them with 'a disagreeable, black, dirty dust'.[3]

Many settlers, having foreseen housing problems when they first reached Swan
River, brought huts and tents which they erected at Fremantle camp and later re-
erected on their agricultural plots. A settler named Smithers actually brought a
portable 'van' which he dismantled and packed for the voyage out and then re-
assembled when he reached the Swan River.[4] Huts of this type, and others made
partly from local materials, were appearing at the Fremantle camp by September
1829. For example, a settler who arrived in *Calista* wrote on September 9 that he
had already built an 'excellent storehouse in the quickest manner . . . the sides of
heath, the thatching reeds and rushes perfectly weather tight'.[5] During the same
week, William Stirling reported that settlers had begun building storehouses.[6]

Stirling himself reported that once the first Fremantle lots had been allocated,
grantees were 'proceeding with alacrity in the preparation of buildings'.[7] Distinc-

175

Pl. 6.1 'View at Swan River. Sketch of the Encampment of Mal^{n} Curling Friend, Esq.,
R.N.', March 1830.   [Courtesy of Mitchell Library]

Pl. 6.2   Settler's Tent at Fremantle.   [Woodcut from a sketch, done on the spot by Jane
Roberts (1830) and reproduced in her *Two Years at Sea* (2nd ed., 1837)]

tion should be made, however, between buildings erected by settlers and later dismantled (e.g. Smithers'), those erected by quasi-permanent settlers, and those erected by merchants who formed the nucleus of the Fremantle community. The second group is represented by Joseph Hardey, leader of the Methodist group. Hardey reached the colony on 9 September 1829 and 'erected a wood house at Fremantle seeing it would take so much [time] getting up into [the] interior'. His brother and wife lived in the house until all the family's goods had been transported up-river to his land at present-day Maylands. By July 1830 his Fremantle hut was still standing, having been converted into a coffee-house which returned Hardey an annual rent of £78.[8] Hardey was also quick to see the commercial opportunities arising from disenchanted settlers who left the colony, for he made 'excellent purchases' from them.[9] James Henty may also be considered a quasi-permanent settler because he stayed at Swan River for just over two years before moving to Van Diemen's Land. Although he intended settling at Swan River, Henty never overcame the initial disappointment of being told by the governor that all good land on the Swan had been taken and that he should go to newly opened agricultural land in the south.

When Twiss, under pressure from the British public to find out whether the first press reports on Swan River were accurate, finally received Stirling's official report, he was able to assure readers that the colonists were 'cheerful' and that there was 'no foundation for the unfavourable reports which have appeared in public journals'.[10] But the settlers at Swan River had little to be cheerful about. By mid-1830 all the good land around the Swan and Canning basins had been allocated and even many of the fortunate settlers who had arrived early enough to be granted such land complained that only the river banks of their plots were suitable for agriculture. The articulate John Morgan probably wrote for many when he told the Colonial Office that 'these miserable estuaries surrounded by *splendid poverty*, cannot excite anything like admiration.—The botanist may sit, and admire, the numerous shrubs, and very beautiful flowers,—but the farmer will be straining his eyes out in search of land,—and the sailor—for a straightforward, unimpeded navigation.'[11] Collie, the surgeon, came to a similar conclusion: 'no one is eager to locate himself amidst sand', and though it might support shrubs and trees, agriculturalists were not optimistic that it would be productive for crops.[12] Thus, as early as February 1830, Henry Camfield was advising settlers not to come to Swan River for at least two or three years when, he said, conditions might have improved.[13]

Under these conditions, the urge to discover agricultural land 'beyond the mountains' was as strong in the hearts of Swan River settlers as it had been in the hearts of New South Wales settlers—stronger perhaps, because of their disappointment at discovering such a small area of fertile land when most had come to establish large agricultural farms. The optimism of some settlers is conveyed by an unknown writer to a South African newspaper dated 25 October 1830. Though he was highly critical of the colony, before leaving it he wrote: 'Beyond the Darling Range . . . a very noble tract of land has been discovered, the possession of which is the only prospect of relief to the misled and unhappy adventurers who seriously begin to entertain thoughts of abandoning the coast.'[14] The first excursion over the ranges was made in June 1829 by Lieutenant Henry of Fremantle's *Challenger*, who observed a 'range of Majestic Mountains'.[15] Another party from *Challenger*, which included James Drummond, the government botanist, went in search of a river 'supposed to run in a south-west direction from the mountains'. Although their reports were inconclusive concerning agricultural land, the discovery of majestic mountains and the search for another river would have been one piece of news, perhaps the only piece, to hearten these settlers, some of whom had already been in their tents at Fremantle for many weeks. Many had not yet discounted the possibility of explorers finding the high mountains and wide rivers predicted by John Barrow.

Whatever settlers thought about these possibilities, the Colonial Office had instructed Stirling to give high priority to exploration of agricultural land thought to exist between Swan River and King George Sound (see page 53). Not only would settlement of this area effectively link the two settlements but it would also make the military's task of protecting settlers from attacks by Aborigines easier than if they were scattered all over the colony. Thus, in November 1829 an expedition by Preston and Collie to the Murray district led to the opening of land there for selection. Then, during March 1830, Stirling, Roe and Lieutenant Dale of the 63rd Regiment explored the area around Leschenault Inlet and, on the basis of their discoveries, it too was declared open for selection. However, even though Stirling, Henty and others took up large holdings in the area, it attracted few of the settlers camped at Fremantle. In May 1830 land north of the Blackwood River (Augusta) was thrown open, having also been examined by Stirling and Roe. A few settlers braved conditions at the isolated outpost, but most of them moved further north to the Vasse, where agricultural land was less heavily timbered.[16] By mid-1830 settlers were expressing more interest in the nature and extent of agricultural land eastward beyond the ranges. Lieutenant Dale made the first exploration of this area during July and August, discovering the Avon Valley, but it was not declared open for settlement, the governor still hoping that settlers would move to the southern areas already opened. Erskine verified Dale's discovery in September and the following month Stirling himself visited the area and, under pressure from settlers, then declared it open. By mid-December, nearly 101 250 ha had been granted, leading in due course to the establishment of York, Northam and Toodyay.

It soon became clear, however, that good land, whether in the Swan/Canning basins or elsewhere, existed only in pockets. By March 1830 Morgan reported to Hay on the variable quality of land so far explored: 48 km of unoccupied land to the Murray River, then 64 km of sand to the Preston and Collie Rivers, 'and so on to the end of the Chapter,—King George's Sound'.[17] Refusing to be discouraged by such forebodings, and with no other alternatives, many colonists, some reluctantly, moved to the newly discovered land.[18] Though their departure from Fremantle to their agricultural plots, and the movement of officials to the capital, Perth, greatly reduced the port's population, it also facilitated fulfilment of Fremantle's major role—a port and landing-place.

While immigrants were entering the colony in large numbers, complaining that

Banksia   Xanthorrhea   Natives Encampment   Xanthorrhea Tuart

Pl. 6.3 Scene on Melville Water near Perth, 1842. [Watercolour by W. Habgood. Courtesy of Rex Nan Kivell collection in the National Library of Australia]

nothing had been done to facilitate their re-settlement, the governor as early as September 1829 in turn criticized those who were 'little accustomed to encounter hardships and in all cases too sanguine in the expectations they had entertained respecting the Country'.[19] It was a judgement that Stirling reiterated time and again. In January 1830 he was more specific. Such persons, he declared, will be 'ruined by their own groundless expectations and helpless inefficiency',[20] and later that year, when he reported the failure of Peel's 'gigantic' scheme, he wrote again that many of the settlers were simply incapable of supporting themselves.[21] Thomas Peel's scheme, as already noted, was crucial for the colony's success. The settlers and equipment he had brought in *Gilmore, Hoogly, Nancy* and *Rockingham*, and the enormous tract of land he expected to cultivate would, it was believed, assure the colony's viability, and the 'ambitiously planned town' laid out at Clarence on Cockburn Sound would, in time, rival the capital itself.[22] Although much has been written on the causes of Peel's failure, the fact that he did fail was a severe blow to the colony's progress.[23] Peel arrived at the colony during December 1829, six weeks after the deadline imposed by the Colonial Office for him to take up the land allocated before he left London. His landing-place, Clarence, was entirely un-suitable as a port, for agriculture or for shelter during the months of transition. Within a year of his arrival Peel had left Clarence for the Murray River, and the governor was obliged 'to liberate all but a very limited number of his people from their indentures'.[24] In May 1830 Henty described Peel's affairs as 'most gloomy' and his people 'wretchedly provided for'. Many of Peel's workers, released from their indentures, drifted away from desolate Clarence mainly to Fremantle town, where they voiced their complaints and disappointments.

It was therefore understandable that Stirling should have been uncharacteristic-ally despondent in his report of October 1830. But this was only momentary. Within three months his confidence in the colony had been restored, for to Rear-Admiral Owen he wrote that all was well, that settlers had actually begun constructing small vessels and exporting timber and that he looked forward to the imminent establish-ment of a whale fishery.[25] Not even the virtual cessation of immigration following reports of the colony's plight appeared to worry him. The colony's need was for 'right' settlers, he declared, not large numbers of 'any' settlers.[26] By March 1831 the governor's optimism was based on the fact that settlers had moved inland, and traders, artisans and officials who stayed in the towns were busily engaged in erect-ing their houses and planting crops. This seemed to be a signal to Stirling that the colony was 'prosperous'. Everything, it seemed, was now going right. Even the severe damage to vessels in the winter storms of 1830 was attributed to the neglect of persons in charge, and though seventy persons had quitted the colony, these in general were persons 'not of a description whose departure could be regretted'.[27] A vessel he had sent to Van Diemen's Land for supplies had returned with flour and grain, which reduced prices in the colony; fresh meat was plentiful, fruit trees were flourishing, fishing was good and the first exports of timber were being loaded at Fremantle aboard the *Edward Lombe*. A considerable proportion of the population was engaged in extracting building materials and already there were 'some very good houses' in Perth and Fremantle. Lieutenant Dale's discovery of further fertile land across the mountains meant that there was 'no longer any doubt entertained of ulti-mate success of the Colony'. And Bannister's explorations to King George Sound had 'much increased the confidence of the community in the future of the colony'.

The governor was determined to retrieve the confidence of potential settlers—confidence which had been lost as a result of adverse publicity in London during January 1830. Yet his report of March 1831 (summarized above), like his letter to Rear-Admiral Owen, was more a catalogue of hopes based on temporary activity associated with re-settlement than on evidence of fundamental economic viability. The *promise* of prosperity actually led him to conclude that 'any rapid increase in population, so much to be deprecated last year, could now be received without alarm'. The difficulties of 1829-30, he implied, were due mainly to too many settlers—not of the 'right kind'—arriving too quickly and there being insufficient facilities for their reception. The breathing-space afforded by the absence of new arrivals after late 1830 provided the opportunity for farmers and merchants to become established. The colony, he believed, was on the threshold of rapid growth and prosperity. Nor was the governor alone in his optimism. By mid-1830, when most settlers who had come to till the land had gone to their plots, frustrations at being 'incarcerated' in tents at Fremantle were replaced by the enthusiasm of bringing farms into production. 'Grumbling . . . which has hitherto been the order of the day, is now quite knocked on the head', wrote one settler in August 1830.[28]

Like so many of the governor's expectations, however, the new prosperity was not achieved. From the time he penned his optimistic report of March 1831 until August 1832, when he returned to England to get a 'new deal' for Swan River, economic conditions deteriorated. The seeds of recession were sown long before March 1831 when it was discovered that many settlers, including presumably those who met the governor's high standards of courage, perseverance and application, were short of money. Until the end of 1830 land had been granted to settlers according to the value of capital goods, and the numbers of workers and livestock brought to the colony (see pp. 143-4). But decisions on the appropriate mix of goods (necessary to achieve sufficient land) and cash (necessary to see settlers through the transition period and the first non-productive season on their allotments), had to be made by settlers *before* they left England and few, if any, were in a position to make an accurate assessment of the appropriate mix. George Fletcher Moore, the advocate-general, whose *Diary of Ten Years Eventful Life of an Early Settler in Western Australia* is a day-to-day record of difficulties he experienced at Swan River, wrote: 'The great mistake committed by settlers has been bringing too many articles of machinery . . . . If I were coming again, I should content myself with grubbing hoes, felling axes, (mine are too long and narrow), spades . . .'[29] Land-grant conditions clearly encouraged settlers to err in favour of goods rather than cash. In addition, the first settlers reached Swan River too late in 1829 to catch the growing season; crops must be sown in May/June to be reaped in December, a fact which might not have been readily appreciated by settlers before they sailed. By the time they had been allocated land—and the delays could not have been foreseen—and cleared small portions of it, farmers would have been lucky to catch the 1830 season. Moore was especially critical of over-sanguine persons who thought that they had nothing more to do than scratch the ground and sow; he also warned of the many difficulties which had to be surmounted and that the proper seasons for growing had scarcely yet been ascertained.[30] Indeed, the majority of settlers did not reach Swan River until early 1830 and therefore could not sow their first crops until 1831. Meanwhile, they had to provide for their own day-to-day needs (vegetables, at least, could be grown quickly), pay workers and provide their keep. Ready cash was soon spent and income could not be earned during the transition period, although a few sold vegetables, stock and hardware in a market that was clearly in the buyer's favour.

The liquidity problem became especially serious after early 1831, when immigration from Britain ceased. In February of that year Robert Lyon identified it as the greatest lack in the colony.[31] 'Gentlemen have become destitute', he wrote. 'The want of money has already reduced many of the settlers almost to a state of pauperism',[32] a view consistent with the increasing incidence of letters received by the governor from settlers seeking loans and grants.[33] Butler, for example, sought a loan of £50 or £60 to complete his stone cottage at Freshwater Bay; Wallace Bickley sought £50 to acquire a horse 'with a view to facilitating his agricultural pursuits', and promised to repay it from proceeds from the approaching harvest. The governor was unable to help them, even though he must have been tempted to break the firm rule against such loans which had been imposed on him by the Colonial Office, to assist V. R. Hall, whose ingenuity and industry he would have applauded.[34] Hall had arranged with the master of a vessel at Fremantle to provide all the timber he could 'for exportation at £3.10.0 per ton on the water side'. As the ship would not remain long in port, Hall sought a modest loan of £20 to pay the wages of men to deliver the timber. Even though he agreed to repay the loan when the master of the vessel paid him before sailing, the governor, though sympathetic, could not comply.

The governor's announcement in mid-1831 that he would buy the next crop at fifteen shillings per bushel encouraged farmers to seed as much land as they could clear.[35] By December the government resident on the Canning reported that crops were producing abundantly but that an even greater acreage would have been sown if the cost of provisions had not been so high.[36] Lacking cash, some settlers could not afford to buy the provisions necessary to pay workers to clear their land. Not only were prices high, but they fluctuated considerably. The arrival of a vessel with supplies from Java, for example, reduced the price level, but a delay in arrival of another raised it.[37] The liquidity problem with associated high and fluctuating prices also prevented settlers from purchasing stock from other colonies,[38] and thus led to worsening unemployment.[39]

Despite encouraging reports on yields at the Canning farms, returns were insufficient to alleviate the colony's serious liquidity problem. By mid-1832 many settlers were dispirited. Morgan, who tended to over-react, described conditions as 'ruinous in the extreme' and declared that he would willingly accept £100 for his 2025 ha property 14 km from Fremantle, so convinced was he of the folly of laying out money in farming activities.[40] Even Stirling admitted to the Colonial Office that Swan River was suffering considerable inconvenience because 'settlers have spent all their money'. Even more important, he confessed to having miscalculated the magnitude of difficulties associated with beginning a new colony.[41] His discouragement, primarily the result of the unforeseen problems noted above, had been exacerbated by the long absence from the colony of *Sulphur,* which he had sent to Van Diemen's Land for urgently needed supplies. By the end of June, acting on the advice of his newly established Executive Council, he sent the small colonial schooner *Ellen* to Mauritius for supplies, on the clear understanding that the goods brought back would be sold at prices yielding neither a profit nor a loss.[42] This was an important concession to settlers who believed that prices should have been effectively controlled at the colony's inception, and especially during the non-productive period.[43]

In his unpublished manuscript, 'Economic History of Western Australia', William Somerville gives the timely reminder that, because the historian of early colonial Western Australia is forced to reply heavily on the diaries and letters of 'the official class', whose reminiscences and impressions of life were those of persons 'in receipt of regular incomes from the British Government', he is in danger of providing his reader with unbalanced interpretation. Since Somerville wrote his lively manuscript, a great deal more information has been uncovered in the form of letters by, and diaries of, ordinary settlers, which helps to balance the views of officials on regular incomes. Even so, Somerville's point is well taken. It is rare to find reminiscences/letters from labourers or indentured workers; the letters of William Dyer, Henty's indentured worker, and his observations on the life-style and capabilities of some settlers tends to confirm wide-spread ineptitude.[44] Adverse economic conditions at Swan River forced settlers (notably Peel) to release many of their indentured workers. This, together with the relative absence of social constraints, gave workers more freedom than they had hitherto experienced in England. G. F. Moore's lament that he could no longer talk with his servants has wider implications than absence of social chit-chat. The workers' new freedom and strength at Swan River during those formative years established a social structure and relationships very different from those in the England whence they had come. Moore also laments that 'Masters here are only so in name . . . . In my absence, *** does nothing, and if I speak to him,—exit in a rage. I could send him to gaol but I do not like this extremity, and yet I cannot afford to lose the advantage of his time . . .' Elsewhere, Moore writes of the insolence of servants, that 'Irish servants are beginning to be just as saucy as the English ones' and 'Indentured servants become Masters, No matter what damage they do, how careless they are, sober or drunken, idle or industrious, impudent or respectful, well or ill, you must keep them and satisfy every demand on the *instant* or off they go to a magistrate and make a complaint.'[45] A settler could lament that large capitalists would ruin the colony by bringing out an ill-assorted medley of labourers, but those same labourers quickly formed a social alliance which had more lasting effects than he ever dreamed.

Somerville is probably also only partly correct in assuming that many settlers avoided putting on paper 'stark disagreeable truths and always made the best of things'. Quotations already used in this book confirm that criticism, especially of those who were responsible for the establishment and government of Swan River, was not lacking. This was manifested most clearly in the early months, when settlers lived under difficult conditions at the Fremantle camp.

But these conditions were transitory. Once settlers moved to their lots, agricultural or town, and erected houses while living in temporary huts, 'the general feeling . . . wholly changed';[46] they left off grumbling and, especially during the prosperity of late 1830, forgot the privations and losses sustained during the first few months at Fremantle. The same theme was adopted by a correspondent to a South African newspaper in December 1831. The writer, a settler, probably an agriculturalist, noted the effects of the new social structure but probably did not understand either its causes or its implications. Settlers who had already gone to their lots and 'set to work' were 'all contented and comfortable'; those who complained were the 'useless class who can only gain existence by shopkeeping' or who 'having no idea of any country but such as Cheapside and Carshilt, are beyond description miserable at finding that nature requires some assistance to put forth her bounties'. Another class—the potential grumblers, were more dangerous—self- imagined statesmen, who because Captain Stirling did not at once invite them to his Council table, became patriots, of course, and the whole purport of their lives was to create dissatisfaction and make everything appear worse than it really was.[47]

The governor had the unenviable task of trying to keep the colony together in those early difficult years. By birth and by upbringing, and now by dint of his land grants, his sympathies, and his support, were clearly with settlers who had gone to their farms 'and set out to work in good earnest'. The behaviour of the 'useless class' and the 'political grumblers' were, he wrote, of negative value to the colony. He seemed not to appreciate, though he may well have understood, the reasons for their behaviour. He thought he had done all he could under the difficult circumstances—for example, by proclaiming the hours servants should work and the rations they should receive,[48] and by exceeding his authority in providing sustenance when it was clearly necessary. By April 1832, in a long report to the Colonial Office, he ruminated on the causes of Swan River's plight. The lack of provisions at Swan River for the maintenance of settlers, he wrote, had been a major difficulty. Settlers had been charged with advancing, and in fact making, the settlement—the local government was there solely to guide and protect. But, he wrote, had the settlers been 'all equally industrious and well provided, as the best of them, there were enough to have accomplished rapidly and successfully the Establishment of a Colony, and the Plan which was adopted would have been fully justified by the Result'.[49] The governor's complaint was that, because so small a proportion had been fit for the task they had undertaken, the venture had been only partially successful; and this had been due 'alone to those whose industry, intelligence and means have established them at this moment to consider themselves not only established but secure in a great measure of the reward of their exertions'. In this report Stirling went on to tabulate losses, unfinished houses and destitution. He never really deviated from his view, formed within months of *Parmelia*'s arrival, that the colony's plight was due to lack of persons with 'industry, intelligence and means'. In those early months he had described three kinds of settlers (see p. 150); now he described settlers as belonging to three new categories: (1) established and doing well; (2) succeeding in part but still struggling; and (3) having achieved little or nothing and for the most part obliged to work for their subsistence. As for the working class in general, it may be said 'that they find their life in this Colony preferable to that which they left. Wages are high both for mechanics and labourers, and though prices are also high, this has been caused by the absence of constant employment, which arises from the scarcity of capital amongst employers.'

What of the colonists' relations with Aborigines during these early years? Aborigines at Swan River had seen three expeditions of white explorers between the French of 1801 and Stirling's arrival with the first settlers in June 1829. Each of the expeditions had reacted cautiously to the Aborigines, partly because they had been conditioned to believe that they were warlike, partly because reception ranged from conviviality to hostility with no seeming explanation, and partly because the Aboriginal culture and way-of-life was so different from their own, and their ability to understand and appreciate it was so limited, that they refrained from contact other than for an exchange of gifts. Charles Howe Fremantle was the link between explorers and settlers during the weeks he established his 'fort' at the Fremantle camp and, as already noted, the kindly but firm behaviour of his men towards Aborigines was directed to making the way easier for European settlers.

While the explorers, and even Fremantle, could muse on the Aborigines' habits—even be impressed by their dexterity, mimicry and stealth—the first settlers, destined to live beside them, took a rather different view. With few exceptions, settlers were repulsed by the Aborigines' way of life, convinced that at the first opportunity they would be attacked by them, and horrified by the suggestion that they initiate meaningful social interaction. The land of the 'savages', in one stroke of a pen, had been ceded to the British Crown and was available to Britons who met the conditions of grant or sale. Once the land was granted, the Aborigines were deemed at worst trespassers and at best tolerated if they caused no trouble.

One of the governor's first acts on reaching Swan River was to read a proclamation for the protection of Aborigines—a worthy act but, as Paul Hasluck shows, protection 'of' soon became interpreted as protection 'against'.[50] The problem was neither new nor confined to Australian Aborigines. On the one hand, many white settlers, superior in arms and believing themselves infinitely superior in culture and intellect, thought little about the traditional rights of a race that had inhabited the land for at least 40 000 years. On the other hand, the Aborigines' inquisitiveness soon changed to hostility when they realized that, unlike earlier visitors, Stirling's settlers, and those who followed them, had come to stay—to disrupt the landscape, disturb and kill animals that were their source of food and to treat them with a hostility and indifference that they keenly resented.

Men like Francis Armstrong, the protector of Aborigines, who took great pains to collect information on their numbers and way of life, and Robert Lyon, who seemed dedicated to converting the tribal leader, Yagan, to Christianity as a lasting solution to race relations, probably held exceptional attitudes towards Aborigines.[51] Those expressed freely by two leading settlers soon after they reached Swan River were probably more widely held and partly explain why relations deteriorated so quickly. To the *Leicester Journal*, Eliza Shaw wrote that the Aborigines were as black as ink, that 'it is not safe for a white woman to be seen by them, as they are perfectly savage, and would take [women] off by force if they could lay their hands on them; even female children are unsafe to be alone'.[52] And to Hay, John Morgan was even more explicit concerning his dislike and disgust: 'a miserable race of animals,—moving upon two legs,—They are considered human beings, but I repeat to say that the link which connects them with the brute, is at all times,—very painfully perceptible.'[53] Shaw and Morgan were impressed by the Aborigines' physical skills—running, spearing and mimicry—but Morgan warned that, although mimicry 'looks like an effort of intellect, a short acquaintance I am sorry to say, very soon shows it to be mechanical'. Fear, abhorrence and disrespect quickly led to violence. One of Peel's overseers was killed by Aborigines apparently in reprisal against a beating inflicted on a Aboriginal caught stealing. At Perth during May 1834 an affray with Aborigines led to intervention by the military, who 'inflicted some wounds', one settler explaining that the Aborigines were quarrelsome if, in large assemblies, they met a few colonists.[54] Although these skirmishes were to increase in frequency and severity over the next few years, culminating perhaps in the infamous Battle of Pinjarra into which the governor led a detachment of troops/settlers and killed fourteen Aborigines, not all settlers took an uncompromising view concerning the need and appropriateness of retribution. One settler explained that they did not exhibit ferocity and were grateful for kindnesses shown, but the problem is 'their extreme curiosity, and like all other barbarians they are greatly addicted to theft'. These traits led settlers to over-react, which in turn 'excited the poor savage to hostile acts'. He also believed that the Aborigines' hostility had been caused by settlers fixing themselves 'along the banks of the rivers to the exclusion of the natives', thus exciting their hostility and jealousy.[55]

There was a sad inevitability about the course to be run as the settlers, with superior arms, emerged the victors. Many, however, refused to go to their inland lots until they could be assured of reasonable protection against attacks by Aborigines, and those already on their lots appealed for protection. In his report of April 1832 to the Colonial Office, Stirling, having applauded settlers whose industry, intelligence and means had made them successful agriculturalists, admitted that he had a problem with the Aborigines. The nature of hostility, he wrote, was a great drawback, for it occasioned the necessity of military posts at considerable expense and even with every precaution, outrages could neither be in all cases prevented nor punished. He said he had made an effort to be friendly and persuaded them not to take things by force. George Fletcher Moore, having lost stock through attack by Aborigines, wrote that his own 'warlike propensities are so much excited that I have arranged my affairs to watch and attack the natives, and kill, burn, blow up or otherwise destroy the enemy as may be the most practicable. The wretches have destroyed £3 worth of my swine's flesh, but after all perhaps these uninformed creatures think that they have as good a right to our swine as we have to their kangaroos, and the reasoning if such there be, may be plausible enough.' It was a reasonable reaction.

II

Before making his 1827 visit of exploration to Swan River, James Stirling was convinced, on the basis of 'professional observation', that a settlement there was justified on the grounds of its favourable location. His visit was necessary only to determine whether Swan River contained safe anchorages and sufficient fertile soil for settlers to live by agriculture. We have already argued that his claim to have discovered both a network of safe anchorages and fertile soil in sufficient quantity was sorely tested, and found wanting, within weeks of the arrival of first settlers. The same settlers also discovered that none of the advantages Stirling had claimed for Swan River because of its favourable location ever materialized.

The China-traders never called. In his report to Governor Darling, Stirling had argued that Swan River was only 'very little out of the Track of Ships bound for China, through the Eastern passages', and that these vessels were lightly laden on their outward voyages because merchants were unable to find cargoes suitable for the China market. Shipowners, he argued, would welcome the opportunity to fill the hatches of their China-bound vessels in England with cargo for the proposed settlement at Swan River. As the colony developed an export trade, the same vessels could refill their hatches at Swan River with seal-skins, ships' timber, trepang and other local goods 'suitable to the wants of the Chinese', thus assuring shipowners of full cargoes for the entire voyage to and from China.[56] All this could be achieved by China-bound vessels making only a 'slight detour' from their normal tracks to include Swan River. His 1827 voyage of exploration to Swan River only confirmed the relevance of this 'advantage'.[57]

Stirling was correct in his assumption that vessels trading with China were lightly laden on their outward voyages. Whether they traded with Indian ports en route to China via the Cape of Good Hope, or sailed directly to China across the Indian Ocean, passing the north-west coast of Australia, their hatches, relative to the homeward voyage, were lightly laden. Prior to 1813 all British trade with India and China was monopolized by the powerful East India Company,[58] although it was mainly a one-way traffic, there being little demand in these countries for European goods.[59] British trade with India comprised mainly military and naval supplies,[60] and 'goods intended for the natives of India', mainly woollens. Because the sale of these commodities was slow, the company did not indulge willingly in the trade, its attitude apparently being that, because vessels were going to India half empty, they might as well carry cloth as nothing. Trade between India and China was also carried on in 'country vessels', which were much smaller than the impressive Indiamen that sailed directly between England and China. At first the Chinese would not accept European articles in exchange for their exports and insisted on payment in Spanish dollars; but they later relented and accepted raw cotton and opium from India.[61] In 1813 the British parliament withdrew the East India Company's monopoly on trade with India, thus providing opportunities for other merchants, especially manufacturers; and in 1833 the company lost its monopoly of British trade with China.[62]

The main, almost sole, purpose of trade with China, whether by vessels sailing via India, or directly across the Indian Ocean, was to acquire tea which, by the end of the eighteenth century, had become a national beverage in England. The increasing encroachment of foreign vessels in the China trade, especially American vessels, had forced the East India Company to change both the style and management of their vessels.[63] Prior to American competition their Indiamen made rather leisurely voyages to China, returning to England with cargoes of tea which invariably were

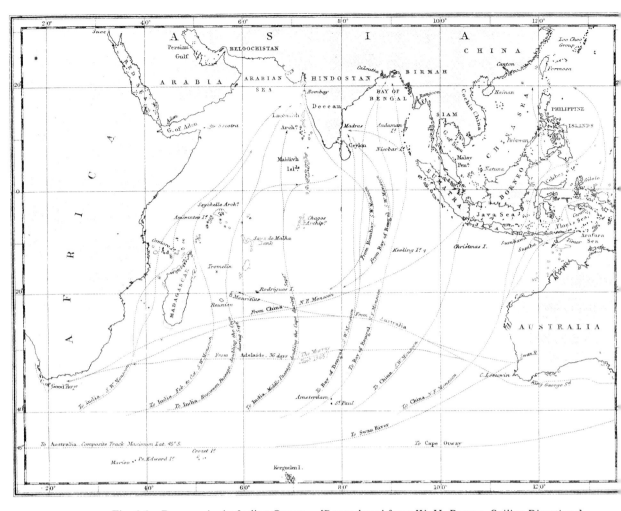

Fig. 6.1 Passages in the Indian Ocean. [Reproduced from W. H. Rosser, *Sailing Directions*]

stored for over a year in Thames warehouses.[64] The smaller American vessels, less concerned with tradition, conveyed tea to Europe much faster than the cumbersome Indiamen, thereby offering it 'fresh' to consumers, an advantage which forced British traders to try to regain their competitive advantage. The building of fast tea-clippers by both British and American shipowners heralded the short but legendary era of tea races.[65]

By 1827, when Stirling was urging Indiamen trading directly with China to 'detour slightly' from their course and trade with the proposed Swan River Colony, the East India Company was enjoying the last few years of its monopoly of British trade with China. The company was therefore probably unwilling to adopt Stirling's suggestion, even though it offered the prospect of full hatches for the entire voyage. Indeed, there is strong evidence to suggest that Stirling's proposal, despite the East

India Company's unwillingness, was impractical. First, the tea-trade with China was seasonal. Vessels began to reach Canton in October and left as soon as they had taken on their cargoes of tea, which was seldom earlier than January.[66] Thus, even if one or two vessels had 'detoured' to Swan River, they would have called there at the same time (perhaps August). This would hardly be a suitable basis for regular trade between England and the proposed colony. Second, it is doubtful whether the detour would have been as slight as Stirling suggested. 'The Indian Ocean', wrote Northcote-Parkinson, 'is a world by itself, with winds peculiar to it.'[67] Its major entrance is around the Cape of Good Hope, and the routes then taken were dominated by winds which were both constant and predictable. Vessels taking the southern route to China, the ones Stirling hoped could be persuaded to detour to Swan River, would stay in latitudes 30° to 40°, where prevailing westerlies blew all year round. 'It is essential to the success of a passage from the Cape to Java', wrote Captain Hall, 'to run to the southward as far sometimes as 40°, in which parallel the wind blows almost invariably from the westward all round the globe. The requisite quantity of easting [i.e., how far east the vessel should travel before turning to the NE], is easily gained although at the expense of some discomfort, for the weather is generally tempestuous. This point once accomplished, the ship's head may be turned to the northward, and all sail made to reach the SE trade, which, now that the ship has gone so far to the eastward, proves a fair wind; whereas had the limits been approached sooner, it would have been directly unfavourable.'[68]

A successful voyage to Java and China therefore depended on choosing the right latitude and picking up the south-east trades at the right time. Captain Hall emphasized that a knowledge of these particulars was essential for a successful voyage, and the 'penalty awaiting the mariner who turned northward too soon, and before he had run his easting down, was to find the trade wind scant and be forced to seek higher latitudes [i.e. go south] again.' A mariner who made an error of only 80 km in his calculation might waste a fortnight searching for the south-east trades.

The regularity of meteorological phenomena, and their rigorous obedience to known laws, was emphasized fifty years later by Rosser (Fig. 6.1).[69] His chart of 'Passages in the Indian Ocean' indicates that vessels taking the eastern passage to China in the south-west monsoon period would turn north only a few degrees east of the island of St Paul (Fig. 1.9), and vessels which turned north to catch the northwest monsoon did so at 91° longitude (some 2960 km west of Swan River), coming close to the Australian coast only at North West Cape. Vessels sailing directly to Swan River (after a settlement was established there) sailed eastward from the Cape on 45° latitude, much further south than the China-bound vessels, and made a slight change of direction towards the colony when they reached a point north of Kerguelen Island.

Stirling's suggestion that Swan River was only a 'short detour' from the tracks followed by China-traders using the eastern passage therefore greatly understated the extra distance vessels would be required to sail. His suggestion was impractical on trade as well as nautical grounds. At the very least, the masters of China-traders would need to be assured that, having made the detour, they could quickly pick up the south-east trades after leaving Swan River. Captain Hall's warning to mariners that failure to turn north at a fairly precise longitude could mean a delay of three or more weeks searching for the south-east trades, would not have been lost on China-traders aiming to reach Canton during early October and thus be among the first to load the valuable cargoes of new-season tea. Rosser's information (1878) that the south-east trades do *not* touch the west coast of Australia, and that the general winds are fully 640 km from the coast—north-north-west to south-south-west according to the season—was probably also known to mariners in 1827.

Stirling seems not to have appreciated the seasonal nature of the China tea-trade. In his 1827 report to Governor Darling, he wrote that the China-traders would find at Swan River 'an anchorage safe and easily approachable *during the greater part of the year* [which] would make their arrival and departure convenient' (our italics).[70] Indeed, it was Swan River's reputation as a dangerous port on a dangerous coast which Stirling had set out to disprove in his 1827 report. And despite his claims to have found a fine harbour inside the mouth of the river, and a protected anchorage at Cockburn Sound, the influential Barrow nonetheless insisted in his critique of Stirling's proposal that the whole range of the western coast, including Swan River, was full of danger and ships would avoid rather than seek it. It needed Stirling's strong personal representation in London during 1828 to convince Barrow that the proposed site of the new colony was safe for shipping. Events during the first two winters supported Barrow's apprehensions rather than Stirling's optimism.

Perhaps the most imaginative advantage Stirling claimed for Swan River because of its favourable location was its potential as a naval and military station 'upon a grand scale'. In his letter to Governor Darling suggesting that he make a voyage of exploration to Swan River, Stirling, on the basis of professional observation, claimed that such a station would not only protect the settlement there and provide settlers with a market for their produce but would also command India, the Malay Islands and all the settlements of New Holland. His example of how a single British vessel could reach Swan River and alert the naval force which, in turn, by sailing on favourable winds, would encounter an enemy fleet on its way to India deserves full marks for ingenuity. In his 1827 report, written after he had visited Swan River, Stirling reaffirmed the potential importance of the site as a 'valuable Naval and Military Station', especially Cockburn Sound, which he wrote was 'superior in convenience and more than equal in safety to Spithead'. But how viable was the proposal? Were there any likely contingencies concerning India and the Malay Islands that the existing India station could not handle? And why was a station 'on a grand scale' necessary to protect the eastern settlements of New Holland?

The British government's naval station at Trincomalee in Ceylon (now Sri Lanka) protected all its interests in the Indian Ocean. It was the station to which Charles Howe Fremantle had hoped to be attached and to which, following his brief stay at Swan River, he was sent for two years where he was 'employed on many interesting errands'.[71] Trincomalee was ideally located both to protect British interests in the area (including clippers active in the tea-trade) and as the headquarters from which diplomats visited neighbouring countries. Captain Fremantle's voyages from that station between 1829 and 1831 aptly convey the importance of the latter role. He was sent by Rear-Admiral Sir Edward Owen[72] to the French settlement at Pondicherry; to Madras to collect specie for conveyance to Calcutta; to Bombay for repairs to *Challenger*'s hull sustained when she had struck rocks in Challenger Passage; to all ports between Bombay and the Red Sea to report on the extent of their trade; and finally, a most important voyage to Canton to deliver an official letter of protest to the Viceroy of Canton concerning his decision to suspend the tea-trade.[73]

It is hard to visualize circumstances under which Swan River could have supplemented, let alone replaced, Trincomalee as a naval station. The British government's parsimonious attitude to expenditure on facilities at Swan River suggests that it was in no mood to proliferate civilian settlements let alone establish expensive naval establishments. And it is just as hard to visualize the proposed station 'commanding all the settlements of New Holland'. In 1827 the eastern Australian colonies were little more than convict settlements containing only a few free settlers, and while the British government would have protected them from an aggressor, this would hardly have required the establishment of a naval station on a grand scale at Swan River. Besides, it would require a very efficient intelligence service to learn of an enemy fleet's presence (presumably moving eastward across the Indian Ocean) and its intentions. Perhaps the main role for such a station would be to protect China-traders taking the eastern passage but, as already noted, these vessels usually travelled in convoy and were protected by a ship of war, and as the trade was highly seasonal the proposed naval station at Swan River would be inactive in this role for much of the year. No one in Whitehall seems to have taken seriously Stirling's claim that vessels established at Swan River could intercept an enemy fleet on its way to India via the Cape and around Madagascar. Barrow did not even refer to it in his critique of Stirling's plan. Swan River 'must be looked at solely in the light of a new colony', he wrote, and then concluded that it was probably more logical to develop the 'many millions of acres of rich country remain[ing] unoccupied on the eastern side' than to establish a new settlement. Whitehall was finally influenced by Stirling's point that the west coast should be annexed, and a settlement established at Swan River, to forestall French ambitions, but only if it were established as a private venture with minimal official expenditure. The British government was not interested in establishing a naval station there on the scale envisaged by Stirling because it could not see any reason for doing so.

Even so, the hope for a 'naval station on a grand scale' was never far from the minds of early settlers, especially after 1830, when their expectations for a large, thriving settlement had not been fulfilled.[74] Many believed that the establishment of a naval station was central to the colony's revival. Such a hope was certainly never far from Stirling's mind, for his early reports return frequently to it.[75] Indeed, William Somerville claims that many of the colony's early difficulties can be attributed to Stirling's decisions being unduly influenced by his ambition for the establishment of a naval station.[76] On his arrival at Swan River in *Parmelia*, Stirling showed 'strong partiality' for Garden Island, the logical site for a future naval station. Not only did he include the whole island in his land grant, wrote Somerville, but he used much of the limited building material brought on *Parmelia* and *Sulphur* to erect houses for himself, some offices and also storehouses and huts for settlers on Garden Island. His selection of Garden Island as 'first priority' in his land grant was, claimed Somerville, influenced by his dream of a naval and military station which, 'if realised would make the splendid anchorage he had discovered of very great value'. In other words, Somerville claims that Stirling's decision to erect buildings on the island, and then to incorporate it into his land grant, was influenced by the anticipated increase in value of the island should a naval base be erected on it.

Stirling's third justification for the establishment of a settlement at Swan River was that it would be of great value as a convalescent station for His Majesty's troops employed in the Indian establishment and for the civil and military servants of the company, rendering long and expensive voyages to Europe unnecessary on the score of health, and while such persons would be highly benefited by such a change of climate, a colony settled there would rapidly spring up into wealth stimulated by the sums of money expended during such visits.[77] He also anticipated that the convalescent troops, and the ships from India would act as the colony's 'guard'. The China ships would convey stores from England at a low rate, and also prisoners, if it were thought proper to make it a penal settlement. These sequential events would, 'in all probability', lead to Swan River becoming self-sufficient.

Stirling's visit to Swan River in 1827 only confirmed in his mind its future as a convalescent station. The 'climate' (which he experienced in March) was 'cool, temperate and healthy', and the various mineral springs he had discovered there would be 'favourable to the removal of Indian complaints'[78]—discoveries which he directed as much to the East India Company as to Whitehall, for Swan River, he declared, should be 'an object of great interest to the East India Company and its servants', and many valuable lives could be preserved if it were adopted by the company as an 'extensive hospital establishment for Europeans and their Civil and Military services'.

Stirling's proposal was warmly supported by Governor Darling. In his letter to the Colonial Office attached to Stirling's report, Darling envisaged Swan River as a staging centre for invalids; instead of sending them directly to England, they could recuperate at a place only a thirty-day passage away, where 'the advantages of an invalid in point of climate would I have no doubt be greater than in England'. Yet despite the governor's support, the proposition was firmly scorned by Barrow. Coupling it with Stirling's expectation that ships would 'seek' Swan River when, wrote Barrow, it was known that the whole coast was 'full of danger', he declared that 'our Indian Gentlemen' would never think of repairing to a *penal settlement* on the west coast of New Holland, 'as Captain Stirling has vainly imagined'.[79] Stirling, by suggesting almost as an aside that the China ships could bring prisoners to Swan River 'if it were thought proper to make it a penal settlement', had inadvertently given Barrow an opportunity to denigrate the viability of what he considered was an important justification for establishing a settlement there. As already noted, the Colonial Office was greatly influenced by Barrow's advice, the letter of rejection from Huskisson of the Colonial Office to Governor Darling containing many verbatim passages from Barrow's report. Even so, Huskisson did not entirely reject Stirling's proposal, indicating that he would inform the East India Company of the circumstances attending the discovery of Swan River 'in case they should consider it advisable to make any settlement there'. Huskisson nonetheless indicated that he was not aware of any 'sufficient motive' to induce the East India Company to 'embark on an undertaking of this nature', and the company ultimately declined the offer despite, as Eddy concludes, 'the benevolent energies of India merchants such as Prinsep, and doubtless Mangles, Stirling's father-in-law'.[80]

Although Swan River Colony never became a convalescent station for 'Indian gentlemen', the hope that it would was never far from the minds of the governor and some settlers. In one of his first reports from the colony, Stirling reported the calling at Swan River of H.M. ships *Cruizer* and *Success* and 'the rapid recovery which her people have made since here from the effects of the Climate of India makes it probable that King's Ships will frequently resort to it for health'.[81] A few months later, a settler, John Henty, expressed the view that Swan River would one day 'become a recuperation place for people from India', and at least one emigrants' guide claimed that Fremantle would become 'the Cheltenham or Leamington to the invalid classes' and was 'well adapted for refreshment of those who are exhausted by naval or military service'.[82] Even after he returned from his mission to England (1835), Stirling referred again to the beneficial effect of Swan River on British subjects wishing to quit India for a time in search of health,[83] and the reciprocal economic benefits for the colony. Indeed, as late as 1867, potential emigrants were being informed that with the impending cessation of transportation of convicts to Western Australia (begun in 1850), it was likely that a sanitorium would be established there for invalids of the Indian Army, a subject which was 'occupying the serious attention of the Indian Government'.[84]

Somerville contends that the convalescence argument has been a 'stock part of Official propaganda' ever since it was raised by Stirling, though with little effect.[85] In those early days, he wrote, the argument had more force. Calcutta or Bombay were only twenty-five days sailing from Fremantle, a fraction of the long voyage around the Cape to Britain. Because of profound ignorance of the nature of, and remedies for, tropical diseases, sickness amongst Caucasians in India was prevalent, and mortality high. 'In those days, when a man suffered from anything from a belly-ache to Bubonic plague, the surgeons bled him, taking large quantities of life blood upon which his strength rested. Hence it was thought that when Englishmen resident in India suffered a breakdown in health, they would take the short journey to a country where their countrymen had settled and which was known to enjoy a healthy and temperate claimate. This, however, was not so. What a sick man wanted then as now was to get to their old home and not to found a new one "on a foreign strand".'

Despite Somerville's reasonable argument, the case for a convalescent station would have been strengthened had Swan River prospered quickly and hence been able to provide the comforts and facilities expected by convalescents. But it did not prosper; it almost failed. Indeed, during the first few years the pioneer settlers just hung on. None of the exogenous stimulants Stirling had envisaged ever eventuated; the China-traders did not call, and neither the naval station nor the convalescent hospitals were established. In the absence of these developments, and the parsimonious attitude of the British government towards provision of social overheads, economic growth had to be initiated from within. Given the conditions at Swan River between 1829-32 (already outlined) initiation was thwarted and progress therefore was painfully slow.

III

When Charles Howe Fremantle left Swan River on 28 August 1829 for the India station (the destination he had hoped for even before leaving England), he could have had no idea of the interesting and exciting service ahead, nor of participation in events which Stirling had hoped would play an important role in Swan River's development. The tea/opium trade with China had been temporarily suspended in 1830-31 because of an Imperial edict banning the import of opium.[86] In April 1831 Lord Bentinck sent a letter of protest to the Viceroy of Canton, and another to the Emperor of Peking (to be delivered only if the former failed in its purpose). These were sent in the first instance to Rear-Admiral Owen at the India station with an order that they be delivered by warship. Owen chose young Fremantle for this mission. At first, the Viceroy refused to receive the letter, requesting that it be delivered through the Hong merchants.[87] Fremantle refused to comply but was prepared to deliver it to a proper envoy of the Viceroy at the southern gate of the city. When this was not agreed to by the Chinese, Fremantle refused to compromise. He had a clear idea of the importance of his assignment and little respect for the Chinese. If it came to a showdown he was confident of the outcome, as he wrote to his Uncle William: 'I shall certainly do what has to be done, take or send a large body of men with it to the Palace which will ensure of its being delivered.' Such stern action was, however, unnecessary. The Viceroy agreed that the letter could be handed to a mandarin outside the city gate, so on the last day of the year *Challenger* moved up-river and the letter was delivered 'with due ceremony'.

It was also during his visit to China that Fremantle explored islands along the coast and reported to Rear-Admiral Owen that the British government should seriously consider taking possession of one of the offshore islands, or part of the mainland, in order to protect their tea/opium interests. 'I am of the opinion', he wrote, 'that the town of Cowloon situated on the Main Land is well adapted for all the purposes that would be required, it is rather a large town possessing a beautiful Harbour formed by the Island of Hong Kong opposite which the passage called the Lyee Moon used by the Vessels from the Northward bound to Canton, its advantageous situation can only be understood by reference to the Chart.'[88] Fremantle further recommended that this proposed station should have at least eight ships of war and 3000 troops. His advice did not go unheeded; in 1841 Hong Kong became a British settlement.

Having received accolades from both the East India Company and Rear-Admiral

Pl. 6.4 Possibly the earliest impression of the first houses in Perth, drawn by C. D. Wittenoom, 1829. [Courtesy of the Battye Library]

Owen for his successful mission to China, Fremantle was ordered to return home via Australia, New Zealand, Tahiti, Pitcairn Island and Valparaiso and 'obtain any information that might be interesting to H.M. Government'.[89] On 5 September 1832 he sailed around Rottnest Island, hauled off for the night, and the following day anchored in Gage Roads. More than interested in the colony's progress since he had left three years before, Fremantle was clearly disappointed. In his Remark Book he wrote that the 'Wrecks themselves lying on the Beach are quite sufficient to stamp the character of this Anchorage'.[90] The port which had been named after him, though sandy and unpromising in appearance, did have several houses, mostly occupied by persons keeping stores and 'if the Colony continue' might in time be a 'place of consequence'. But the capital, Perth, with very few houses and these mostly of wood and very small, was 'scarcely worthy of the name'. He was, however, impressed by progress made by settlers who had taken up grants on the river.

Pl. 6.5 'My house and garden in Western Australia, September 1833'. [Watercolour by H. W. Reveley. Courtesy of Rex Nan Kivell collection in the National Library of Australia]

He singled out Edward Barrett-Lennard as having done more than any of the settlers—cleared a great deal of land, fenced it and acquired a good stock of cattle—and was full of praise for the way he had invested in improvements to the land rather than in a 'fine house', a decision which Fremantle believed assured him ultimate success. Though his views were no doubt influenced by Peter Broun, the colonial secretary who accompanied him up-river, and by settlers like Moore, Bull and Irwin, who had brought their allotments into production and confidently expected that the colony's needs for wheat would be fully met for 1833, Fremantle was astute enough to see that progress had been very uneven and many settlers were, in fact, badly off. The first manifestation of this came on the third day of his visit when Lieutenant-Governor Irwin (acting in Stirling's absence) asked him for all the provisions *Challenger* could spare because the colony was 'in much want'.[91] Those worse off, observed Fremantle, were the poor people (presumably the unemployed farm-workers), many of whom had not tasted even a piece of salt meat for many weeks.

He shared Stirling's view, which was also probably the view of many settlers, that the absence of private money in the colony, and the constraints preventing the governor from spending government funds, was a main cause of their plight—a plight from which he saw 'no means of their extricating themselves'. Even the salaries paid to the few officials were, he wrote, 'so low (relative to prices) that it is quite impossible they can live on them'. He shared the views of settlers that unless the government made a grant of money available,[92] then the 'best thing that can be done for the Colony is to make it a penal settlement; the labour of the convicts would be most valuable as there is everything to do and no means of completing anything'. Unless there was a significant change along at least one of the lines he had suggested, then it would be a long time before the colony made any headway.

Charles Howe Fremantle's greatest disappointment was the 'very bad understanding' between settlers and Aborigines, which had resulted in skirmishes and deaths on both sides. Three years earlier he had expected to find warlike savages whom he would try to placate with gifts from the Cape; instead, he found interesting, friendly, humorous people in whom he took a keen, if condescending, interest. So serious had relations between the races become that it was considered dangerous for settlers to move about the colony alone or unarmed. 'It is laughable', he recorded, 'to see a Shepherd with a Musket instead of a Crook, and every flock is obliged to have two if not three men to guard it.' Perhaps because of his birth and upbringing, Charles Fremantle showed little sympathy for the lower classes of settlers, whom he blamed for the affrays. Some of them were waging a war of extermination, shooting Aborigines 'whenever they are fallen in with'. Instead, his sympathy was with the Aborigines.[93] 'We take possession of their country, occupy the most fertile parts, where they are in the habit of resorting to for nourishment, destroy their fishing and kangaroo, and almost drive them to starvation, and they naturally consider themselves entitled to our sheep and stock whenever they can get hold of them.' Though they were cunning and sly—as he had discovered during his first visit—he deeply regretted the 'awful warfare' which had taken place between the races.

Before leaving Swan River, after only a short stay of one week, Fremantle supported another of Stirling's complaints—that many of the first settlers little understood the kind of life they had embarked on; that they were not accustomed to hard work; and that they had no knowledge of farming and, as a result, 'gave way to their disappointment [and] consumed their provisions without making the slightest exertion to support or establish themselves'. He still considered Gage Roads a dangerous anchorage and he doubted whether Britannia Roads (Owen Anchorage), with banks on both sides, was any safer. Though Cockburn Sound was the only harbour secure from all winds, the entrance through Challenger Passage, as he had discovered in 1829, was both dangerous and difficult to keep buoyed. Even while visiting the colony he learned that its buoys had been washed away yet again, and saw little chance of their being replaced until *Sulphur* returned to the colony.[94]

Charles Howe Fremantle sailed from the port bearing his name on 11 September 1832, never to return. Though delighted to be on the road home, 'where all are the same and happy *save Reform Bills, Cholera etc*!' (his emphasis), it would be a clear nine months before he reached England. From his diary it appears that Pitcairn Island was the most enjoyable sojourn during the long voyage. Here he made enquiries concerning Fletcher Christian's descendants, paid his respects to the Queen and ordered two Englishmen—'bad characters not capable of assisting the Natives in any way'—from the island. As at Canton and Swan River, his sympathy was for the natives, and his criticism for undesirable whites who 'put notions in their heads with respect to what is done in other parts of the World, and thereby have introduced Vice and immorality'. Before leaving Pitcairn he prepared a list of articles most needed by the islanders, and on his return to England, arranged for supplies to be sent out.

The young Fremantle had revealed fine qualities of leadership, and could point to an impressive list of achievements during the four and a half years' voyage which ended at Portsmouth during early June 1833. A decade was to pass before he left England again—on an equally long voyage to the Caribbean and Mediterranean. His most impressive achievement, however, came a few years later when, as rear-admiral, he ran the entire naval transport service for the Crimean War from Balaclava. It was a difficult assignment, which he handled with great distinction. 'By hard work', writes Ann Parry, 'Fremantle brought order out of chaos', a judgement supported by *The Times* of the day when it referred to his 'perfect capacity for the duties of a post which requires no ordinary application and ability', which brought the harbour of Balaclava 'into as good order as any dock in London or Liverpool'.[95] It was no mean achievement. By September 1855 he had established a system which facilitated the entry into Balaclava of 90 000 men, 20 000 horses and donkeys as well as grain, straw and other supplies essential for the armies engaged in that frightful war.[96]

In July 1858 he was appointed to the command of the important Channel Squadron, which had recently acquired steam-powered, screw-propelled ships. Though these ships were fully rigged, and used steam only as auxiliary power, Fremantle, by showing the same perception and adaptability he had displayed at Swan River, Canton and Balaclava, soon mastered the new technology. Several years later he was transferred to the command of the Devonport Squadron and promoted to the rank of admiral.

After 1868 he took no active part in Navy affairs. He was, as Ann Parry concludes, worn out by a life of responsibility. Knowing no other life, he refused to retire from the Navy and so, in due course, reached the top of its list. In later years his memory lapsed and at home in Swanbourne he was 'apt to fancy himself still at sea and to give strange orders'.[97] Though he had always yearned for the chance to emulate his famous father's deeds at Trafalgar, the glory of battle was never his. The Napoleonic Wars were over when he joined the Navy, and at Crimea he was assigned an administrative post, the importance of which he seems never to have recognized or appreciated. Likewise, the historic significance of his main act at Swan River—annexation of the whole western coast—seems to have escaped him. He was reluctant to go there and eager to leave. He resented using *Challenger* to convey animals and goods from the Cape, and using his sailors to erect huts and clear land while awaiting the arrival of the first settlers. This was not young Fremantle's idea of naval activity. Ann Parry is therefore probably correct in her judgement that Charles Fremantle would be astonished to know that the two periods of his career of most interest to posterity are his services at Crimea and Swan River.

IV

Economic conditions at Swan River deteriorated markedly during 1832. Immigration had virtually ceased following publicity in England during 1830 of the colony's plight, so that by April 1832 the total resident population was a mere 1507 persons, of whom 87 per cent lived in Perthshire (and 51 per cent in the towns of Fremantle and Perth), and the remainder were scattered on farms in the Murray, Sussex (Augusta/Vasse), Yorkshire and Plantagenet (King George Sound) areas.[98] As Charles Fremantle had noted, the liquidity problem prevented settlers from purchasing anything other than essential goods, and there was neither capital from abroad, nor the necessary infrastructure within the colony, to exploit for export its considerable natural resources (e.g. timber and whaling).[99]

Settlers therefore strongly supported a proposal that the governor himself should return to London at the earliest opportunity to try to obtain a new deal for settlers on the Swan. Thus on August 12, three weeks before Charles Fremantle returned to the colony on his way back to England, James Stirling left the colony armed with memorials in which settlers had set down their views on its difficulties and their suggested solutions.

On reaching London, Governor Stirling lost no time in presenting the colonists' case to the British government. In a long and important letter to Hay, written in London on 22 December 1832, Stirling not only tabulated the colony's difficulties but also made it quite clear that a large share of responsibility for the colonists' plight rested with the British government.[100] He reminded Hay that when he (Stirling) had first pointed out the suitability of the territory for settlement, and the existence of a port, the government would not take measures for its occupation. It was only when the government became apprehensive concerning French intentions for the region that it hurriedly despatched Captain Fremantle to take possession of the west coast, and then asked Stirling to take charge of a settlement to be established there, and furnish a plan for its development. Though his plan was 'thrown aside' at first, it was subsequently acted upon under the persuasion of commercial interests. For these reasons, argued Stirling, the British government was responsible for the colony's development, and it was largely because it had not shouldered these responsibilities that the colony was now in great difficulties. Accepting that every new settlement experienced some difficulties, he nonetheless claimed that these had been exacerbated at Swan River by the 'countenance of Government' having never been given to it in earnest. Lacking official backing, the colony could not be fully explored, and its local government had neither sufficient authority to preserve peace and administer justice nor clear instructions concerning expenditure. Unsatisfactory land regulations had resulted in widespread distribution of population, and settlers, 'allured by the liberal distribution of Land flocked rapidly in with great if not groundless hopes, and notwithstanding *the declarations of Government in the full assurance that everything usually done for new Colonies would be done for theirs'* (our italics).

Stirling's important letter, to which he attached the memorials from settlers, made it quite clear that many of Swan River's problems were of the British government's making: not only had it failed to provide clear instructions concerning expenditure by the governor, but when instructions did arrive in January 1832 they put limits on the expansion of the civil establishment and the mode of granting land for sale, and ordered the imposition of taxes. Such restrictions, claimed Stirling, could not have come at a worse time. The settlers were too few in numbers, and too low in means, 'to render the Country they had chosen a very prosperous or pleasant residence'. Furthermore, the virtual cessation of immigration after 1830 had greatly reduced the market for their products. The government's announcement that it would not grant any more land and would limit its expenditure to a very small amount, and its instruction that the colony was to bear the charge of its own establishment, opened the settlers' eyes 'to the fact that they were to be thrown upon their own resources'. As a result, those with money restrained from spending it, and those with none could not get credit or employment, thus causing distress 'in some instances proceeding from the want of hope, in others from the want of means'.

If the British government wanted to keep possession of Swan River, he concluded, it would have to assist those already there and invoke policies to attract new settlers and capital. Swan River settlers were not appealing for charity so much as to 'the policy of the Government', and if the government undertook appropriate measures, there was no reason to doubt its success and prosperity. If it did not, Swan River would be a constant charge on the public purse, or would have to be abandoned.

Governor Stirling was quite explicit concerning necessary government action:

(1) Make a declaration of intention to maintain in the colony a civil and military establishment and appoint more settlers to the legislature. Such action, he argued, would engender confidence in the future and resolve all doubts about the permanency of the establishment.
(2) Rescind the regulation preventing settlers from disposing of land, and allow settlers to count the improvements they made on one tract of land towards *total* improvements, including tracts not improved.
(3) Arrange the immigration of labourers on the principles adopted by the Emigration Committee, with the stipulation that the colonial government provided passage money and employment.
(4) Allow potential settlers reimbursement of deposits on land if they paid their own passage money.

Stirling had no doubts whatever concerning the position, soil, products and ports of the colony and the scope afforded for an extensive system of colonization in future years. Indeed, if only to uphold his credibility as the colony's founder, and especially the basis upon which it was finally settled, he refused to comment on widespread criticism in England during 1830 and 1831 concerning the accuracy of his 1827 report. Swan River, he emphasized, was a valuable asset of the Crown, but it required assistance 'to place it at once on its legs and enable it to maintain itself'. Van Diemen's Land had proved to be a major source of wool for British manufacturers; Swan River, given government support during its formative years, would prove no less valuable.

In his reply to Stirling of 2 January 1833, Hay set the tone for discussions which lasted until Stirling finally returned to Swan River during June 1834. The government rejected Stirling's version of its initial interest in Swan River, and told him that the settlers there were to pay for their own services; the government would not support them further, save establishment posts and minor expenditure:

> You are quite correct in stating, that the scheme for forming a Settlement on the West Coast of Australia, which the Government contemplated, in consequence of some *false rumours* respecting the intentions of France *was given up entirely on the grounds of economy*, and this project would not have been resumed had not a Party of Adventurous Gentlemen come forward, who proposed, at their own risk, to undertake a scheme of this sort, for which they were to receive in compensation extensive Grants of Land, and a certain degree of protection, and assistance for a limited period.
>
> It was never, however, contemplated that the greater part of the expenses attendant on the founding of a new Colony was to be incurred by the Government, and accordingly the *whole of the Civil Establishment was fixed upon the most economical footing*, even to the extent of sending out the Officer in Command . . . and some of those under him, without any other advantages whatever than a promise of land . . . the origin of the Settlement must *not* be attributed to the Government, but was rather a concession to the representations of certain Individuals [our emphases].[101]

Hay's letter undermined the very basis of Stirling's case. Not only had the government never intended providing the services and support that Stirling claimed they should, but they had no intention of now changing their policy to alleviate the plight of settlers. While Hay accepted that many settlers may well have believed that the government was 'a party to the scheme', he reminded Stirling that the 'Notice to Emigrants' of 5 December 1828 conveyed quite clearly that assistance for emigrants could not be expected beyond a very limited period. All the issues raised by the governor were rejected: his claim that the delay in granting his commission had impeded the colony's progress; complaints concerning the land grant system; and his claim that unless the colony was granted more resources it would have to be abandoned.

In his reply to Hay of 5 January 1833, Stirling completely rejected Hay's interpretation of the government's involvement in Swan River. Had he known that it would not be supported by the government he would not have accepted appointment as lieutenant-governor:

> I took a view wholly different . . . I had been employed on the Coast of Australia as the Captain of a Ship of War. It occurred to me while there that the *most valuable position in New Holland* remained unoccupied, and I felt it to be

my duty to ascertain whether the reports which had been made by French and Dutch Navigators as to the absence of Soil, Water and Ports were correct, or not. It was my fortune by coming later to discover the existence of those qualities in the Territory which are essential to successful colonization. Having done so, it was no less my duty as a Public Officer to lay this information before the Government. And it was natural that I should wish to see that place become a British Possession. This may account for my having accepted, even under the most unfavourable Circumstances, the charge of the Expedition [our emphasis].

His views were noted, but they did not persuade the Colonial Office, which held to the view that those 'adventurous gentlemen' and their supporters who had initiated the colony's establishment must also be largely responsible for its upkeep and development. The governor, however, did not give in. On 5 February 1833 he appealed to Lord Goderich, the colonial secretary.[102] Although his letter contained many of the same points he had put to Hay, Stirling had already accepted that the government would not change its mind concerning relief for settlers or expenditure on social overheads. Instead, he emphasized a need which *only* the government could provide: a ship-of-war to be stationed at Swan River. The colony's long coastline was scarcely known and a ship-of-war could not only explore and survey it but, on grounds of *economy*, be more efficient and adaptable than a military force. He had suggested the idea to Hay; he now put the proposal strongly before Goderich.

The vessel would ply between the two fine harbours on the coast: Cockburn Sound and King George Sound, and its presence, or expected presence, would

> control Ships and their Crews, . . . and any import duties, which might be imposed . . . secure the several small settlements upon it from being plundered by the Boats and Vessels occasionally carried off by desperate characters from the Neighbouring penal Settlements, and would enable the Colonists to consider themselves and their Wives safe from the visits of these and other piratical Vessels.[103]

Though no white settlers had been so plundered by piratical vessels, Stirling could cite Lockyer's report concerning the activities of sealers on the south coast, especially their abduction of Aboriginal women.[104] The ship-of-war would have other uses. Because the colony was still in its infancy it had not been possible to chart its seas. Even in the part most frequently visited,

> rocks exist whose position is undetermined, one of which situated 10 or 12 miles off Cape Lewin [*sic*] occasioned the loss of a Ship bound to India in 1830—The further exploration of the adjacent Coasts, the Survey of the Ports, the examination of Shark's Bay; the determination of the fact as to whether a second Mississippi does or does not exist on the N.West Coast, and the inspection of the Shore of the Great Australian Bight are also amongst the objects which might be accomplished by the Boats and Seamen of a Ship stationed in that Country.

Further, if the vessel was commanded by 'the Officer administering the Government' (that is, by Governor Stirling), its crew could be used to help erect block-houses at the ports, to buoy channels and assist with the establishment of a pilot service. There was certainly no doubt that some assistance was needed with the latter two functions. Stirling did not envisage the arrangement as permanent. Indeed, he suggested that an appropriate vessel might be made available from the India Command, and because the 'Interests of the India Company appear to be involved in the success of the Colony', the company might be asked to pay for all or part of the expense.

The following day he provided Hay with a detailed cost of the proposal,[105] pointing out that if it were adopted *Sulphur* could return home. A month passed before Lord Goderich replied not only to Stirling's letter of 5 February 1833 but also to his many other letters written before and after his return to London, and to the memorials Stirling had brought from the colonists. Methodically dealing with all the issues, Lord Goderich's letter of 8 March 1833 must be regarded as the British government's definitive position on Swan River.[106] Containing passages identical to those written by Under-Secretary Hay in earlier letters to Stirling, it represents official refutation of the major proposals put forward by Stirling and the settlers at Swan River. Though the governor must have been greatly discouraged, he probably expected the government to take a hard line. Even his ship-of-war proposal was dismissed as 'impractical'; the most the government would do was to try to arrange for a ship-of-war to visit the colony once every six months. He was told to consider arming the colonial vessel and vesting its officers 'with the necessary authority for repressing outrages on the part of the Crews of Merchant Vessels, and for upholding the Revenue Laws, in aid of the Officers of Customs . . .'[107]

More serious for Stirling than the dismissal of his 'pet scheme' was the government's refusal to play a leading role in resolving the colony's economic problems. Goderich agreed to augment the military establishment and to approve the addition of more settlers to the Legislative Council, but he bluntly refused the request for government assistance to establish a bank and to import livestock, on the grounds that such undertakings must be left to private enterprise. Though he did not oppose the suggestion that the colonial government might advance the passage money of labourers (it was already being done by other Australian colonies), he could not see how this could be adopted until the colony accumulated the necessary revenue. Instead, he suggested that successful land settlement schemes organized by private developers was a more appropriate solution to Swan River's labour problems. It was fallacious, he argued, to suppose (as settlers had) that sale of Crown lands would deter emigrants from proceeding to the colony. It might keep away 'persons of small means', but 'experience proves that the greatest drawback upon the progress and prosperity of new Colonies, arises from such a facility in obtaining Land, as tends to destroy all supply of labour for wages, and to convert each Settler into a small and impoverished Landowner'. Nor would Lord Goderich support the settlers' request that surplus expenditure on occupied grants be counted towards unoccupied grants. Instead, he suggested that settlers should surrender part of their estates in return for an immediate title (free from any restriction as to alienation) for the remainder. The revenue obtained from sale of 'surplus' land, and from sale of land held by colonists who left Swan River, could be placed in a fund and used to bring out new settlers and provide the much-needed social overheads. Lord Goderich thought the settlers very inconsistent in their demands that recently imposed duties be removed and that they remain free from taxation for some time to come. The government, as Hay had reminded, never contemplated that it should incur the chief expense of forming the colony. The colonists themselves must bear the cost of their services; he was merely suggesting ways in which this could be done. To emphasize the government's intentions, he informed Stirling that there would be a slight *reduction* in its new estimates of expenditure for the colony.

Finally, he reminded Stirling of what the latter had written in his first report from Swan River concerning the 'character' of the majority of emigrants, rather than the paucity of their numbers, being the chief drawback to the success of the undertaking. The reminder was deliberate. It must be 'distinctly explained' to the settlers that the British government considered that it had fulfilled the pledge it gave at the outset by continuing to maintain the civil establishment and increasing the detachment of troops. Any further expenditure not provided for in the parliamentary estimates would have to be defrayed out of funds within the settlement. His message was loud and clear. The alternatives for Swan River were not, as had been suggested, increased government support or abandonment. A third alternative—greater effort and sacrifice from the settlers already there—was the appropriate solution. All reports had shown Swan River to be a colony with a future. Its location, he concluded, 'points it out as an important Station, with reference to Commercial objects, and it can scarcely be doubted that in process of time, it will become a place of much resort for the Traders in the Eastern Seas'. Charles Howe Fremantle had made a similar prediction during his second visit to the colony.

Goderich's letter was quickly followed by another from Downing Street in which was outlined a proposal for revenue-collection at Swan River that could be implemented 'without any assistance whatever from this Country'. Tariffs were proposed on imported luxury goods and the governor was forbidden to increase salaries of officials without obtaining the Secretary of State's approval, or to embark on public works exceeding £200 without the approval of his Council.[108]

Stirling returned to Australia in 1834, arriving at King George Sound on 23 June 'after the longest sea voyage ever known', with little to show the settlers for his long journey to, and strenuous efforts in, London.[109] The Colonial Office had made a few minor concessions, but they also had made it quite clear that Swan River had to resolve its own problems and not rely upon the British government for financial support. If nothing else, however, Stirling's disappointing news let the settlers know where they stood. The problems were clear enough, as were the solutions: large numbers of immigrants and associated capital were needed to clear virgin land for agriculture, to exploit the considerable natural resources and thereby provide revenue for the government to establish adequate infrastructures and services.

James Stirling stayed at Swan River only 3½ more years, during which he did his best to persuade settlers that the future rested entirely with them. Neither during this period, nor for many years thereafter, were settlers able to achieve the objectives so firmly laid down by the Colonial Office. The difficulties experienced by the first settlers, and especially the failure of Peel's enterprise, had given the colony a reputation which continued to discourage immigrants. By and large, the problems Stirling had enunciated in London remained unsolved and the settlers just hung on. The governor's decision to retire from colonial administration and return to active naval service is not difficult to understand. Though an enthusiastic colonizer, he was also a tried and tested naval man who had entered its ranks at a very young age, distinguished himself in battle and now seemed anxious to return to the service.

His announcement nonetheless stunned the colonists. Though he had been criticized by many, and was the target of their frustrations and failures, George Fletcher Moore recorded that, during the governor's last few weeks at the Swan, he became 'more and more popular every day, and we cling to him with the greater tenacity in proportion as the time approaches for his departure'.[110] The farewells were predictably, and rightly, effusive and emotional. An 'address by the people' emphasized his warm and ready sympathy towards individual distress, the high general tenor of his administration and the fact that his private life had been an example worthy of his high position.

Stirling's naval service and promotion thereafter is remarkably similar to Fremantle's. He commanded *Indus*, a 78-gun warship attached to the Mediterranean station, then *Howe*, a 120-gun warship. In 1851 he was promoted to rear-admiral, and between 1854 and 1856 he was commander-in-chief of the East Indies and China station, which brought Swan River Colony under his protection. Though he sailed extensively across his huge domain, he never returned to the Swan, even though he could have easily arranged to do so. By 1862 he was a full admiral and three years later, on 22 April 1865, he died at Woodbridge, Surrey, aged seventy-four years.[111]

7

Epilogue

He stands like a colossus across the first pages of the history of European settlement at Swan River. For centuries, predecessors had shunned its dangerous shores, seeing no reason to annex, let alone settle, the western coast of New Holland. But James Stirling, unlike his predecessors, was at once a visionary and a man who recognized a commercially viable proposition, and then set about methodically applying his great talent to persuade a reluctant British government first to annex the 'western third', and then establish a settlement at Swan River with himself as its governor.

In James Stirling's strength lay his weakness. As Emerson had believed that nothing great was achieved without enthusiasm, so Balfour had lamented that few enthusiasts could be trusted to speak the truth. Stirling was their composite example. Flying in the face of centuries-long experience, he alone advocated the annexation and settlement of Swan River. All that was known about the place was critical in nature, at best negative; surrounding seas were riddled with reefs that were a danger to all (and especially cumbersome) sailing-ships; the coastline was barren and yielded nothing edible to mariners who had been at sea for many weeks before reaching its isolated shores; the Aborigines, though unseen, were considered pathetically backward; and even the Swan River itself, though beautifully serpentine, with pendulous foliage along its banks and unique bird-life on its waters, was more an object of scientific interest than of commercial exploitation.

Sent by the British government to Australia for other reasons, Stirling soon revealed a personal plan to establish a British settlement at this desolate place. It is probable that, before leaving England, Stirling discussed his plan many times with his father-in-law, a director of the British East India Company, whose trade monopolies in the Indian Ocean encompassed the unclaimed western coast. Thus, only a few days after reaching Sydney, Stirling, through well-prepared and clever argument, was able to convince Governor Darling that Swan River, because of its favourable location, possessed political and economic advantages that had been entirely overlooked by others who had been more concerned about its reputed physical deficiencies. It was essential, he concluded, that a British officer investigate the place, not to confirm its political and economic advantages—these were irrefutable—but simply to find out whether the area also possessed sufficient good soil to support a settlement, and had safe anchorages for naval and merchant vessels. Troubled by the presence in Australian waters of French vessels with unknown intentions, Governor Darling willingly acceded to Stirling's request that the latter be the British officer to make the investigation. Darling appears not to have questioned either the facts or the logic which had led Stirling, through 'professional observation', to conclude that Swan River was an ideal location for a naval station, convalescent hospital and trading-post for ships bound for China. Indeed, Darling willingly loaned Stirling the services of Charles Fraser, his government botanist, to assist in assessing Swan River's agricultural potential.

A two-week exploration of Swan River by Stirling and Fraser in 1827 was mainly an exercise in confirmation of expectations. It was too short in duration and lacking in expertise to adequately answer the questions that had been posed by Stirling. Fraser's qualifications as soil scientist and agriculturalist were, at best, doubtful; yet he wrote a report that effusively articulated the agricultural potential of land around Swan River, and beyond. Stirling's qualifications, and those of his officers, to identify safe anchorages were adequate, but the time allowed to complete what is normally a long and tedious exercise was, like the time at Fraser's disposal to delineate soils, hopelessly inadequate. As a consequence, their reports—and especially the expectations that they aroused—caused great hardship for hundreds of Britons who comprised the foundation population. The question must be asked: had the persuasive Stirling unduly influenced—not maliciously but seductively by his boundless enthusiasm—Charles Fraser to pen words that did little credit to his professional and administrative standing?

On the basis of the reports, Governor Darling was convinced of the viability of a settlement at Swan River and said so in a covering letter to the Colonial Office. One is tempted to conclude that wiser heads at the Colonial Office prevailed when the recommendation was not supported. But the most influential head in that decision was not at the Colonial Office at all but at the Admiralty—John Barrow, the acknowledged expert on the antipodes. He had never been there, but was wonderfully dextrous at pulling the strings that decided what the British government would do in that remote part of the world. Almost certainly angered when he heard that Stirling had been given permission by Darling to go off and explore Swan River when the prime purpose of his visit to Australia had been to transfer a settlement from one part of northern Australia to another (his current pet project), Barrow appears to have been not a little vindictive in his initial criticism of Stirling's report on Swan River—criticism that the Colonial Office fully accepted, and transmitted almost verbatim to Darling. Perhaps a wise head did not prevail at the Admiralty either. Barrow's objections were based on no more objective research than had been applied to the reports themselves. Whether Stirling recognized this vulnerable trait in Barrow's psyche cannot be confirmed, but he certainly found, and found quickly, a way of completely changing the implacable Barrow's mind. Indeed, Barrow's enthusiasm for Swan River matched, and may have surpassed, Stirling's and became an embarrassment which had serious consequences for the first settlers. Not only was Stirling able to resolve all of Barrow's considerable doubts about establishing a settlement at the Swan but he also put his name to articles in influential journals which carried the advantages of settlement well beyond those provided by Stirling and Fraser. Misinformation was therefore compounded and the expectations of potential settlers greatly distorted. From being a place to be avoided, Swan River, in a few months, became paradise on earth, and the interest understandably generated in it by potential settlers was so strong that it was dubbed 'Swan River mania'.

Stirling's talent of persuasion did not end with Barrow. He was instrumental in bringing together members of a syndicate whose financial backing was essential for the success of the Swan River enterprise. He persuaded high officials of the British government to appoint him first superintendent and then lieutenant-governor of the new colony; to send out the first official party and the military detachment in two vessels when only one had been provided; and progressively to obtain one concession after another (though not all he had sought) between time of appointment and sailing. His departure from England in the *Parmelia*, the vanguard of many vessels to Swan River with expectant settlers, was rightly a farewell of effusive congratulations. In a few months he had been instrumental in completely changing his government's mind. His arrival at Swan River, however, almost ended in tragedy. As Bryan has aptly written, he sailed 'triumphantly, a modern Caesar, right up to the very shores of the country he was to command'. His over-confident pilotage, as Stirling himself later admitted, soon put the *Parmelia* onto a sandbank that still bears her name, and began for James Stirling eight years of leadership dogged with difficulties and disappointments caused mainly by his initial excessive enthusiasm which, he soon learned, is no substitute for careful research and planning.

Charles Howe Fremantle, the youthful naval captain who had been sent to Swan River a few months before Stirling, and whose main ambition seemed to be rapid promotion in the Navy, was a cool head in the crisis on that near-fateful day when the euphoria of great expectations turned, in a moment, to the hard fact of reality. Without his quick and able assistance, Swan River's day of foundation could have been a day of great disaster. Fremantle then did all that he could to resettle the new arrivals, and stayed at the Swan much longer than planned, but his assistance was transitory. He sailed on to other tasks in the knowledge of a job well done; James Stirling was committed to staying and building a colony.

The difficulties he faced, personally and as administrator, were many and complex. Nothing had been done to receive settlers, and the first settlers were quickly followed by over one thousand more who were literally dumped on the mainland beaches with baggage, equipment and livestock, where they lived in great hardship for up to several months. They may have accepted this as an inevitable price had the large tracts of fertile land described by Stirling, Fraser and Barrow actually existed, and had the safe and capacious harbours not been 'conditioned' by natural hazards and barriers that the colony had neither the capital nor manpower to rectify. These realities set the keynote for years to come. Stirling gave strong and sympathetic leadership during those difficult years, and within (and occasionally without) his constraining terms of appointment, took many initiatives to try and make things easier for settlers whom he respected. He set high standards of perseverence and, as a disciplined navy man who had tasted battle at an unusually early age, expected no less from others. He would not, and probably could not, condone frailty of spirit and purpose, and readily classified his subjects, laying the blame for many difficulties at the feet of grumblers and those who had come with 'groundless expectations'. While he showed concern and gave encouragement for those who reached, or at least respected, his own standards, he never tempered his criticism of the 'idle and useless' classes with acknowledgement of his own part in the dissemination of misleading information. Optimism was his byword. In official reports to the Colonial Office he never faltered in a policy of highlighting achievements and discounting difficulties. When first settlers were demonstrably shattered by what they found at Swan River, Stirling described them as 'cheerful and confident'. With few exceptions, he consistently recorded that the colony was making good progress when, given the severe economic constraints, progress could be only slow and fitful.

Having agreed to establish a colony at Swan River, the British government insisted that their financial outlay on it would be minimal. Land grants were made on the basis that settlers themselves would provide a great deal of infrastructure. Thus when the reality of Swan River was soon realized; when settlers ran out of money; when production of crops and exploitation of natural resources were impeded by lack of capital equipment and, in some cases, by inability of settlers to retain their indentured workers—the governor's task became almost impossible. Nor, in his judgement, was it made easier by the tenor of independent reports being sent to the Colonial Office by Morgan, Lyon, Dance and others. Simple logic and persuasive argument were insufficient to resolve these fundamental economic problems, but, to his great credit, the governor provided the kind of leadership he believed necessary under these circumstances. The propriety of his decisions to change his own land grants as news was received from explorers of better land than he had already chosen can be questioned; and, with Somerville, we might also question his motives for including the whole of Garden Island (and a small lot on top of strategically placed Arthur Head) in his grant. But set against the man's achievements in a period of difficulty and distress, in a colony as isolated as any of Britain's colonies could be, his place in Australian history is assured.

But as with Phillip, the foundation governor of New South Wales, the baptism of fire took its toll. At the settlers' request he returned to London in 1832 to try and get a new deal for the colony but by then the British government would have no part in his new plans. He faced determined and aggrieved Colonial Office officials, and even harder-nosed Treasury officials, who stood immovable against the financial and other concessions he sought. So Stirling returned to the Swan empty-handed and clearly dispirited. He stayed for several more years, then returned to naval service. That he never returned to the colony when the opportunity to do so was, for many years, readily available is probably significant. He may well have had enough of the colony and its people, and would therefore not deliberately seek to be reminded of the brave experiment which turned sour on the very day it was begun. He well knew that the advantages he had depicted for Swan River because of its favourable location were illusory. This, together with the inadequacy of so many settlers, and the responsibility he must have felt for the contents of his 1827 report, was reason enough to stay clear of Swan River.

Notes

ABBREVIATIONS

AA	Aylesbury Archives
ADB	*Australian Dictionary of Biography*
BL	J. S. Battye Library of West Australian History
CSO	Colonial Secretary's Office Correspondence
GD	Governor's Despatches
HRA	*Historical Records of Australia*
PRO	Public Records Office
SRP	Swan River Papers
WAHSJ	*Western Australian Historical Society Journal and Proceedings*

CHAPTER 1: DISCOVERY

1. O. H. K. Spate, *Australia* (London, 1968), p. 30.
2. Henry Handel Richardson, *The Fortunes of Richard Mahoney*, Book II: *The Way Home* (Melbourne, 1946), p. 392.
3. Griffith Taylor, *Australia* (London, 1940), pp. 40-2.
4. David Edgeworth, *Explanatory Notes to the Geological Map* (Sydney, 1932), cited by Taylor, p. 42.
5. Spate, pp. 25-6.
6. Taylor, p. 48.
7. J. T. Jutson, *The Physiography (Geomorphology) of Western Australia*, Geological Survey Bulletin No. 95 (Perth, 1950), pp. 3-6.
8. Taylor, pp. 84-5.
9. D. J. Mulvaney, *The Prehistory of Australia* (rev. Pelican ed., Melbourne, 1975), pp. 152, 280.
10. Ronald M. and Catherine H. Berndt, *The First Australians* (Sydney, 1954), p. 43.
11. Mulvaney, p. 15.
12. Berndt & Berndt, pp. 39-40.
13. Sylvia J. Hallam, *Fire and Hearth* (Canberra, 1975), passim.
14. Berndt & Berndt, p. 26.
15. Mulvaney, p. 61.
16. Berndt & Berndt, p. 48.
17. *Ibid.* p. 21.
18. Mulvaney, p. 42; C. M. H. Clark, *A History of Australia,* Vol. 1 (Melbourne, 1963), pp. 5-11.
19. Mulvaney, p. 42.
20. *Ibid.* p. 45.
21. Clark, pp. 6-7.

22. Mulvaney, pp. 24-8; Kenneth Gordon McIntyre, *The Secret Discovery of Australia* (London, 1977), pp. 71-3.

23. Mulvaney, pp. 29, 39; Berndt & Berndt, pp. 137-8. See also, I. M. Crawford, *The Art of the Wandjina* (Melbourne, 1968), passim.

24. George Collingridge, *The Discovery of Australia* (Sydney, 1895), pp. 26-7.

25. *Ibid.* p. 25.

26. *Ibid.* p. 29.

27. McIntyre, p. 69; Collingridge, p. 27.

28. McIntyre, pp. 69-70, although most dictionaries indicate that it is a word of Portuguese origin.

29. J. H. Parry, *Europe and a Wider World 1415-1725* (London, 1964), p. 36.

30. McIntyre, passim; Ian McKiggan, 'The Portuguese Expedition to Bass Strait, A.D. 1522', *Journal of Australian Studies* 1 (June 1977), pp. 2-32; K. G. McIntyre, 'Portuguese Discoveries on the Australian Coast', *Journal of the Royal Historical Society of Victoria* 45, 4 (November 1974), pp. 201-28; B. C. Rennie, 'The Dauphin Map', *Journal of Australian Studies* 3 (June 1978); Ian McKiggan, 'The Dauphin Map—a Reply', *ibid.*

31. Günter Schilder, *Australia Unveiled: The share of the Dutch navigators in the discovery of Australia* (Amsterdam, 1976), pp. 54-7.

32. *Ibid.* pp. 58-9. See also Michael Langley, 'John Harrison: The Hero of Longitude', *History Today* (December 1976), pp. 818-23; John F. Bailey, 'Longitude and the Sea Clock', *History Today* (June 1970), pp. 410-18.

33. Schilder, p. 60.

34. *Ibid.*

35. The most comprehensive account of the *Batavia* incident is H. Drake-Brockman, *Voyage to Disaster* (Sydney, 1963).

36. G. Arnold Wood, *The Discovery of Australia* (London, 1922), p. 267; see also pp. 225, 239, 242-3, 248 and 256; Collingridge, p. 272; Schilder, pp. 91 and 94; Willem C. H. Robert, *The Dutch Explorations 1605 to 1756, of the North and Northwest Coast of Australia* (Amsterdam, 1973). p. 141.

37. Schilder, p. 77.

38. *Ibid.* pp. 105-6.

39. *Ibid.* pp. 106-7. See Wood, pp. 338-9 for a summary of the ideas contained in Purry's book.

40. Schilder, p. 107.

41. Wood, pp. 285-8; translation by J. E. Heeres, *Abel Janszoon Tasman's Journal . . .* (Amsterdam, 1898; facsimile, Los Angeles, 1965), p. 152. See also Andrew Sharp, *The Voyages of Abel Janszoon Tasman* (London, 1968).

42. See Chapter 3.

43. See Chapter 3, G. G. Schilder, *De ontdekkingsreis van Willem Hesselsz de Vlamingh in De Jaren 1696-1697* ('s-Gravenhage, 1976).

44. Spate, p. 30.

45. John Dunmore, *French Explorations in the Pacific* (Oxford, 1965), Vol. 1, pp. 1-7.

46. *Ibid.* p. 47; R. H. Major (ed.), *Early Voyages to Terra Australis . . .* (London, 1859), p. vii; James A. Williamson (ed.), *A Voyage to New Holland by William Dampier* (London, 1939), p. xi.

47. O. H. K. Spate, 'De Lozier Bouvet and Mercantilist Expansion in the Pacific in 1740', in John Parker (ed.), *Merchants and Scholars* (Minnesota, 1965), pp. 223-37; James Burney, *A Chronological History of Voyages & Discoveries in the South Seas* (London, 1803-17; facsimile, London, 1967), Vol. V, p. 30.

48. Dunmore, p. 208.

49. *Ibid.* pp. 203-13. See also Kate Caldwell, 'The Voyage of François Alesne De Saint

Allouarn, 1771-72', *WAHSJ* 2, 16 (1934) pp. 6-8.

50. K. A. Austin, *The Voyage of the Investigator 1801-1803* (Adelaide, 1964), p. 158; Williamson, Introduction; John Masefield (ed.), *The Voyages of Captain William Dampier* (London, 1906).

51. Dunmore, pp. 250-82. See also Olive Wright, *Introductory Essay to New Zealand 1826-1827 from the French of D'umont D'urville* (Wellington, 1950).

52. D'Entrecasteaux first visited Tasmania, then sailed north in the Pacific Ocean to New Caledonia, and westward via Timor, after which he was blown well out into the Indian Ocean. He then sailed southward and towards the west coast of New Holland before reaching Cape Leeuwin. Dunmore, pp. 283-311; G. H. Hogg, 'D'Entrecasteaux; an account of his life, his expedition, and his officers', *Papers and Proceedings of the Royal Society of Tasmania* 1937, pp. 53-74.

53. Rev. P. V. Henn, 'French Exploration on the Western Australian Coast', *WAHSJ* 2, 15 (1934), p. 9.

54. Jacques Julien Houten de Labillardière, *An Account of a Voyage in Search of La Pérouse . . .*, trans. by Debrett (London, 1800), p. 458. See also Hogg, p. 61.

55. Captain George Vancouver, *A Voyage of Discovery to the North Pacific Ocean and Round the World*, Vol. 1 (London, 1801), pp. 103, 118.

56. *Ibid.* p. 143.

57. *Ibid.* pp. 168-9.

58. Edward Smith, *The Life of Sir Joseph Banks* (London, 1911); Austin, pp. 30-2; Ernest Scott, *The Life of Captain Matthew Flinders, R.N.* (Sydney, 1914), p. 174.

59. Scott, pp. 173-4; Austin, p. 32; Sir Gavin de Beer, *The Sciences were Never at War* (London, 1960).

60. Scott, pp. 180-1.

61. James D. Mack, *Matthew Flinders 1774-1814* (Melbourne, 1966), pp. 43-5.

62. Matthew Flinders, *A Voyage to Terra Australis . . .* (London, 1814), Vol. 1, pp. 61-2.

63. *Ibid.* p. 73; Scott, p. 207.

64. Dunmore, Vol. II, p. 9.

65. *Ibid.* pp. 9-11.

66. Christine Cornell (trans.), *The Journal of Post Captain Nicolas Baudin* (Adelaide, 1974), p. 3.

67. *Ibid.*

68. F. Péron, *A Voyage of Discovery to the Southern Hemisphere . . .* (London, 1809; facsimile, Melbourne, 1975), Book 2.

69. *Ibid.* p. 141.

70. Cornell, pp. 502-3.

71. Dunmore, Vol. II, pp. 9-40.

72. Marnie Bassett, *Realms and Islands: The World Voyage of Rose de Freycinet, 1817-1820* (London, 1962), p. 2.

73. *Ibid.* p. 2. See also J. Arago, *Narrative of a Voyage Round the World, in the Uranie and Physicienne Corvettes . . .* (London, 1823), pp. i-ii.

74. J. S. Battye (ed.), *The Cyclopedia of Western Australia*, Vol. 1 (Perth, 1912), p. 82.

75. See p. 32.

76. *ADB* Vol. 2, pp. 61-4.

77. Phillip P. King, *Narrative of a Survey of the Intertropical and Western Coasts of Australia* (London, 1827), Vol. 2, pp. 163-7.

78. *Ibid.* pp. 229-32.

79. Dunmore, Vol. 2, p. 180; Wright, Introduction.

80. Dunmore, p. 182.

81. Lord Bathurst to Governor Darling, 1.3.1826 (official letter), SRP3.

82. *Ibid.*

83. *Ibid.*
84. See Chapter 1.
85. Bathurst to Darling, 1.3.1826.
86. See Chapter 3, p. 99.
87. Eris O'Brien, *The Foundation of Australia* (London, 1937), p. 3.
88. Bathurst to Darling, 1.3.1826.
89. *Ibid.* 11.3.1826. See also Geoffrey Blainey, *The Tyranny of Distance* (Melbourne, 1968), pp. 89-92.
90. Darling to Bathurst, 10.10.1826, *HRA*, Series 1, Vol. 12, pp. 640-1.
91. *Ibid.* 24.11.1826, pp. 700-1.
92. *Ibid.* p. 701.
93. Marnie Bassett, *The Hentys* (London, 1955), pp. 78-9.
94. Darling to Hay, 4.12.1826, *HRA*, Series 1, Vol. 12, p. 730.
95. Blainey, p. 83.
96. See p. 9.
97. J. J. Eddy, *Britain and the Australian Colonies 1818-1831: The Technique of Government* (Oxford, 1969), p. 235.
98. Malcolm Uren, *Land Looking West,* (London, 1948), p. 41.
99. *Ibid.* p. 42.
100. *Ibid.*
101. *Ibid.*
102. *Ibid*

CHAPTER 2: JAMES STIRLING

1. *ADB* Vol. 2, pp. 484-8; Uren, pp. 14-20.
2. Further details of *Success* are in 'The Story of H.M.S. Success', *Swan River Booklets*, No. 1 (Perth, 1935).
3. Bassett, *The Hentys*, pp. 78-9.
4. Uren, pp. 4, 20.
5. William Somerville, 'An Economic History of Western Australia' (University of Western Australia and BL), Vol. 1, p. 13.
6. Darling to the Colonial Office, 18.12.1826, SRP1.
7. Stirling to Darling, 14.12.1826, SRP1.
8. Horsburgh's detailed charts of winds and currents in the Indian Ocean would have been known to Stirling. See A. C. Staples, 'Maritime Trade in the Indian Ocean, 1830-1845', *University Studies in History* IV, 4 (1966); James Horsburgh, *Directions for Sailing to and From the East Indies, China, New Holland, Cape of Good Hope, and the interjacent ports* . . . (Printed for the Author, 1809-11).
9. Blainey, Chapter 3.
10. Darling to the Colonial Office, 18.12.1826.
11. See Figure 2.1.
12. Blainey, p. 40.
13. J. J. Eddy claims that Stirling mentioned coal and iron 'as incentives to the governor'; Eddy, p. 126.
14. Stirling to Darling, 14.12.1826, indicates that Stirling carried French charts of Rottnest Island and Swan River.
15. *Ibid.*
16. Stirling refused to accept that the Swan River was a river in its lower reaches. It was an estuary (which he called Melville Water). He limited the name Swan River to 'that

stream which, joining the Sea at the islands below Fraser's Point, concludes its career as a River'.

17. Stirling had served in American waters, blockading the Mississippi River during the War of 1812.

18. Lockyer's Report to Alexander McLeay, Colonial Secretary, Sydney, 18.4.1827, SRP1. See also R. M. Stephens, 'Major Edmund Lockyer', *WAHSJ* 2, 19 (1936).

19. Lockyer kept a diary covering his stay at King George Sound but not during his journey aboard *Success*, nor did Stirling.

20. Darling to Bathurst, 21.4.1827 (enclosing Stirling's report) and *ibid.* 3.5.1827 (enclosing Lockyer's report), SRP1.

21. Stirling to Bathurst, 15.5.1827 (written aboard *Success* in Sydney and enclosed with Darling's letter of same date).

22. Darling to Hay, 15.5.1827.

CHAPTER 3: SWAN RIVER OBSERVED

1. Schilder, p. 75. Heeres, p. 16, wrote that Dedel apparently drew a map of the area but its whereabouts is unknown. He also wrote that Houtman thought the land was probably gold-bearing as well as fertile.

2. Schilder, p. 76.

3. Lous Zuiderbaan, 'The Vergulde Draeck. Historical Background', Chapter 1 in Jeremy N. Green, *Jacht Vergulde Draeck. Wrecked Western Australia 1656*, Part 1 (Oxford, 1977), p. 44.

4. *Ibid.* pp. 43-7.

5. C. R. Boxer, 'The Vergulde Draeck', *History Today* (London, March 1968).

6. H. Drake-Brockman, *Voyage*; and 'The Wreck of the Batavia', *Walkabout* (1955). See also Hugh Edwards, *Islands of Angry Ghosts* (New York, 1966).

7. Zuiderbaan, p. 49.

8. *Ibid.* p. 52.

9. *Ibid.*

10. Harry Turner, *The Gilt Dragon Incident* (Nedlands, 1963), pp. 85-6.

11. Zuiderbaan, p. 53.

12. Turner, p. 95.

13. C. de Heer, 'My Shield and My Faith', *Westerly* (April 1963), p. 35.

14. Turner, pp. 96-8.

15. Zuiderbaan, p. 55.

16. 'Daily Register Kept by the Skipper Samuel Volckersen on the flute the "Waekende Boëy" sailing from Batavia to the South Land 1658'. Translated by de Grys, Nedlands, W.A., held by H. Turner. Hereafter referred to as 'Daily Register'.

17. Zuiderbaan, pp. 55-7.

18. Extracts from Leeman's journal have been taken from the *Westerly* article cited above and 'Daily Register'.

19. Frederick A. Pottle, *Boswell and the Girl from Botany Bay* (London, 1938).

20. See also Collingridge, pp. 283-5.

21. *Ibid.* p. 284.

22. *Ibid.*

23. Major, pp. 61-2.

24. Hallam, passim.

25. Zuiderbaan, pp. 58-60.

26. *Ibid.* p. 60.

27. Missive by the Directors of Committee of XVII to Governor General, 16.3.1696, in Willem C. H. Robert, *The Explorations, 1696-1697, of Australia by Willem de Vlamingh* (Amsterdam, 1972), p. 159.
28. C. Halls, 'The loss of the Ridderschap van Holland', *The Annual Dog Watch* 22 (1965).
29. Extract of Resolution, 10.12.1695, in Robert, *Explorations*, p. 159.
30. *Ibid.* p. 11.
31. Schilder, *De Vlamingh*, Vol. 1, pp. 134-40.
32. Robert, pp. 15-16, 28-9.
33. *Ibid.* p. 11.
34. *Ibid.* pp. 161-3.
35. *Ibid.* pp. 165-6.
36. *Ibid.* p. 25.
37. Discussions with officials at Fremantle Maritime Museum.
38. An exception, of course, is Rottnest Island. The governor-general in Batavia did not accept Volkersen's invitation to name the island (see p. 69) but Vlamingh named it on account of the large number of 'rats' seen there.
39. Günter Schilder, 'A continent found by mistake', *The Geographical Magazine* (London, February 1978), p. 342.
40. W. Stark, 'Literature and Thought: The Romantic Tendency, Rousseau, Kant', *The New Cambridge Modern History* VIII (Cambridge, 1965), p. 55.
41. Peter Gay, *Age Of Enlightenment* (Nederland, 1966).
42. Dunmore, Vol. 1, p. 109.
43. Smith, pp. 6-7.
44. *Ibid.* p. 87.
45. *Ibid.* p. 110.
46. Péron, pp. 14-15.
47. Correspondence (in English) from Baudin expedition, Bibliothèque Nationale (Paris), Marine BB4997.
48. Cornell, pp. 441-2.
49. Greenwood, p. 109.
50. Cornell, p. XII.
51. *Ibid.* p. 1.
52. *Ibid.*
53. *Ibid.* p. 3.
54. Péron, p. 11.
55. Cornell, p. 3.
56. Péron, pp. 9-12.
57. Cornell, p. 3.
58. Letter from Baudin to the 'Ministre de la Marine et des Colonies', 5.10.1801, BL 282.
59. Cornell, p. 162.
60. *Ibid.* p. 8.
61. *Ibid.* pp. 1-6.
62. *Ibid.* pp. 42, 178, 181, 452, 509.
63. *Ibid.* p. 510.
64. Péron, p. 59.
65. *Ibid.* pp. 62-4.
66. *Ibid.* pp. 67-8.
67. Cornell, p. 165.
68. Baudin letter, 5.10.1801.
69. Péron, pp. 80-1.
70. Cornell, pp. 186-97.
71. *Ibid.* pp. 194-5.

72. *Ibid.*
73. Péron, Chaps X and XI.
74. *Ibid.* p. 139.
75. *Ibid.* p. 145.
76. Paper No. 7, BL 407A.
77. Péron, p. 146.
78. BL 282A.
79. Péron, p. 141.
80. BL 282A (15) No. 11.
81. Péron, p. 143.
82. *Ibid.* pp. 144-5.
83. *Quarterly Review* (London) XXXIX (January and April 1829).
84. Péron, p. 149.
85. *Ibid.* p. 150.
86. *Ibid.* p. 152.
87. Cornell, p. 503.
88. *Ibid.*
89. *Ibid.* pp. 511-12.
90. *Quarterly Review* IV (1810), pp. 42-60; XVII (1817), pp. 229-248; XII (1814-15), pp. 1-46.
91. George Seddon, *Swan River Landscapes* (Nedlands, 1970), p. 74.
92. George Seddon, *Sense of Place* (Nedlands, 1972), Chapter 3.
93. Seddon, *Swan River*, pp. 80-1.
94. *Ibid.* p. 52.
95. Sylvia J. Hallam, 'Population And Resource Usage On The Western Littoral', ANZAAS, 1977, Section 25A, Vol. 2, pp. 16-36.
96. Hallam, *Fire*, pp. 5-7.
97. Hallam, ANZAAS, p. 22.
98. *Ibid.* p. 25.

CHAPTER 4: DECISION AND PREPARATIONS

1. W. B. Kimberly (compiler), *History of West Australia* (Melbourne, 1897), p. 39; *ADB* Vol. 2, p. 485.
2. Somerville, Vol. 1, pp. 1-29, makes a great deal of this point, claiming that the boom provided the motive for potential settlers who thought they saw the opportunity of acquiring landed estates in Australia.
3. *Ibid.* p. 30; and Darling to Hay, 15.5.1827, SRP1. Darling's action was approved: Hay to Darling, 6.11.1827, SRP3.
4. Uren, p. 44. See pp. 42-7 for details of Stirling's achievements at Raffles Bay.
5. *Ibid.* p. 48.
6. Stanley to Stirling, 29.11.1827, SRP3. Also Uren, pp. 48-9.
7. *HRA*, Third Series, Vol. VI, p. 585. Uren, p. 72, shows that the letter informing Stirling that the government declined his offer was not received by Stirling until he was about to sail on *Parmelia* during early February 1826.
8. Eddy, p. 235.
9. *Ibid.* pp. 241-2.
10. Barrow to Horton, 15.10.1827, SRP3.
11. Huskisson to Darling, 28.1.1828, SRP3.
12. *Ibid.*
13. *Ibid.* 30.1.1828.

14. Eddy, p. 243.
15. *Ibid.* p. 3.
16. *Ibid.* pp. 16-18.
17. *Ibid.* p. 19. Cygnet in 'The Story of the Birth of Perth', *Swan River Booklets,* No. 4, p. 2, writes of Murray as 'the greatest brain on the Peninsula after Wellington'! Uren, p. 49, notes that Murray was a fellow Scot and a friend of the Stirling family.
18. Eddy, p. 19. Hay was appointed first permanent under-secretary of the Colonial Office in July 1827, *ibid.* p. 25.
19. *Ibid.* p. 32.
20. Stirling to Hay, 30.7.1828, SRP3. He apparently wrote this letter after seeing Hay.
21. Barrow to Twiss, 2.8.1828, SRP3.
22. Stirling and Moody to Hay, 21.8.1828, SRP3. See Somerville, Vol. 1, pp. 31-7. The charter granted to Penn in 1681 established 'a semi-professional kingdom making Penn supreme Governor with power to make laws only limited by the provision that they were not to be repugnant to the laws of England'. Such a system would have gone far beyond the mere granting of land as in the case of the Australian Agricultural Company in N.S.W. and the Van Diemen's Land Company.
23. Eddy, p. 243.
24. Hay to Barrow 3.10.1828, C.S.O. 324/86/68; Murray to Admiralty, C.S.O. 202/23075.
25. Stirling to Twiss, 22.10.1828, SRP3.
26. Bassett, *The Hentys*, p. 86; and Uren, pp. 55-8, especially the observations of J. S. Roe on rumours in official circles concerning whether or not a settlement would be established.
27. Ann Parry (ed.), *The Admirals Fremantle* (London, 1971), pp. 74-5.
28. *Ibid.*
29. When Fremantle obtained command of *Challenger*, he was asked by both Cockburn and Lord Brechnock to give preference to certain applicants for midshipmen positions: Charles Howe Fremantle to his uncle William Fremantle, 7.9.1828, correspondence found in AA.
30. Parry, *Fremantle*, p. 140.
31. BL 16A.
32. Lord Cottesloe (ed.), *Diary and Letters of Admiral Sir C. H. Fremantle, G.C.B.* (London, 1928), p. 10.
33. Parry, *Fremantle*, p. 141.
34. C. H. Fremantle to William, 23.10.1828, AA. While waiting at Portsmouth, Fremantle took trouble to avoid seeing persons who were associated with the Winchester affair. He was especially concerned about newspaper publicity when it was announced that he had been promoted to command *Challenger* (*Ibid.* 7.9.1828).
35. *Ibid.* 12.11.1828. So hurried was the preparation of *Challenger* that Fremantle could not leave Portsmouth to attend a family reunion, having pledged himself to Cockburn not to lose any time, 'and asking for leave would appear careless' (*Ibid.* 23.10.1828).
36. *Ibid.* 16.11.1828.
37. *Ibid.* 21.11.1828.
38. Barrow to Schomburg, 2.12.1828, SRP3.
39. C. H. Fremantle to William, 4.12.1828.
40. *Ibid.*
41. *Ibid.*
42. Basset, *Realms*, p. 86.
43. C. H. Fremantle to William, 19.12.1828. *Pallas* was the vessel Fremantle had helped refit at Portsmouth while waiting for *Challenger* to return from Canadian waters.
44. C. H. Fremantle to his mother, 14.12.1828 and 7.1.1829, from Madeira, AA.

45. *Ibid.* 18.3.1829, from Simon's Town. Fremantle also kept a diary during the early part of his voyage which is now held in the family home at Swanbourne, Buckinghamshire. After leaving Swan River he lost interest so there are many 'gaps'. (See Plate 4.4).

46. *Ibid.*

47. A letter from an anonymous member of Challenger's crew held by BL. Collie, Dance and others on *Sulphur* and *Parmelia*, which reached the Cape only weeks after *Challenger* had sailed, record similar rumours and fears by Cape residents.

48. C. H. Fremantle to his mother, 18.3.1829, from Simon's Town.

49. *Ibid.* Cleaɪ evidence that Stirling and Fremantle had known each other for many years. *Brazen* was Stirling's first command in 1812. (See Chapter 2, p. 37.)

50. Schomberg to Crocker (Admiralty), 2.3.1829. *Challenger* was three crew short having invalided seven hands at the Cape.

51. C. H. Fremantle to his mother, 18.3.1829.

52. Unpublished part of Fremantle's Diary, held at the family estate, Swanbourne, Buckinghamshire.

53. Cottesloe, Part II. This volume contains parts of Fremantle's personal diary relating to his visit to Swan River.

54. C. H. Fremantle to Crocker (Admiralty), 8.10.1829; Cottesloe, pp. 23-7.

55. Péron, p. 144.

56. Cottesloe, pp. 38-40, 41.

57. Cygnet, 'The Story of Foundation Day', *Swan River Booklets*, No. 2, p. 5, assumes that the ditch was being dug to guard against any sudden raid by Aborigines.

58. Fremantle's Log, 26.6.1829, after *Parmelia* had arrived.

59. Presumably the bull brought from the Cape. It was originally landed on Garden Island but later brought to the mainland where there was more feed.

60. Lord Cottesloe notes that the spring was marked on the Chart of 1827, but not on subsequent charts.

61. A 'bomb' was a small warship on which was mounted bombs or mortars for use in bombardments. When *Sulphur* was refitted for the voyage to Swan River her bombs were replaced by guns (six 24-pounders and two 6-pounders). See E. S. Whiteley, 'H.M.S. Sulphur', *WAHSJ* 6, 6 (1961), p. 45.

62. Murray to Admiralty and Twiss to Barrow, 12.11.1828, SRP3.

63. Barrow to Twiss, 15.11.1828, SRP3. It cost the Navy £3100 to fit out *Sulphur* for the voyage and £1403 for stores, *Swan River Booklets*, No. 5, p. 6. See also Somerville, pp. 38-41; and Uren, p. 59.

64. Lord Hill to Murray, 3.12.1828, SRP3; Somerset to Twiss, 24.12.1828, SRP3; Hay to Crocker, 27.12.1828, SRP3.

65. Hay to Stirling, 31.12.1828, SRP3.

66. Uren, p. 63.

67. Admiralty to Hay, 29.12.1828; Seppings, Legge and Boyle (Agents) to Hay, 29.12.1828, SRP3.

68. Murray to Stirling, 30.12.1828, SRP3.

69. Murray to Darling, 12.1.1829, SRP3.

70. *Swan River Booklets*, No. 5, p. 7.

71. Admiralty to Dance, 24.1.1829, SRP3.

72. Peel and others to Murray, 14.11.1828, SRP3.

73. Thus 10 000 settlers at £30 per head = £300 000 x 1s 6d per acre would yield a grant of four million acres (1 620 000 ha).

74. Peel to Twiss, 30.11.1828, SRP3.

75. Uren, p. 76.

76. Alexandra Hasluck, *Thomas Peel of Swan River* (Melbourne, 1965), passim.

77. Twiss to Stirling, 29.1.1829, SRP3.

78. Murray to Stirling, 23.12.1828, SRP3.
79. Peel chose land south of Swan River.
80. Stewart to Hay, 11.12.1828, SRP3.
81. Stirling to Twiss, 16.1.1829, SRP3.
82. Twiss to Stirling, 29.1.1829. On 3.2.1829 another set of regulations for persons propos-
    ing to go to Swan River: Hay to Dawson, 31.12.1829, SRP3.
83. Dance to Hay, 14.1.1829, SRP4.
84. Collie to Dance, 16.1.1829, SRP3.
85. Parker to Earl of Northesk, 17.1.1829, SRP3.
86. Earl of Northesk to Parker, 18.1.1829, SRP3.
87. Sabine (Horticultural Society), to Hay, 20.1.1829, SRP3.
88. Hay to Stirling, 22.1.1829, SRP3.
89. Edward Shann, *An Economic History of Australia* (Cambridge, 1948), Chapter 1.
90. Hay to Stirling, 14.1.1829, SRP3; Navy Office to Stirling, 24.1.1829, CSO, Vol. 1, p.
    20.
91. Stirling to Twiss, 5.2.1829, SRP3.
92. Hay to Dawson, 31.12.1828, SRP3.
93. *Regulations for the Guidance of those who may propose to embark as Settlers, for the
    New Settlement on the Western Coast of New Holland* (London), 13 January 1829.
94. Hay to Stirling, 16.1.1829, SRP3; *Swan River Booklets*, No. 5, p. 8.
95. Murray to Stirling, 30.12.1828, SRP3. The exact date of departure is not certain
    although J. S. Roe, the main chronicler of the voyage, entered 5.2.1829.
96. J. S. Roe, a letter written aboard *Parmelia*, 6.2.1829, held by J. Roe; *Swan River
    Booklets*, No. 7, p. 7; Uren, Chapters VIII to XI.
97. Extract of a letter from a gentleman on board *Parmelia*, 23.3.1829, published in the
    Sunday Times (London), 21.6.1829.
98. *Ibid.*
99. Stirling to brother John, from the Cape, 25.4.1829, BL 449A/19. Other aspects of the
    voyage to the Cape are reported in Kimberly, pp. 40-2.
100. Stirling to Twiss, 29.4.1829, SRP3.
101. Confirmed in his personal letter to John of 25.4.1829, BL 449A/19.
102. *Swan River Booklets,* No. 5, p. 8; Dance to Twiss, 6.5.1829, SRP3, also records details
     of the drowning—that they had taken on board a replacement Assistant Surgeon
     William Milligan.
103. Dance to Twiss, 6.5.1829, from the Cape, SRP4.
104. Kimberly, pp. 41-2; Stirling to brother John, 25.4.1829.
105. Kimberly, p. 41. In his letter to brother John (see n. 104). Stirling had already decided
     to appoint William Stirling as Registrar, 'which hereafter may be a profitable office to
     be paid by fees'. He had also decided to appoint George Mangles as Superintendent of
     Government Stock.
106. P. Broun, Journal of Events Connected With the Public Service, 9.9.1829, SRP4, p. 8;
     Swan River Booklets, No. 2, pp. 3-4.
107. SRP4, p. 8.
108. See Chapter 1, p. 33.
109. The sequence of events on that morning is not clear from Fremantle's terse diary
     entries. When he first saw *Parmelia* from Carnac Island he also 'Observed the boat
     board her from the River; and she stood for the Islands.' Uren, pp. 90-1 believes that
     this was the boat in which Currie had gone ahead and found 'sufficient water' and that
     Fremantle then 'raced to Parmelia hoping to be in time to give a warning of the dangers
     ahead. But he was too late; the other boat was fast and he just arrived to hear Captain
     Mark Currie assure Stirling that the way was clear. To Fremantle's disgust, Stirling
     acted on this and the ship proceeded and in five minutes was on shore.' Fremantle

records having boarded *Parmelia* and met Stirling, followed by the sentence that Stirling 'sent to sound over the inner bank and Captain Currie, . . . *found a passage* . . .', Cottesloe, p. 58. This could be interpreted as Currie finding the passage after Fremantle boarded *Parmelia*. It could also be interpreted that Fremantle was aboard when *Parmelia* struck, but this is unlikely.

110. Luscombe to Stirling, 14.7.1829, CSO, Vol. 1, pp. 4-5.
111. See Graeme Henderson, 'Problems Encountered By Shipping At The Port of Fremantle 1829 to 1850' (M.A. thesis, University of Western Australia, 1971).
112. Stirling to his brother Walter, BL 449A; Stirling to Twiss, 25.8.1829, SRP3.
113. *Swan River Booklets*, No. 2, p. 7.
114. Cottesloe, p. 67. The decision to enter the Sound was 'very much in consequence of the advice given by the Lieutenant Governor to the Master of the Parmelia'.
115. In his official report from Trincomalee (Cottesloe, p. 24), Fremantle wrote that 'it was not until the next morning with all the exertions of this Ship's Crew and Boats that she was extricated from her perilous situation after she had received much damage'.
116. Cottesloe, pp. 60-1.
117. Morgan to Hay, 18.3.1830, from Garden Island, SRP6. Alexander Collie's Diary confirms the confusion recorded by Fremantle and Morgan.
118. Dance to Twiss, 9.9.1829.
119. Cottesloe, p. 61.
120. See Henderson, part 3, for details of correspondence between Stirling and Luscombe.
121. Stirling to his brother William, 7.9.1829, BL 449A/20.
122. Fremantle to the Storekeeper, Trincomalee, 30.10.1829, Cottesloe, pp. 92-3.
123. Fremantle to Schomberg, 20.10.1829, Cottesloe, pp. 81-2.
124. Stirling to his brother Walter, 7.9.1829.
125. Stirling to Twiss, 25.8.1828, SRP3.
126. Jane Currie's Diary, 1829-1832, BL 329A. See also Cross, p. 12. Captain Dance wrote, 'The Gun-room Officers gave a grand dinner to the Governor and his Lady, Fremantle and Officers of the *Challenger*, all the Colonial Officers: about forty in number sat down to dinner, and day dawned before the company departed.'
127. Stirling to Fremantle, Garden Island, 10.8.1829. Original held in family archives, Swanbourne, Bucks.
128. Fremantle to Stirling, aboard *Challenger*, 15.8.1829, Cottesloe, pp. 77-8.
129. Cottesloe, p. 69.
130. Fremantle to Stirling, CSO, Vol. 2, p. 7.
131. Officers of *Challenger* to Broun, 21.8.1829, CSO, Vol. 1, pp. 145, 149, 150; 25.8.1829, Vol. 2, p. 2; 24.8.1829, Vol. 2, p. 18.
132. Lyon to Secretary of State for Colonies, 20.12.1832, SRP11. Somerville, pp. 55-7, agrees that the allocation of 'great estates were a very important factor contributing to the stagnation' of the colony.
133. Stirling to his brother Walter, 7.9.1829: 'all [Fremantle's] officers have become proprietors and are charmed with the country' (p. 4).
134. Bassett, *Hentys*, p. 93.
135. Fremantle, in his letter to the Admiralty from Trincomalee (8.10.1839, SRP5), did not mention that the future port had been named after him. He merely noted that it was 'to be built at the mouth of the River for the convenience of the Shipping in Gages Roads near the Spot where the party from this Ship first established themselves'.

CHAPTER 5: REALITY

1. Stirling to Twiss, 25.8.1829 (from Garden Island), SRP3, confirmed in Cottesloe, pp. 23-7.

2. Stirling to brother William, 7.9.1829.
3. *Ibid.* See also Henderson, part 3, p. 4; Uren, pp. 93-4.
4. Stirling to Twiss, 25.8.1829; Cottesloe, p. 61.
5. Cottesloe, p. 61.
6. *Ibid.*
7. Uren, p. 94; Somerville, p. 46.
8. Cottesloe, p. 25. See also CSO, Vol. 1, p. 1: A report showing the number of working parties in Garden Island during July 1829. The Storehouse had been built by August 10, other 'temporary' residences were for Stirling, Broun, Morgan, Currie and Drummond. Stirling to the Colonial Office, 13.3.1831, and enclosure H: Civil Engineer's Statement of Public Works executed at Garden Island, SRP7.
9. Cross, pp. 8, 10.
10. Bassett, *Hentys*, p. 92.
11. Morgan to Hay, 18.3.1830, SRP6. His reference to destruction of property may also refer to goods landed on the mainland by settlers who arrived in *Calista, Marquis of Anglesea* and other vessels.
12. Stirling to his brother Walter, 7.9.1829.
13. Named after the family name of his wife.
14. Stirling to Twiss, 25.8.1829.
15. Cottesloe, pp. 67-8.
16. J. M. R. Cameron, 'Swan River Mania, 1829-1830: A Study of the Relationship Between Migration and Information', mimeo. See especially Figure 2, 'Requests to the Colonial Office for Information about Swan River Colony', which shows a peak of interest of 40-60 per month during January-March 1829, followed by a gradual decline to 25 per month at year's end.
17. *Quarterly Review* XXXIX (January and April 1829).
18. J. M. R. Cameron, 'Information Distortion in Colonial Promotion: The Case of Swan River Colony', *Australian Geographical Studies* 12 (1974).
19. Circular regarding settlement at Swan River by H. C. Semphill, SRP5.
20. *South African Commercial Advertiser*, Editorial, 25.4.1829.
21. Pamela Statham, Ph.D. thesis in preparation, University of Western Australia.
22. Cameron, 'Swan River Mania', p. 20; Pamela Statham, 'Swan River Colony, 1829-1850', a chapter in a forthcoming volume, *The New History of Western Australia,* ed. C. T. Stannage.
23. Statham, 'Swan River Colony'.
24. J. M. R. Cameron, 'The Colonization of pre-convict Western Australia' (Ph.D. thesis, University of Western Australia, 1975), p. 110.
25. *Sussex Advertiser*, Editorial, 15.6.1829.
26. *Leicester Journal* 16.10.1829.
27. *Hull Advertiser* 11.9.1829.
28. *Sussex Advertiser* 15.6.1829.
29. *Leicester Journal* 16.10.1829.
30. *Brighton Gazette* 20.5.1839, written from Swan River, 1.11.1829.
31. *Hull Rockingham* 3.7.1830, written from Swan River, 14.2.1829, by Harley, mate of *Tranby*, and Georgiana Molloy.
32. *York Chronicle* 17.6.1830, written from Swan River by P. H. Dod of *Atwick*.
33. J. M. R. Cameron, 'The Near Collapse of Swan River Colony: Review and Reappraisal', *Social Science Forum* 1, 1 (August 1973), p. 21.
34. *Ibid.*
35. *Ibid.*
36. Bassett, *Hentys*, p. 94.
37. I. L. Berryman, *The Swan River Letters* (forthcoming), pp. 77, 82.

38. *Ibid.* p. 86.
39. Henty to anon, 1.5.1830, SRP6.
40. *Globe* 27.1.1830, letter written 9.9.1829.
41. *Hampshire Chronicle* 29.3.1830, letter written 25.11.1829.
42. J. Cross, *Extracts of Letters from Swan River, Western Australia* (London, 1830).
43. *Leicester Journal* 24.9.1830, letter written 10.3.1829.
44. Mrs E. Shenton, 'Reminiscences of Perth, 1830-1840', *WAHSJ* 1, 1 (1927), p. 1.
45. Stirling to Murray, 10.9.1829, SRP4.
46. Cameron, 'Colonization of pre-convict Western Australia', p. 119.
47. CSO, Vol. 2, p. 66.
48. T. B. Wilson, *Narrative of a Voyage Round the World . . .* (London, 1835), p. 223.
49. Stirling to Twiss, 26.1.1830, SRP 4.
50. 'The Diary of Mary Ann Friend', *WAHSJ* 1, X, p. 3.
51. Cameron, 'Near Collapse', p. 24.
52. Henderson, part 3, p. 7. Also, A. H. Chate, *An Account of the Cowcher Family* (Perth, 1953), p. 14.
53. Jane Roberts, *Two Years at Sea* (London, 1843), p. 47.
54. Wilson, p. 192.
55. Roberts, p. 47.
56. 28.8.1830 (from Augusta), SRP 8(9), p. 116.
57. *Globe*, letter from Swan River, 27.1.1830.
58. 28.8.1830, p. 116.
59. *Ibid.*
60. Statham, 'Swan River Colony'.
61. Cross, p. 34.
62. *Ibid.*
63. Statham, thesis in preparation.
64. Irwin, p. 46.
65. Cross, pp. 24-5.
66. *Brighton Gazette*, A. H. Stone, 10.6.1830.
67. CSO, Vol. 5, p. 135.
68. *SRP* 8(9), 28.8.1830, p. 116.
69. *The Times* 1.6.1830, James Henty from Fremantle, 15.11.1829. See also letter from Fremantle, 13.11.1829: 'Either from the Caroline or the Atwick has a single individual got upon his land', Camfield Letters, BL HS/587, p. 1. *Caroline* had arrived 12 October, and *Atwick* 19 October. See also *Brighton Gazette* 1.4.1830: 'there is not one of the settlers (at least those we brought out) who is not grumbling at the unexpected delay of grants'.
70. Lyon to Secretary of State for the Colonies, 20.12.1832, SRP10; *Courier* 14.12.1832. Though a supporter of Stirling, Purkis criticized his early decision to give so much land to officers of *Challenger*.
71. Statham, thesis in preparation; Cameron, 'Near Collapse', p. 24; *Brighton Gazette* 10.6.1830; *Doncaster Gazette* 20.5.1831.
72. *Glasgow Courier* 13.2.1830, written from *Sulphur*, 12.9.1829.
73. *Brighton Gazette* 1.4.1830, letter from a 'young man who left Brighton last May', written 26.11.1829.
74. *South African Commercial Advertiser* 17.4.1830, written February 1830.
75. *Ibid.*
76. *Hampshire Telegraph and Sussex Chronicle* 23.8.1839, written 24.1.1830.
77. *Royal Devonport Telegraph and Plymouth Chronicle* 9.10.1830, written 2.4.1830. This letter supported an editorial in the Van Diemen's Land paper of 30.3.1830, that wheat would not grow at Swan River because the soil was too sandy. 'Hundreds will be totally

ruined by this mad attempt of Stirling', contended the editorial.

78. *Courier* 4.5.1831, written 16.8.1830.
79. Bassett, *Hentys*, p. 103. The young correspondent from Brighton (n. 73) claimed that land (south of the river) for '6 miles' (to Canning) was not worth farming. On the north side it was no better. See also *Leicester Journal* 24.9.1830, written from Swan River, 10.3.1830.
80. Eddy, p. 32.
81. Morgan to Hay, 18.3.1830, SRP6.
82. J. M. R. Cameron, 'Prelude to Colonization: James Stirling's Examination of Swan River, March 1827', *The Australian Geographer* XII, 4 (1973), pp. 309-27.
83. Cameron, 'Colonization of pre-convict Western Australia', p. 47.
84. *Ibid.* p. 50.
85. Cameron, 'Information Distortion', p. 60.
86. *Ibid.* p. 63. See also *South African Commercial Advertiser* 7.11.1827, for a severe criticism of the licence taken by Barrow.
87. Barrow to Hay (private letter), PRO, 323/149, pp. 135-6.
88. *South African Commercial Advertiser* 7.11.1829. The same paper renewed its attack 25.11.1829 when first news was received from the colony.
89. Stirling to brother Walter, 7.9.1829. This letter was published in Hull, 13.2.1830.
90. Stirling to Twiss, 25.8.1829 (from Garden Island), SRP3.
91. *Hull Advertiser* 30.4.1830, letter from William Stirling, 21.11.1829; *Courier* 23.6.1827, written 25.1.1830.
92. *Brighton Gazette* 20.5.1830; *York Chronicle* 17.6.1830.
93. *Southampton Mercury* 26.6.1830, written 30.1.1830. See also Bassett, *Hentys*, p. 94.
94. Morgan to Hay, 18.3.1830, SRP6.
95. Berryman, *passim*.
96. Lyon to Secretary of State for the Colonies, 20.12.1832, SRP10.
97. Stirling to Twiss, 25.8.1829. In this report Stirling also said, 'there is a passage of 4½ fathoms' and that it would not be difficult to navigate when 'we shall have buoyed it or established competent Pilots'.
98. Cross, p. 18. Rutherford writes that *Calista* and *Marquis of Anglesea* 'arrived from England . . . but anchored in Gage's Roads'. See also Henderson, part 3, p. 2.
99. Cross, p. 18; Stirling to Twiss, 25.8.1829.
100. The word 'equinoxial' was used by William Stirling, Cross, p. 36.
101. Dance to Twiss, 9.9.1829, SRP4. He sent a similar account to the *Courier*, published 27.1.1830.
102. *Globe* 27.1.1830, written from Swan River, 9.9.1829.
103. *Brighton Gazette* 1.4.1830, written from Swan River, 26.11.1829.
104. Rutherford's observation, Cross, p. 19.
105. *Ibid.* p. 19.
106. *Morning Journal* 28.1.1830, written from Swan River, 10.9.1829.
107. Stirling to brother Walter, 7.9.1829.
108. Lloyds to Board of Trade, 5.1.1829, PRO (microfilm); Despatches; correspondence to the Secretary of State.
109. Morgan to Hay, 18.3.1830, SRP6.
110. *South African Commercial Advertiser* 13.2.1830.
111. Cross, p. 15.
112. Berryman, pp. 29-32.
113. *Challenger* had sailed for India on 28 August, but mail taken by her would reach England after mail taken aboard *St Leonard*.
114. Berryman, Introduction, passim.
115. *Ibid.* p. 48.

116. *Ibid.* p. 49.
117. *Leicester Journal* 5.3.1830.
118. *South African Commercial Advertiser* 25.6.1831.
119. Berryman, p. 48.
120. Moore, p. 92.
121. Letters to his brother, 1.2.1830 and 5.9.1830, Camfield Letters, BL H/S 587.
122. Tanner to Stirling, 11.7.1839, SRP9; Tanner to Brown, 11.7.1832, CSO 23, p. 2.
123. Various accounts were given of the accident. William Stirling, the governor's cousin, seemed to discount the seriousness of it in letters sent to the *South African Commercial Advertiser* 10.3.1830 and 17.4.1830. Cygnet, *Swan River Booklets*, No. 1, wrongly records that the vessel ran on a sandbank which was later named after it.
124. The account given by a passenger is the main source of the following narrative: *South African Commercial Advertiser* 10.3.1830.
125. Remark Book of His Majesty's Ship Challenger commencing 1 January 1832 and ending 12 June 1833. Held at Hydrographer's Office, Taunton, Somerset under Remark Book 1829-1833.
126. CSO, Vol. 5, p. 43.
127. Jervoise to Stirling, 7.7.1830, CSO, Vol. 7. See p. 143 regarding difficulties experienced obtaining suitable timber; Jervoise to Stirling, 7.4.1830, CSO, Vol. 6, repeating his request for lemon juice to reduce scurvy on board.
128. Henderson, part 3, p. 9.
129. Jervoise to Stirling, 25.11.1830; and Commander-in-Chief to Stirling, 9.3.1831, CSO, Vol. 10.
130. Jervoise to Morgan, 23.12.1830, SRP8.
131. Henderson, Introduction, p. 1.

CHAPTER 6: REASSESSMENT

1. *Brighton Gazette* 20.5.1830, letter from A. H. Stone, passenger aboard *Caroline*.
2. Roberts, p. 47.
3. *Ibid.* pp. 47, 51.
4. *Royal Devonport Telegraph and Plymouth Chronicle* 1.8.1829.
5. *The Times* 2.2.1830.
6. Cross, *Extracts of Letters*, p. 23.
7. Stirling to Murray, 10.9.1829, Enclosure 1, SRP4.
8. *Doncaster Gazette* 20.5.1831, Hardy's letter written from Fremantle.
9. *Ibid.*
10. Berryman, Introduction.
11. Morgan to Hay, 18.3.1830, SRP6.
12. BL 332A.
13. Henry Camfield to his brother (Fremantle), 2.1.1830, BL H/S 587.
14. *Zuid Africaan*, 10.12.1830.
15. Stirling to Murray, 10.9.1829, Enclosure 5.
16. J. Cross (ed.), *Journal of Several Expeditions made in Western Australia* . . . (London, 1833), lists expeditions of 1829, '30, '31 and '32 under the sanction of James Stirling.
17. Morgan to Hay, 18.3.1830.
18. Stirling to Twiss, 25.8.1829, SRP3. He described the communication as a 'slight sketch of our present position' rather than a report.
19. Stirling to Murray, 10.9.1829.
20. Stirling to Twiss, 26.1.1830, SRP4.

21. Stirling to Secretary of State, 18.10.1830, SRP5.
22. SRP (passim), and especially the document 'A Mirror of 1830'.
23. Hasluck, *Thomas Peel*.
24. Letters from Henry Camfield, 12.10.1829, BL H/S 589; Bunbury, pp. 170-4.
25. CSO (Outward), Vol. 3, 10.1.1831.
26. *Ibid.*
27. Stirling to Murray, 13.3.1831, SRP7.
28. *South African Commercial Advertiser* 25.12.1830, letter from Swan River dated 20.8.1830.
29. Moore, p. 26.
30. *Ibid.* p. 24.
31. Lyon to Secretary of State for the Colonies, 11.2.1831, SRP8.
32. *Ibid.*
33. CSO, Vol. 13, p. 48ff. The governor's capacity to assist settlers was constrained by the small gold reserves that had been sent to him from London aboard *Sulphur* and which were to be used to pay a few officials and obtain essential supplies from the Commissariat Store. After 1830 additional revenue was obtained through land sales (which replaced the land grant system) and through imposition of excise/customs tax on luxury goods. Some revenue was obtained from pilot services and shipping dues, but this was used to pay for the services (Stirling to Secretary of State, 20.1.1830, SRP4).
34. CSO, Vol. 13, p. 48ff.
35. Morgan to Hay, 23.6.1831, SRP8.
36. CSO, Vol. 20, p. 9.
37. Moore confirms the effect of supply vessels on the price level.
38. In February 1832 the Western Australian Agricultural Society reported that a demand for hundreds of cattle and thousands of sheep could not be met because settlers were unable to charter vessels in which to import them.
39. On 10.7.1832 Scott, the Harbour Master, received a petition from mechanics and labourers who pointed out that the high cost of provisions had led to unemployment and suggested that public works be begun to employ them (CSO, Vol. 23, p. 53). Robert Lyon also reported that the high cost of labour had led to retrenchment (CSO, Vol. 23).
40. Morgan to Hay, 8.3.1832, SRP14.
41. Stirling to Hay (private), 26.6.1832, SRP9.
42. Executive Council Minutes, 2.3.1832, SRP17.
43. Somerville, p. 100. See also Moore, pp. 60, 63, 93.
44. Dyer Letters, BL 1598A.
45. Moore, pp. 60, 87, 142.
46. *Courier* 16.8.1830 and 8.10.1830.
47. *South African Commercial Advertiser* 21.12.1831.
48. CSO, Vol. 5, p. 4.
49. Stirling to Goderich, 2.4.1832, SRP9.
50. Paul Hasluck, *Black Australians* (Melbourne, 1942), p. 69.
51. Lyon to Secretary of State, 1.1.1833, SRP10.
52. *Leicester Journal* 24.9.1830.
53. 18.3.1830, SRP6.
54. *Courier* 4.5.1831.
55. *Zuid Africaan* 10.12.1830.
56. Stirling's 1826 report, SRP1. Stirling would have known that American shipowners had traded seal-skins with the Chinese. See F. R. Dulles, *The Old China Trade* (New York, 1970), pp. 50-65.
57. Stirling's 1827 report, SRP1.

58. Auguste Toussaint, *History of the Indian Ocean* (London, 1966), p. 194.
59. K. M. Panniker, *Asia and Western Dominance* (London, 1959), pp. 52-3.
60. C. Northcote-Parkinson, *Trade in the Eastern Seas 1793-1813* (London, 1966), pp. 75-7.
61. Toussaint, pp. 171-2; Panniker, p. 53.
62. Panniker, p. 95; Northcote-Parkinson, p. 94; Alexander Michie, *The Englishman in China during the Victorian Era* (London, 1900), Vol. 1, p. 42ff.
63. Dulles, *passim*; Northcote-Parkinson, pp. 160-3; Toussaint, p. 203; Michie, pp. 214-15.
64. Michie, p. 175.
65. Dulles, pp. 115-21.
66. Northcote-Parkinson, p. 257. In times of war, vessels taking the direct route to China (i.e. across the Indian Ocean and around the north-west coast of Australia), travelled in convoy and were accompanied by a ship of war all the way to Canton and back (*ibid.* p. 308).
67. *Ibid.* p. 98.
68. *Ibid.* p. 102.
69. W. H. Rosser, *Short Notes on the Winds, Weather, and Currents, Together with General Sailing Directions and Remarks on Making Passages; To Accompany a Chart of the Indian Ocean* (London, 1878).
70. Stirling's 1827 report.
71. Parry, *Fremantle*, p. 149.
72. After whom Owen Anchorage in Cockburn Sound was named.
73. Parry, *Fremantle*, pp. 149-60.
74. Morgan to Hay, 18.3.1830. Cockburn Sound could be a secure anchorage for 'ships of war of heavy burthen . . . it will be an anchorage of the very first national importance, particularly in the event of war with France, and America united'. See also Morgan to Hay, 28.1.1833, SRP15, where the argument is re-stated and 26.7.1835, SRP12. Four settlers wrote to the Secretary of State claiming that Cockburn Sound was a safe depot for His Majesty's ships cruising in the Indian Ocean in all seasons. In time of war the value would be ascertained and properly appreciated (Lewis, Morrell, Lamb and Nairn Clark to Secretary of State, 26.7.1832, SRP14).
75. E.g. Stirling to Glenelg, 22.12.1835.
76. Somerville, p. 56.
77. Stirling's 1826 report.
78. Stirling's 1827 report.
79. Barrow to Horton, 15.10.1827, SRP3.
80. Eddy, pp. 241-3.
81. Stirling to Twiss, 26.1.1830.
82. J. Cross, *Hints on Emigration to the New Settlements on the Swan and Canning Rivers* (London, 1829).
83. Stirling to Aberdeen, 23.7.1835, GD, Vol. 1, No. 64. See also Stirling to Glenelg, 12.7.1836, GD, Vol. 1, No. 127.
84. James Baird, *The Emigrants' Guide to Australasia* (London, 1868), p. 65.
85. Somerville, pp. 27-8.
86. Parry, *Fremantle*, pp. 156-7.
87. Traders in Canton who were the sole intermediary for foreign trade.
88. In a letter to Uncle William, written aboard *Challenger* at Macao, 23.12.1831, he said, 'It is truly absurd their fears, the style of their letters, their little knowledge of the art of War and their general blustering manner' (Parry, *Fremantle*, p. 157).
89. *Ibid.* pp. 159-60.
90. *Ibid.* p. 161.

91. Remark Book 1829-1833.
92. He suggested loans to settlers with land under cultivation at 5% interest, payable in instalments.
93. In China he had sympathized with the people who suffered the effects of opium, while immense fortunes were made by the English. 'A dirty Master of a Merchant Ship . . . told me this morning that his fee on the opium alone that went in and out of his ship was £5,000 annually', he wrote to his brother (Parry, *Fremantle*, p. 158).
94. *Sulphur* had taken Stirling to the Cape where he would transfer to another vessel bound for England.
95. Parry, *Fremantle*, pp. 181-2.
96. Cecil Woodham-Smith, *The Reason Why* (London, 1953).
97. Parry, *Fremantle*, p. 197.
98. Stirling to Goderich, 2.4.1832, SRP9; Western Australian Association, First Report, SRP9, p. 17.
99. Statham, thesis in preparation.
100. Stirling to Hay (private), 22.12.1832, SRP10.
101. Hay to Stirling, 2.1.1833, SRP16.
102. Stirling to Hay, 5.1.1833, SRP12.
103. *Ibid.* 12.12.1833.
104. Major E. Lockyer, 'Report on the Newly-founded Settlement at King George's Sound' (BL, 1827).
105. Stirling to Hay, 13.2.1832, SRP13.
106. Goderich to Stirling, 8.3.1833, SRP16.
107. *Ibid.*
108. Stanley to Stirling, 28.7.1833, SRP16.
109. Stirling to Hay, 23.6.1834, SRP13.
110. Uren, p. 245.
111. *Ibid.* pp. 246-8.

Select Bibliography

OFFICIAL DOCUMENTS AND PUBLICATIONS

Colonial Secretary's Office Records (CSO).
Governors' Despatches (GD).
Public Records Office (PRO). Microfilms from originals in London, held by BL.
Swan River Papers (SRP). Copies held by BL.
Historical Records of Australia (HRA), Series 1 and 3.
Lockyer, Major E. 'Report on the Newly-founded Settlement at King George's Sound,' 1827. BL.

GENERAL TEXTS

Arago, J. *Narrative of a Voyage Round the World, in the Uranie and Physicienne Corvettes* . . . London, 1823.
Austin, K. A. *The Voyage of the Investigator 1801-1803.* Adelaide, 1964.
Baird, James. *The Emigrants' Guide to Australasia.* London, 1868.
Bassett, Marnie. *The Hentys.* London, 1955.
———. *Realms and Islands. The World Voyage of Rose de Freycinet, 1817-1820.* London, 1962.
Battye, J. S., ed. *The Cyclopedia of Western Australia.* Vol. 1. Perth, 1912.
Beer, Gavin de. *The Sciences were Never at War.* London, 1960.
Berndt, Ronald M. and Catherine H. *The First Australians.* Sydney, 1954.
Berndt, Catherine H. and Ronald M. *Pioneers and Settlers. The Aboriginal Australians.* Melbourne, 1978.
Blainey, Geoffrey. *The Tyranny of Distance.* Melbourne, 1968.
Burney, James. *A Chronological History of Voyages and Discoveries in the South Seas.* London, 1803-17; facsimile: London, 1967.
Chate, A. H. *An Account of the Cowcher Family.* Perth, 1953.
Clark, C. M. H. *A History of Australia.* Vol. 1. Melbourne, 1963.
Collingridge, George. *The Discovery of Australia.* Sydney, 1895.
Cornell, Christine, trans. *The Journal of Post Captain Nicolas Baudin.* Adelaide, 1974.
Cottesloe, Lord, ed. *Diary and Letters of Admiral C. H. Fremantle, G.C.B.* London, 1928.
Crawford, I. M. *The Art of the Wandjina.* Melbourne, 1968.
Cross, J. *Hints on Emigration to the New Settlements on the Swan and Canning Rivers.* London, 1829.
———. *Extracts of Letters from Swan River, Western Australia.* London, 1830.
———, ed. *Journal of Several Expeditions Made in Western Australia.* London, 1833.
Cygnet. *Swan River Booklets.* Perth, 1935.
Drake-Brockman, H. *Voyage to Disaster.* Sydney, 1963.
Dulles, F. R. *The Old China Trade.* New York, 1970.

Dunmore, John. *French Explorations in the Pacific.* 2 vols. Oxford, 1965.

Eddy, J. J. *Britain And the Australian Colonies 1818-1831.* The Technique of Government. Oxford, 1969.

Edwards, Hugh. *Islands of Angry Ghosts.* New York, 1966.

Flinders, Matthew. *A Voyage to Terra Australis . . .* London, 1814.

Gay, Peter. *Age Of Enlightenment.* Nederland, 1966.

Hallam, Sylvia J. *Fire and Hearth.* Canberra, 1975.

Hasluck, Alexandra. *Thomas Peel of Swan River.* Melbourne, 1965.

Hasluck, Paul. *Black Australians.* Melbourne, 1942.

Heeres, J. E., trans. and ed. *Abel Janszoon Tasman's Journal . . .* Amsterdam, 1898; facsimile: Los Angeles, 1965.

Jutson, J. T. *The Physiography (Geomorphology) of Western Australia.* Geological Survey Bulletin No. 95. Perth, 1950.

Kimberly, W. B. *History of West Australia.* Melbourne, 1897.

King, Phillip P. *Narrative of a Survey of the Intertropical and Western Coasts of Australia.* 2 vols. London, 1827.

Labillardière, Jacques Julien Houten de. *An Account of a Voyage in Search of La Pérouse . . .* Translation by Debrett. London, 1800.

McIntyre, Kenneth Gordon. *The Secret Discovery of Australia.* London, 1977.

Mack, James D. *Matthew Flinders 1774-1814.* Melbourne, 1966.

Macknight, C. C. *The Voyage to Marege.* Melbourne, 1976.

Major, R. H. *Early Voyages to Terra Australis. . .* London, 1859.

Marchant, Leslie R. *The French and Western Australia 1503-1826.* Forthcoming.

Masefield, John, ed. *The Voyages of William Dampier.* 2 vols. London, 1906.

Michie, Alexander. *The Englishman in China during the Victorian Era.* Vol. 1. London, 1900.

Mulvaney, D. J. *The Prehistory of Australia.* Rev. Pelican ed. Melbourne, 1975.

Northcote-Parkinson, C. *Trade in the Eastern Seas 1793-1813.* London, 1966.

O'Brien, Eris. *The Foundation of Australia.* London, 1937.

Parry, Ann, ed. *The Admirals Fremantle.* London, 1971.

Parry, J. H. *Europe and A Wider World 1415-1715.* London, 1964.

Panniker, K. M. *Asia and Western Dominance.* London, 1953.

Peron, F. *A Voyage of Discovery to the Southern Hemisphere. . .* London, 1809; facsimile: Melbourne, 1975.

Pottle, Frederick A. *Boswell and the Girl from Botany Bay.* London, 1938.

Pike, Douglas, general ed. *Australian Dictionary of Biography.* Melbourne, 1966-   .

Regulations for the Guidance of Those Who May Propose to Embark as Settlers, for the New Settlement on the Western Coast of New Holland. London, 1829.

Richardson, Henry Handel. *The Fortunes of Richard Mahoney.* Melbourne, 1946.

Robert, Willem C. H. *The Explorations, 1696-1697, of Australia by Willem de Vlamingh.* Amsterdam, 1973.

―――. *The Dutch Explorations 1605 to 1756, of the North and North-west Coast of Australia.* Amsterdam, 1973.

Rosser, W. H. *Short Notes on the Winds, Weather, and Currents, Together with General Sailing Directions and Remarks on Making Passages; To Accompany a Chart of the Indian Ocean.* London, 1878.

Schilder, Günther. *Australia Unveiled: The Share of the Dutch Navigators in the Discovery of Australia.* Amsterdam, 1976.

―――. *De Ontdekkingsreis Van Willem Hesselsz: De Vlamingh In De Jaren 1696-1697.* 2 vols. The Hague, 1976.

Scott, Ernest. *The Life of Captain Matthew Flinders, R.N.* Sydney, 1914.

Seddon, George. *Swan River Landscapes.* Nedlands, 1970.

————. *Sense of Place*. Nedlands, 1972.

Sharp, Andrew. *The Voyages of Abel Janszoon Tasman*. London, 1968.

Smith, Edward. *The Life of Sir Joseph Banks*. London, 1911.

Spate, O. H. K. *Australia*. London, 1968.

Taylor, Griffith. *Australia*. London, 1940.

Toussaint, Auguste. *History of the Indian Ocean*. London, 1966.

Turner, Henry. *The Gilt Dragon Incident*. Nedlands, 1963.

Uren, Malcolm. *Land Looking West*. London, 1948.

Vancouver, George. *A Voyage of Discovery to the North Pacific Ocean, and Round the World*. 6 vols. London, 1801.

Williamson, J. A., ed. *A Voyage to New Holland by William Dampier*. London, 1939.

Wilson, T. B. *Narrative of a Voyage Round the World*. London, 1922.

Woodham-Smith, Cecil. *The Reason Why*. London, 1953.

Wright, Olive, ed. *New Zealand 1826-1827 from the French of D'umont D'urville*. Wellington, 1950.

Zuiderbaan, Lous. 'The Vergulde Draeck. Historical Background'. Chapter 1, in Jeremy N. Green, *Jacht Vergulde Draeck Wrecked Western Australia 1656*. Oxford, 1977.

ARTICLES

Bailey, John F. 'Longitude and the Sea Clock'. *History Today* (June 1970).

Boxer, C. R. 'The Vergulde Draeck'. *History Today* (March 1968).

Buckley, Nora C. 'The Extraordinary Voyages of Admiral Cheng Ho'. *History Today* XXV, 7 (July 1975).

Caldwell, Kate. 'The Voyage of François Alesne De Saint Allouarn, 1771-72'. *WAHSJ* 2, 16 (1934).

Cameron, J. M. R. 'Swan River Mania, 1829-1830: A Study of the Relationship Between Migration and Information'. Mimeo. Proceedings of the Indian Ocean International Historical Congress, Reunion, 1972.

————. 'The Near Collapse of Swan River Colony: Review and Reappraisal'. *Social Science Forum* 1, 1 (8/1973).

————. 'Prelude to Colonization: James Stirling's Examination of Swan River, March 1827'. *The Australian Geographer* XII, 4 (1973).

————. 'Information distortion in colonial promotion: the case of Swan River Colony'. *Australian Geographical Studies* 12 (1974).

de Heer, C. 'My Shield and My Faith'. *Westerly* (April 1963).

'The Diary of Mary Ann Friend'. *WAHSJ* I, X (1931).

Drake-Brockman, H. 'The Wreck of the Batavia'. *Walkabout* (1955).

Hallam, Sylvia, J. 'Population And Resource Usage On The Western Littoral'. ANZAAS. 1977.

Henn, Rev. P. V. 'French Exploration On The Western Australian Coast'. *WAHSJ* 2, 15 (1934).

Hogg, G. H. 'D'Entrecasteaux: an account of his life, his expedition, and his officers'. *Papers and Proceedings of the Royal Society of Tasmania* (1937).

Langley, Michael. 'John Harrison the Hero of Longitude'. *History Today* (December 1976).

McIntyre, K. G. 'Portuguese Discoveries on the Australian Coast'. *Journal of the Royal Historical Society of Victoria* 45, 4 (November 1974).

McKiggan, Ian. 'The Portuguese Expedition to Bass Strait A.D. 1522'. *Journal of Australian Studies* 1 (June 1977).

————. 'The Dauphin Map—a Reply'. *Journal of Australian Studies* 3 (June 1978).

Rennie, B. C. 'The Dauphin Map'. *Journal of Australian Studies* 3 (June 1978).
Schilder, G. 'A continent found by mistake'. *The Geographical Magazine* (London, February 1978).
Shenton, Mrs E. 'Reminiscences of Perth, 1830-1840'. *WAHSJ* 1, 1 (1927).
Spate, O. K. H. 'De Lozier Bouvet and Mercantilist Expansion in the Pacific in 1740'. In John Parker, ed. *Merchants and Scholars*. Minnesota, 1965.
Staples, A. C. 'Maritime Trade in The Indian Ocean, 1830-1845'. *University Studies in History*, (Perth, 1966).
Stark, W. 'Literature and Thought: The Romantic Tendency, Rousseau, Kant'. *The New Cambridge Modern History* VIII (Cambridge, 1965).
Statham, Pamela. 'Swan River Colony, 1829-1850'. In C. T. Stannage, ed. *The New History of Western Australia*. Nedlands, forthcoming.
Stephens, Robert. 'Major Edmund Lockyer'. *WAHSJ* 11, 19 (1936).
Whiteley, E. S. 'H.M.S. Sulphur'. *WAHSJ* 6, 6 (1961).

NEWSPAPERS AND JOURNALS

Brighton Gazette
Courier
Glasgow Courier
Globe
Hampshire Chronicle
Hull Advertiser
Hull Rockingham
Leicester Journal
Morning Journal
Quarterly Review, Vols IV, XII, XVII, XXXIX
Royal Devonport Telegraph and Plymouth Chronicle
South African Commercial Advertiser
Southampton Mercury
Sunday Times
Sussex Advertiser
The Times
York Chronicle

UNPUBLISHED DIARIES AND LETTERS

Baudin letters, held by BL.
Camfield letters, held by BL.
Daily Register of Samuel Volkersen on the flute the 'Waekende Boëy' sailing from Batavia to the Southland 1658. Translated by de Grys, Nedlands and held by H. Turner.
Fremantle family letters, held by AA.
Jane Currie's Diary, BL.
Remark Book of His Majesty's Ship Challenger, commencing 1 January 1832 and ending 12 June 1833, held at Hydrographer's Office, Taunton, Somerset.

UNPUBLISHED THESES AND MANUSCRIPTS

Berryman, I. L. 'The Swan River Letters'. (Publication under negotiation.)

Cameron, James M. R. 'The Colonization of pre-convict Western Australia'. Ph.D. thesis, University of Western Australia, 1975.

Henderson, Graeme. 'Problems Encountered by Shipping at the Port of Fremantle 1829 to 1850'. M.A. thesis, University of Western Australia, 1971.

Somerville, William. 'An Economic History of Western Australia'. 2 Vols. University of Western Australia and BL, 1952.

Statham, Pamela. Ph.D. thesis in preparation, University of Western Australia.

Index

Dryade, 169, 170
du Camper, Nourquer, 31
d'Urville, Dumont, 30, 33, 38, 111
Dutch East India Company, 14, 15, 16, 18, 66, 70, 103
Dutch East Indiamen, 14, 38
Dutch traders/interests, 12, 14, 15, 16, 18, 19, 21, 23, 35, 55, 73, 78, 80, 84, 87, 97, 99, 100, 101, 106, 161
Dyer, William, 183

East Indies, 11, 12, 14, 35, 38, 58
Eddy, J. J., 193
Edward Lombe, 180
Eendracht, 15, 58
Eendrachtsland, 58, 87
Egyptian, 150
El Edrisi, 11
Eliza, 170
Emeloort, 19, 61, 63, 64, 68, 69, 104
Encounter Bay, 27
Entrée Moreau, 49. *See also* Moreau Entrance
Erskine, Lieut. Archibald, 178
Espérance, 23, 31, 33
Esperance Bay, 23
Euclonia, 1

Faivre, Jean-Paul, 86
Fauré, Pierre, 93
Five Fathom Bank, 139
Flinders, Matthew, 25, 27, 28, 31, 35, 52, 100, 101
Fly, 33
Fort Dundas, 35
Fort Wellington, 107
Francis Freeling, 170
Fraser, Charles, 46, 49, 51, 55, 108, 111, 125, 145, 159, 161, 163, 171, 207, 208
Frederik Hendrik Bay, 86
Freeling, Sir Francis, 169
Fremantle, 16, 19, 67, 103, 122, 137, 139, 142, 148, 149, 150, 151, 154, 155, 157, 158, 167, 169, 173, 175, 177, 178, 180, 181, 182, 183, 185, 193, 199
Fremantle, Charles Howe, 112, 114, 115, 116, 117, 118, 119, 121, 122, 123, 124, 125, 126, 134, 135, 136, 137, 138, 139, 140, 141, 142, 143, 150, 167, 172, 173, 178, 185, 190, 194, 195, 196, 197, 198, 199, 204, 205, 208
Fremantle, William, 115, 116, 117
French interests, 7, 18, 21, 23, 25, 27, 28, 29, 31, 32, 33, 37, 44, 46, 49, 50, 52, 54, 55, 76, 84, 85, 86, 87, 89, 91, 93, 97, 100, 101, 104, 105, 109, 111, 117, 119, 126, 127, 132, 143, 145, 161, 185, 191, 199, 206
Freshwater Bay, 76, 182
Freycinet, Louis de, 28, 32, 87, 91, 93, 95, 96, 98, 99, 100, 101

Gage, Rear-Admiral, 129
Gage Roads, 49, 51, 53, 164, 167, 168, 170, 172, 173, 195, 197
Gama, Vasco de, 12
Garden Island (Ile Buache), 21, 46, 49, 71, 84, 96, 99, 101, 103, 118, 119, 122, 125, 130, 134, 135, 136, 137, 139, 140, 141, 145, 148, 149, 150, 158, 164, 174, 191, 192, 209
Geelvinck, 19, 70, 71, 73, 75, 80, 82
Géographe, 27, 46, 55, 85, 86, 87, 88, 93, 96, 99
Geographe Bay, 27, 50, 53, 89, 91, 93, 99, 100, 130, 145
Geraldton, 16, 38
Gerrit-Collaert, 70
Gerritsz, Hessel, 18, 58
Gilmore, 170, 179
Globe, 169, 170
Goderich, Lord, 110, 202, 203, 204
Goede Hoop, 59, 61, 66
de Gonneville land, 21, 23
Gonneville, Paulmier de, 21
Gros Venture, 21
Guildford, 104
't Gulden Zeepaerdt, 16

Hall, Capt. V. R., 182, 189, 190
Hallam, Sylvia, 5, 7, 104
Hamelin, Capt. Emmanuel, 86, 93, 95, 100
Hardey, Joseph, 147, 177
Harris, Capt., 131
Hartog, Dirck, 15, 16, 58, 80
Hasluck, Paul, 185
Hawkesbury River, 57, 145
Hay, Robert, 53, 110, 111, 128, 131, 158, 159, 163, 168, 185, 199, 201, 202, 203, 204
Heathcote, G. G., 49
Heirisson, Sub-Lieut. François, 46, 96, 104
Heirisson Island, 83, 97, 119
Henderson, Graeme, 174
Henry, Lieut John, 122, 124, 178
Henry the Navigator, 12
Henty family, 148, 149, 155, 158, 177, 178, 180, 183, 193
Hercules, H.M.S., 37, 170
Hill, Lord, 126
Hobart, 46, 53
Holland, 35, 82, 106
Holland, John, 168, 171
Hong Kong, 194
Hooghly, 170, 179
Hope, A. D., 1, 19
Horton, R. W., 35
Hotham, Vice-Admiral William, 116
Hottentots, 73, 83, 105
Houtman Abrolhos, 16, 18, 19, 59, 99
Houtman, F. de, 55, 58
Howe, 205
Hull Rockingham, 135